Skills Mania

"Bob Davis understands that the current testing, combined with an upgrading of skills but a downgrading of convictions, is a new way of sorting winners and losers in an increasingly class-based society. A classroom teacher and an innovative thinker, he gives both an insight into the ideology behind this change and a practical guide to its alternative."

— Maude Barlow, National Chairperson, The Council of Canadians,
author of *Class Warfare: The Assault on Canada's Schools*

Skills Mania

Snake Oil in Our Schools?

Bob Davis

Between the Lines
Toronto, Canada

To Meredith MacFarquhar
and the best years
of our lives

Skills Mania

© 2000 by Bob Davis

First published in Canada by
Between the Lines
720 Bathurst Street, Suite #404
Toronto, Ontario
M5S 2R4

Every reasonable effort has been made to identify copyright holders. Between the Lines would be pleased to have any errors or omissions brought to its attention.

Canadian Cataloguing in Publication Data

Davis, Bob, 1934-
      Skills mania : snake oil in our schools?
ISBN 1-896357-33-4

1 Education—Philosophy. 2 Education—Aims and objectives. I. Title.
LB41.D318 2000   370'.1   C99-933112-4

Text design by Margie Adam, ArtWork
Page preparation by Steve Izma
Printed in Canada by union labour

Between the Lines gratefully acknowledges assistance for its publishing activities from the Canada Council for the Arts, the Ontario Arts Council, and the Government of Canada through the Book Publishing Industry Development Program.

THE CANADA COUNCIL | LE CONSEIL DES ARTS
FOR THE ARTS | DU CANADA
SINCE 1957 | DEPUIS 1957

Canadä

Contents

Acknowledgements

Thanks to Margie Adam, Maude Barlow, Scott Bates, Keren Brathwaite, David Cayley, Lai Chu, Haydée Davis-Spinks, Rick Dewsberry, Marcela Duran, Eleanor Duckworth, Paul Eprile, Bill Goldfinch, Tim Grant, Don Gutteridge, David Hartman, Larry Kuehn, Porter Halyburton, Lilith Hanson, Steve Izma, Carl James, Ken MacKenzie, Mary McMillan, Jim McQueen, George Martell, Camille Natale, Doug Noble, Ken Osborne, Odida Quamina, Satu Repo, Paul Safarian, Peter Steven, Sheldon Taylor, Peter Thompson, Gary Trudeau, Neil Walker and Pat Wright. Thank you also to all my students whose work appears in this book.

A special thanks to Wally Seccombe for help on the science chapters, to Jamie Swift and Carroll Klein for key editing help and to my brother, Arthur Davis, for extensive editing and helpful conversation.

Writers differ about how much they need advance reader-critics. I have a friend who doesn't give his writing to anyone till he thinks it's ready to go to press. *I* hunt for a reader for every new paragraph. This blow-by-blow help came from Dave Owen and Gayle Gibson, and I thank them dearly for it. Finally, to Meredith MacFarquhar, my partner and fellow school trenches survivor. Your support and love during the ten years I've been writing this book have kept me on track. Thank you, love.

We are the hollow men
We are the stuffed men
Leaning together
Headpiece filled with straw.

— T.S. Eliot, "The Hollow Men"

Introduction

"All means prove but a blunt instrument if they have not behind them a living spirit."

— Albert Einstein

The Making of a Skills Opponent

My connection with schools goes back to 1939 when I started kindergarten in the English enclave in Quebec City, the same month as the invasion of Poland by Nazi Germany. World War II mainly survives in my mind as the time when my mother's brother was killed in North Africa and she took years to get over it. Schooling for those twelve years in Quebec was very traditional, but not difficult for a well-behaved Anglican preacher's kid who listened and did his homework. But "traditional education" did not end for me with elementary and high school in Quebec. It continued to be my experience of education right through university and then back in high school, where I taught in the early 1960s.

In my English Quebec elementary and high schools I got 70s and 80s. (That was before the advent of letter grades.) Like many students I remember only a few teachers I liked. One high school teacher was in charge of the compulsory cadet corps which in the late 1940s I took very seriously, but what I remember best about him was that he had been a prisoner of war in Hong Kong in World War II and was on fire with the meaning of history for reconstruction after the war. Yes, he expected his students to memorize the four causes of this and the five results of that, but he also insisted upon open and far-reaching discussion about where postwar history was heading and should head. He made us think.

One of the classic features of all elementary classrooms in those days was the handful of tall, rough boys in the back rows who had failed several times and now qualified mainly for running errands and cleaning the blackboards at the end of the day. A few qualified for regular strapping.

In high school I took Latin, which meant I was in 9A. Students in 9B took music, 9C took woodshop (boys) and home economics (girls) and 9D was the commercial stream. This streaming, or tracking, was a reflection of the class differences in the population; those tall boys from elementary school ended up on the bottom of the heap.

From 1952-1956 I studied at Dalhousie University, Halifax, under philosopher George Grant and historian George Wilson. Both provided a very focused challenge to my minister father's Christian conservatism. Grant, in the end, gave me a thoughtful version of this same Christian conservatism, but Wilson passed on a sense of history's sweep and of humanity's weakness. Wilson's view better reflected the feelings in my bones at the time.

George Grant was preoccupied with the modern world's worship of skills and technique. In those days he called it "social engineering." So I suppose you might say the suspicion I now have of skills education comes partly from him.

I certainly know it was his philosophy and my father's that I wished to defend when I got to King's College, Cambridge, for further study in history in 1956. English rationalism became Public Enemy #1, and I strove unsuccessfully to keep up in reading and wit with all those young Eton boys who, I thought, must have been taught witty put-downs at their mothers' knees.

Following Cambridge, after failing an audition for the Covent Garden opera chorus, I went off for two years teaching history at — today it shocks me — an American military academy in Sewanee, Tennessee. More of this later in the book.

The years at Dalhousie, Cambridge and Tennessee were also "traditional schooling" in some of the best senses. Education was not the kind of smorgasbord where students took a little of this and a little of that, with no core program and no mentors to guide you.

Pacman, Not Hockey

During my first Canadian teaching job I got my initial taste of skills-obsessed education. When I started in a North York, Ontario, high school in 1961, students had to take history from grade 9 to grade 12, and, if you were heading to a B.A. program at university, you had to take it in grade 13 as well. The subdivisions of that breakdown into five courses were all pieces of the history of North America and Western Europe, with their origins in Greece, Rome and Israel. Canada was presented as a creature of the French and British Empires — with the slant on modern Canada putting us solidly in the arms of the U.S.A.

Some of us who were totally committed to this yearly compulsory history began (with the lobbying help of many newly local constituencies) to ask about missing ingredients: Where was the history of women? Where were new immigrants? Where were visible minorities? Native people? Labour and social history? We did not want to create a cafeteria of histories (Black Studies, Women's Studies); we wanted the whole compendium expanded to unify the origins and development of our country and our world. The textbook changes the publishers responded with were not impressive — a mention of Nellie McClung added to the mention of Laura Secord, a nod to the Winnipeg General Strike, a new black face on page 436. However, an excellent collection of new small books from all educational publishers on the topics we were talking about flooded the market in the late 1960s and early 1970s.

But we optimists who thought we were helping to produce a new inclusive history were not, in fact, on the same wave length as the authorities. By the early 1970s history itself had nearly disappeared from the curriculum. Five compulsory histories in 1961 had been replaced with one compulsory history in 1971. We thought we were revising the subject; they knew they were wiping it out. We thought the game we were playing was an old one like hockey, but it turned out to be a new-style Pacman. The new curriculum advisors said we should no longer teach history; we were to teach how to *do* history (history skills), in case you ever needed it in your job or wanted to do it in your spare time — and one course was enough for this shrunken purpose.

This was my baptism as a critic-in-embryo of the new skills education. I was naive in thinking we could usher in a world where the cause of the common people and of multicultural Canada was about to flower in our schools. But the skills emphasis (learning how to do history rather than actually doing it) was new, and we didn't understand that this concept would dominate education in the last few decades of the twentieth century — and appear in sound health and "robustiousness" in the year 2000.

Back in the mid-1960s the discovery of this new direction in education led me outside the official school system.

Progressivism, Country Experiments and High School Smorgasbord

In 1966 I helped found Everdale, an experimental school on a hundred-acre farm where fifty students had to do their chores and turn up at the weekly community meeting, but didn't have to go to classes. Some students tended the farm animals, others worked in a big vegetable garden, one group of fifteen travelled to Milwaukee to attend the trial of thirteen draft-card-burning priests, another fifteen spent six weeks in Montreal boarding with French families and going to a French high school. Very few students did traditional academic classes and many spent most of their time struggling with their personal relationships and listening to their favourite rock songs. Our experiment impressed the federal government enough to provide us with five Company of Young Canadians salaries for three years. For youth it was an experimental time.

It was also an experimental time for a group of progressive teachers like myself who, from 1966 to 1971, put out what became the biggest quarterly in North America, *This Magazine is About Schools*. So I experienced this stage of progressive education in mint form. The regular high school versions of this progressivism was vast expansion of credit choices (the cafeteria-choice school), looser discipline and the absence of standards-testing across the system.

This was my brief period of working outside the official school system. Even today I'm reminded of that period when conservative school critics describe most current North American schools as if they are still "progressive," by which they mean child-centred instead of teacher-centred, with miserable standards, run by education bureaucrats and teacher unions. This is part of the reason I consider this book so necessary. Few schools ever operated like this progressive caricature the conservatives present. And as we accept the simplistic pendulum-swing theory of education changes — that conservatives are taking us back to "old ways" — we miss completely the novelty of the Information Age skills system.

Where the New Conservative Education Comes From

The conservative education reaction is a very important political force. What was behind it? I believe it went something like this: With the fiscal difficulties and changes in Western economies since the 1970s, and the resulting shrinkage of the industrial manufacturing work force, the jobs of the new lower middle class and upper working class have disappeared or become very precarious. These workers are the first generation of parents since the end of World War II whose children are worse off than they are. The elders blame the schools for this: "My kid is not getting a good job because she's not been properly taught." Private school enrollment has gone way up in recent history, but many of the parents I'm talking about cannot afford private schools.

The conviction that schools are to blame led to the formation of key political lobby groups, often with the word "quality" in their name — the Quality Education Network and the Organization for Quality Education. The redneck tone was evident in their early pamphlets: "How can my kid learn in a class full of every language and disability known to man?" Then they got more sophisticated advice. "Mark Holmes and I are trying to get the quality groups to add the disadvantaged to their concerns," Dennis Raphael told me in the early 1990s. These men were both University of Toronto professors — one in education and one in social work — and they helped to do the stickhandling for Ontario, working with by Dr. Joe Freedman of Alberta, who led the national movement.

These leaders, following their American forebears, developed the whole enemy/demon theme of a soft progressive education system with no standards, held hostage by education bureaucrats and teacher unions. Even more significantly they helped to transform a populist conservative critique of schools ("We must mobilize parents to turn back the clock to the time when education was done properly") into an Information Age/global capitalism pitch from the corporations about the need for a skills-based educational system.

I do not mean to imply that the conservative critics had no valid claims. Who can defend report cards that said "Harry gets along very well with his peers," but said nothing about how he was doing in reading and mathematics? What I want to emphasize in this book is that the Information Age skills people are now in charge, not the conservative populists. Can one imagine genuine old conservatives like George Grant agreeing to dismantle the study of history? Can one imagine traditional conservatives dropping all reference to character building as an aspect of the study of great novels, drama and poetry? The current conservatives have hopped on the skills bandwagon, compromising traditional conservative thinking on the purpose of education. We will understand current education better if we keep this in mind.

Learning about Skills Mania and Responding to It

The third period of education, then, and the one this book is about — skills mania — crept in slowly at first in the 1970s. It arrived full blast in the 1980s, prompting Rob Greenaway, then executive vice-president of the educational publishing house Prentice-Hall and a man who knew what books schools were demanding, to call the 1980s "the decade of skills."[1] The 1990s were even more so, and there's every sign that the early 2000s will continue to be skills obsessed. Skills are the cornerstone of this theory, but other pillars are also important: the focus on "outcomes" or "expectations," and standardized performance testing. The jargon can change, but the skills foundation remains; in the year 2000 it is solidly in control of conventional wisdom in education. Education is not alone in this. We are inundated by pronouncements on parenting skills, reading skills, reading-readiness skills, dating skills, social skills, coping skills — and the broad notion of life skills.

Education for the Information Age

Everyone has heard the Information Age's educational pitch: content is obsolete today because it goes out-of-date so fast and because students forget it so quickly. It's also mostly propaganda, many skills experts say. We therefore must emphasize not *what* to learn but *how* to learn. We must start off with basic skills — numbers and words — teaching reading, writing and mathematics well as a foundation for everything else. I agree completely. What this book is challenging is the next stage, the plan for senior elementary and high school: the move to something called generic skills, especially portable and critical-thinking skills such as creative problem solving, weighing evidence, probing possible explanations, understanding classification systems, knowing the complexities of teamwork, etc.

People and Skills in the New Global Economy, (a 237-page government report prepared by a committee of seven politicians, five academics, three trade unionists and nineteen company presidents!) explains this position clearly:

> With the advent of new information-based technology and the shift to a more flexible and multiskilled workforce, employers are finding that generic workplace skills are becoming increasingly important relative to job-specific skills. Generic skills are those which workers can use in many jobs. They include analytical, problem solving, workplace interpersonal skills and broad technical skills that may be found in the skilled trades or in the operation of personal computers.[2]

This is the Ontario version of an education and training philosophy popular throughout the English-speaking world. It is essentially the education and training philosophy of American economics pundit Robert B. Reich, Clinton's former secretary of Labor. In *The Work of Nations: Preparing Ourselves for 21st Century Capitalism*, Reich says that "Each nation's primary political task will be to cope with the centrifugal forces of the global economy which tear at the ties binding citizens together — bestowing even greater wealth on the most skilled and insightful, while consigning the less skilled to a declining standard of living."[3]

Armed with these transferable thinking skills, the Ontario pundits continue, student graduates will probably have to change jobs ten or twelve times in a lifetime, but each new job will be as interesting as the last (*not* Reich's conclusion, incidentally). Meanwhile we will have armed them further with non-vocational thinking skills like media literacy ("literacy" has come to mean knowing the skills in a certain field) and political literacy, which replaces the dead old subject of citizenship training. For their non-work hours we will also have passed on social skills, coping skills and life skills — although the latter, on close examination, has crept back into the vocational category, since it's about filling in forms and how to dress for a job interview.

The need for this educational revolution is said to be the arrival of the new information-oriented global capitalism, with its vast computer and robotic systems, its shrinkage of industrial jobs and its increase of high-tech and service jobs.

Three main groups are pushing this new education. First, the CEOs of the biggest corporations work through their lobbies like the Conference Board of Canada — although it has always seemed ironic that even while they insist that the new way of schooling is skills education, these CEOs continue to send their own children to elite private schools where they are taught the old liberal arts. A second key group comprises the many concerned middle-class and upper-working-class parents I talked about earlier. Finally, many liberal and even leftist thinkers have taken a shine to "critical thinking skills," which, they feel, enables them to teach students a critical view of current society without having to preach to them.

What Is Missing in Skills Mania?

I will begin with my answer to these liberal and left thinkers because so many of them are my colleagues. The answer I develop in this book is that their use of the skills philosophy works so long as the teacher passes on to her students her own passion for certain principles and convictions. In that case, analyzing media or politics in her class is a serious affair. If student/teacher discussions are not anchored by such passion and principles (which offer a search for truth and justice at least as perceived by the teacher) then students are armed only with media literacy premises, which encourage them to see through everything and owe allegiance to nothing.

Of course there are people today who say that student allegiances are none of the school's business, but rather the prerogative of family and church, or something for individuals to work out on their own. There are others like some of my colleagues who are sceptical of all beliefs, who believe the school should bend over backward to avoid teaching principles since one can always ask *whose* principles are being taught. My view is that giving nothing but skills in school does not solve this "problem," since an exclusively skills-based education is itself a message to students that techniques can solve all of life's problems. This is technocracy. Education, I believe, cannot avoid passing on principles. We are involved in this exchange, and it is taken on by the most serious teachers "in fear and trembling," to use Kierkegaard's phrase. But the equally sacred liberal corollary is that everything must be debated and nobody will be forced to hold any particular views or get better marks for holding them.

I'm not claiming that either traditional or progressive education is preferable to skills mania. Both philosophies have failed in teaching non-middle-class children just as skills mania has. But I *am* saying that if we right this neglect of a proper education for working-class children, then some combination of the best of traditional and progressive education would be vastly superior to skills mania and would improve the standard of education for the entire student population. It's not the stress on skills I object to. It's the current neglect of what these skills should be anchored in: content, conviction, allegiances, real human beings and, in general, a commitment to helping students understand history, learn about the world and consider ways to make it a better place to live.

Faulty Optimism about Jobs

I also believe that the optimistic job predictions of the skills zealots are a cruel joke in the light of honest economic analysis. The real truth seems to be that portable thinking skills do indeed lead to one interesting job after another, but only if you're one of the few technically sophisticated, university-trained experts. To the great mass of high school graduates, the skills program is a pig in a poke. The best and most thorough debunking of this "jobs for everyone" theory can be found in D. W. Livingstone's *The Education-Jobs Gap: Underemployment or Economic Democracy*: "Education systems can always be improved. But it is not inadequate education that is the primary cause of the education-jobs gap. The basic problem is the lack of decent jobs."[4]

Although my book does not develop this theme, it completely assumes it as one necessary premise in support of my own argument. I am arguing that one of the disasters of technocratic skills education is its increasing abandonment of proper citizenship and humane education. Livingstone's massive proof that education is not responsible for the jobs gap must be kept constantly in our minds while reading this book.

Finally, I shall be arguing that despite the fields of media and political literacy, this new approach has effectively turned all education into vocational training. This is a particularly unfortunate and ironic development in light of the failure of skills mania to come through with the jobs it promises.

Consider one sign of this movement of education towards an increasing vocationalism: over the last two or three decades, history has shrunk drastically as a high school subject, and English has increasingly emphasized language over literature and film. Math and language are now considered the key subjects in school, the Queens of the Sciences, the magisterial subjects, to use the old terms. Unlike times past, when theology or classics or history or English and history were considered the key subjects through which all other subjects made sense, we now affirm that all other subjects make sense not because of anything in their content or their rootedness in human experience, but only as being common tools or techniques. Techniques, simple or fancy, are today's queens. Since techniques lend themselves more to sorting out work than citizenship or deep human relations (e.g., social skills can easily become pure manipulation), even the major skills educators consider media and political literacy to be icing on the schooling cake, often dispensible. Besides, the most successful of the media and political literati don't care for any principles except raw competition, and they say to people (especially the wealthy): "Tell us what you want to accomplish with television or a political campaign, and we'll give you the media and the political skills to do it." This precise nature of technique—to leave out the quality of its purposes—has therefore led the skills philosophy largely into a vocational emphasis. In such a vision the major liberal arts subjects themselves become vocational.

Understanding, Surviving and Responding to Skills Mania

Since that brief period outside the regular school system in the late 1960s and early 1970s, I have worked within the system. For four years I taught postgraduate education at the University of Toronto; then I returned to high school teaching in 1975, where I remained until my retirement in 1996. My specialty, apart from history teaching, was teaching students in "lower streams" and, for my last four years, teaching black history to mostly black students. During these years, I completed a Ph.D. and wrote a book entitled *Whatever Happened to High School History? Burying the Political Memory of Youth.*[5]

I want to examine with you the way Information Age skills work and don't work. Remember that some of the issues I have raised about traditional and progressive education suggest that the skills people were not the first to arrive on the scene with fresh and challenging education ideas. The fact that many people today think skills are paramount shouldn't make us buy their view that education thinking must now somehow start over from scratch: as if all the old schooling battles that have animated conservatives, liberals and radicals since 1800 are now somehow obsolete. Skills like learning to read and do math, of course, have been part of that battle from the beginning, but the deeper issues like *who* will be educated, and for what politics, work, character and reverence, must be the deeper anchors that skills are rooted in. Traditional education still has profound things to teach us about focus, mentoring, purpose and reverence. Liberal progressivism is indispensible on the subject of the human persons with whom we must establish contact for education to be meaningful. And the radical tradition must be central for those of us who fight against unequal schooling and try to teach our students how they might contribute towards a more just society.

But to understand what inventive new combinations we can gradually put together for schools, we must first understand, live through and respond to skills mania.

CHAPTER 1

How the Skills Philosophy Thrives in New Fields

Child Care, Conflict Management and Media Literacy

I am aware that the concept of "skill" itself is not what is new. Hephaestus in Greek legend was a skilled metalworker. Athena was a great weaver. Common wisdom knows that doctors, fast typists, good spellers, skilled carpenters, fine cooks and inspired gardeners are all skilled — though their pay varies from very high to nothing. Everyone knows it's a skill to design bridges that stay up and tunnels that don't cave in; to put miniature ships in bottles or walk tightropes; to do flips in the air or skate like the wind; to draw likenesses or play the piano. In relatively modern times, hundreds of skilled trades, through their craft unions, carved out a dignified position of strength and culture by virtue of their skilled knowledge, which gave them bargaining power with the financial elite.

Skills have often had snob appeal, like rich and middle-class kids learning ballet, but sometimes the skills of the ruling class were immensely practical. A medieval prince who learned theology might please his priest or his bishop; when he learned the skill of jousting, he could defend himself in the next war — as long as his opponents didn't hide behind trees. An upper-class Roman youth who learned Virgil's *Aeneid* might please his teacher; when he learned the "gift of the gab" (Rhetoric 101 from that same teacher), it opened political doors.

So if skills are not new, why are they so controversial now? It is, first, that skills have supposedly become the only education game in town, and second, that they have become very specific types of skills — the mysterious "mental" ones. In the public's mind (with a little help from computer companies) the mental skills are needed to operate computers. For a vast number of politicians, promising a computer on every school desk has become as important as kissing babies. This mechanical — and expensive — solution has never been the view of the venerable skills gurus, however. The grand old founders of creative skills mania and the knowledge worker theory, people like Edward de Bono and Peter Drucker, believe they are presenting us with a whole new purpose of education, where the existing division into subjects is completely out-of-date. These are people who make a very comfortable living addressing CEOs about the kind of creative thinking all of us presumably need in a "knowledge society."

But the most famous guru *within* education is William Spady. To Spady all old subdivisions of education are obsolete and the field should now be organized into six "domains of competency": "Verbal (communication skills), Quantitative (calculating skills), Technical (mainly computer skills), Strategic (problem-solving skills), Social (personal life skills), and Evaluative (aesthetic skills)."[1] Notice that history has evaporated under these new headings — or, more accurately, it has been subsumed under Strategic (problem-solving skills). Chapters 4 to 10 of this book are all organized under traditional subject headings: English, history, citizenship, sociology, psychology and science (two chapters). I know that over time knowledge has been organized under different headings. But I suggest we should not rush to embrace the "domains of competence" theory as the correct way to organize knowledge. And while actual school programs still teach most of the old subjects, this period, when the skills philosophy is questioning the very foundation of these traditional subjects, is an excellent time for us to examine whether we want these divisions or not.

Eight Units of My Own Teaching

This book is not just a critique of skills mania. It is also eight extended units of my own teaching, where I try to keep skills in the bursting framework of history, humankind, animal kind and the earth; war and peace; protest and self-knowledge; contemplation and the design of blueprints for change. In these teaching accounts I resist this era's claim that curriculum content and student conviction be kept out of school, that education is about facts and skills and that the mind (as distinct from a bundle of mental skills) can now be handed over to business, the family and the churches.

In one sense this sounds fancier than I intend. In chapters 4-10, I describe lessons in English, history, citizenship, sociology, psychology and science. Although in this chapter I will look at the "new" skills of childcare, conflict resolution and media analysis, it is in the mainstream school subjects that today's students encounter the full blast of skills mania. It therefore seemed important to examine, through real teaching examples, what it means to see English *not* being turned into language skills only, history *not* merely as "doing history," sociology *not* primarily as "skills for examining society," and science *not* only as skills for the "smartest" students who will train in the higher reaches of physics, chemistry and biology. As I describe the teaching units I have selected, I say a great deal about skills. I talk about teaching them. I talk about stressing them. I talk about testing students' knowledge of them. But I also emphasize the context of these skills, the content, the convictions and the probes they are meant to serve.

There is also a large multicultural emphasis in these lessons. In fact, five of the eight units of teaching were developed when teaching two black history courses to high school students. For four years I specialized in teaching two history courses: "Africa and the West Indies" and "Canada and the United States since Slavery." The teaching methods I used, of course, can be applied to all courses, but the content of black history will perhaps remind readers that my critique of skills cannot be neatly dismissed as a right-wing defense of solid old European content, principles, etc.

I am also aware that some readers will rightfully ask why a white teacher appeared to be acting as an authority on teaching black students and African and diaspora history. I am not an authority. I am merely describing what I did in my classes and why. It will be up to readers to decide whether it makes sense. I told each of my black history classes — where African Canadian students predominate — "I can't teach you what it's like to be black; *you* can teach *me* about that — but I do know some history, so let's hope some of you find that beneficial."

But I am also happy to introduce my students and lessons in this book because I believe that skills mania is a bill of goods being sold to the multicultural community as supposedly the best they can get from the system. I think that members of minorities should be leery of this misrepresentation, although I can understand the attraction of an education that appears to remove the usual racist biases that accompany conventional schooling — a new education that supposedly clears away all the biased overlay and offers only the objective skills underneath.

Unfortunately "the objective skills underneath," if that's all we offer, are themselves, as I mentioned in the introduction, a seductive pitch call technocracy. I learned from educators Dr. Barbara Sizemore and Dr. Asa Hilliard that any honourable educator has two tasks, not one: first, to help students master the existing rating system that gets them into university, and second, to teach those cultural, scientific and humanistic truths that will give students power and dignity in the broader world of people and politics.[2] These leaders never suggested there was any great magical objectivity about the skills and testing approach. They merely cautioned against boasting about your new black history course and neglecting how well your students were progressing in the system as it exists.[3] Some skills mania zealots in the multicultural communities felt they had found the great bias-free system, and then became disillusioned when they found their own children spending an inordinate percentage of school time learning "life skills," i.e., how to fill in job applications and groom themselves and show up on time for interviews. The skills curriculum is just as susceptible to inequality as the old curriculum.

And let's be sure we don't get swept away by the latest buzzwords of educators. Someone told me recently: "You know, skills are now old hat. Even 'outcomes' are old hat. Nowadays it's 'expectations.' We're supposed to be clear on what we expect children to know at the end of the line."

Sounds a lot like outcomes to me. And when I asked if these expectations are facts to be memorized or student convictions about what this world needs to become a better place, I was told: "No, no no, it's skills — problem solving, literacies in the modern sense."

The new emphasis, it seems, is not that new.

Please note as well that the curriculum I have chosen to discuss in this book is not meant to show the broad sweep I'd expect from a total English, history, citizenship, sociology or psychology program. There is not much in this book, for example, about First Nations history and culture, but there was in my actual curriculum. In the black history units I describe here, I did not choose to feature an African Canadian unit. In the graduation year course, African Canadian history is prominent in my work. Units have been chosen for this book with an eye to their special link to the topic of skills training and skills mania.

Such, then, is what the subject sections and my personal lessons will be about.

New Fields Where the Skills Philosophy Has Been Most Comfortable

Though most of this book will emphasize the effects of skills mania on traditional curriculum subjects (chapters 4-10), we cannot shirk the fact that the skills approach has taken its firmest holds in new fields that do not coincide with traditional subject headings. That same Bill Spady spirit of giving education an entirely new rationale infuses all of the skills emphasis at its most honest and its most passionate.

I therefore close this first chapter with three such new fields: childcare skills, conflict management skills and media literacy skills. Chapters 2 and 3 will then consider another of these new fields, collaboration skills. Partly I am beginning outside the traditional subjects to suggest that we should face up to skills mania at its best.

Child Care Skills. I began thinking about skills in the childcare field after an experience during a class presentation for my Childhood, Schools and Society course at Atkinson College, York University. A young daycare worker told our class that the main purpose of her work was to help children with their motor skills, listening skills, communication skills and cognitive skills. Yes, she told me afterwards, she had learned these ideas in the Early Childhood Education course at Seneca Community College, and, yes, she also believed in them herself.

This young woman was raised and was still living in a very close Portuguese Catholic home where the language about being with children would have been very different from the skills language. Partly, I thought, she might use that new language to stand for older ideas. "Social skills," for instance, may have meant "getting along with people," or "learning fairness." Let us assume that for my student there might have been plenty of this translating going on. Perhaps, I thought for a moment, the difference was just words.

But I couldn't let this go. I noticed that my student had not been taught the following: Daycare is meant to provide a community where love and justice will be caught as well as taught, but which is also an end in itself, i.e., a happy place for a child to be while parents are working. This way of putting it is different from the skills language in a few very significant ways. For one thing, it puts emphasis on the daycare *community*, which the skills language does not. The words love and justice assume principles beyond teaching some technical knowledge or skill for some unstated purpose. Justice could include "being fair" and "sharing," surely two very important things for children to learn. But the skills language appears not to deal with thorny traditional questions like why be fair? or why share? (questions that children themselves ask, and for which the modern daycare centre is surely not willing to accept "because I say so" as an adequate answer).

Gradually I realized out that because the new language had this clinical, scientific tone, it seemed to imply that everyone shared a belief in a set of objective skills and a common purpose for teaching them. But along with the common purpose, this skills list also implied that in a wonderful, free world, different children will use these objective and "value-neutral" skills in their own individual way. But this made no sense to me. Why, for example, could the basis of social skills teaching not be learning the clever and sensitive manipulation of people?

A story about children will illustrate this last point. A friend of mine with a six year old was courting a single woman who had children aged nine and four. The courtship brought these three kids together quite often, and on one occasion when the five were out together, the three kids wanted the adults to buy some candy. They were out of earshot of their parents, but the story came out later. "My dad won't give us the money," my friend's six year old said. "Go tell your mother she's the best mum in the world and she'll give it to us." It worked. The kid had social skills. William Hart, in his essay "Against Skills," has this to say about social skills:

> I have no particular objection to the term "social skills" as applied to the manoeuvring of a society hostess or to the adroitness with which the professional salesman sounds out and then softens up a prospective client. It is in its application to those who love us, our friends and close family, which I find grotesque.[4]

Gradually the underlying implications behind the skills language became clearer to me. The development of an apparently value-free skills language is rather like the habit of blaming all special learning problems on "learning disabilities." Nobody, it seems, needs to feel guilty any more for causing these disabilities. These days they're all sup-posedly caused by the brain. Also we are meant to assume that these disabilities can be objectively diagnosed and that there is a correct method of teaching to correct each disability.

Similarly with skills language: we can talk as if childrearing and teaching are mostly a matter of training in a set of individual techniques which we imply are ethically, psychologically and politically neutral and which we assume prepare people for "normal" mainstream participa-tion, however it may be defined. But then again, if kids choose alterna-tive ways, we have supposedly given them the tools to do that instead. So we pretend that we have avoided having to define the contexts within which the skills are conceived when in fact we teach such skills based on large assumptions about normal mainstream life.

Back in the summer of 1973 a group of us began occupying the Campus Community Cooperative Day Care Centre #2, a protest we continued for six months, twenty-four hours a day. From those days I still remember best my two year old talking about the "picket lion" and hearing one of our chants at demonstrations as "Day Care, Yes! Please, No!" when it was actually "Day Care, Yes! Police, No!"

The six-month struggle was an exhausting effort, so on certain days, to help speed up the decision by the University of Toronto to allow us to use the building legally, we divided into two crews, one to keep the building occupied, the other to go with our children to protests in various sensitive parts of the campus and city. One example was dis-rupting University of Toronto graduation ceremonies on the lawn of University College. About forty of us wheeled our kids in strollers through the centre of the awards ceremony.

Were we teaching our children "protest skills"? Were we manipu-lating the children? Were the children learning communication skills? Or perhaps adult manipulation skills? Could official Early Childhood Education courses include such activities in the course content? I ask these questions knowing, of course, that such a departure from *normal life* would not get into Early Childhood texts, thus proving that the skills are not as neutral as they appear.

So the appearance of cooled-out neutrality in the skills language is strictly appearance. The implied psychology, ethics or politics may be buried, and the language may have a quiet non-judgmental tone to those raised with too much imposed morality. Even my daycare worker student might use the skills language partly to avoid always calling chil-dren good or bad. But I decided that the purpose behind this language, which becomes clearer as children move to later educational institutions, is present even in the daycare-as-skills-training approach. The so-called *normal life*, which is the unstated endpoint, context, purpose or anchor of daycare skills training, is the secret hidden from daycare workers who are taught that they are merely helping individual children to be personally happy — as if even what makes people happy is simple and obvious.

Let me switch to schools and give you two other brief examples. While I'm focusing now on schools, I'm still looking at topics that are not traditional subjects of study. The examples are conflict management skills and media literacy skills.

Conflict Management Skills. Elementary school systems in particular have taken this new set of techniques seriously, although such high school programs as Positive Peer Culture show this approach is in the secondary system as well. Two Canadian books where the philosophy can be examined are *Children As Peacemakers*[5] and *Managing Conflict*.[6] Who can be against teaching interested students to look coolly at the tangles in some fights in order to settle matters? This relatively new phenomenon — new in the sense of teaching a *formalized* set of techniques — would demand lengthy treatment for a proper analysis. Here I will make only a general point.

In a time when teaching skills and techniques is increasingly seen as the correct approach to most branches of school life, proponents of this conflict management field should be clear what kind of conflict their largely individual and localized techniques can solve and what kind they cannot. As with childcare skills, when the objective tone of conflict management language is demystified and it is made clear what conception of peace and order is behind these skills, then certain kinds of conflicts are amenable to these approachs, i.e., ones where no larger forces such as mental disorder, racism or class hatred are central to the battle. (If a school has programs and policies to contend with these larger things, excellent, but to save disillusionment, we should know what is solving what.) Is it the new courses offered in black history and the African dance offered in Physical Education that are giving the black students more ownership of the school, or is it the conflict management program in the schoolyard? It could be both, but not necessarily. Both could still be very useful. But some people still talk as if they are not aware of this distinction: i.e., working to have a more just and equal curriculum and school policy as compared to solving individual conflict in the schoolyard.

You may say that these distinctions are very obvious. Maybe they are, but I have heard some exponents of conflict management skills suggest that those of us not employing their methods, regardless of how badly various student groups and individual students were affected by race, poverty or mental instability, are depriving our school of a technique that would create peace and harmony.

I remember in Chicago in the late 1960s being at a marathon group therapy session for teachers which went on continuously for thirty-six hours. It was a very positive experience and I remember it fondly, but what sticks out most from the weekend is a remark made towards the end by one of the enthusiastic leaders. "Just imagine if world leaders like Richard Nixon and General Westmoreland were all to have this experience!" He had false hope for his method.

Much as we should praise the creation of more genuine harmony in our schools, we should not mislead ourselves when some conflict management proponents present a very focused and limited technique or skill as a panacea for school peace in the midst of widespread social war. Two schools in Metro Toronto (Downtown Alternative School and Downsview Secondary School), which practise very successful conflict management programs, both have their programs integrated with school-wide policies that make student participation central in conflict resolution and link battles on large conflict issues like racism and class hostility to changes in school curriculum and special events. Managing individual acts of conflict is not seen as a panacea in itself.

Another way of putting this challenge is to pose the question of when we must take a stand on "no justice, no peace." Now of course it is obvious that on the level of the average day in a North American school, we must often promote and accept peace without sorting out all the issues of justice. But at the same time, we must maintain that expending monumental energy on the techniques of peace may lead us to a deep cynicism if we do not face the more intractable issues of violence, justice and madness. Which all suggests that once again the central issue for the skills philosophy is to delve into what philosophies of life the particular skills or techniques are meant to serve.

Media Literacy Skills. For me the media literacy skills people are the most interesting of all skills enthusiasts. Many of them are very critical of big corporations, whereas most skills proponents are promoters of business. Media literacy has become an important subject in Ontario under the leadership of Barry Duncan, a teacher with the Etobicoke Board of Education and principal author of *Media Literacy*,[7] Ontario's official guide to analyzing media. As a school subject media literacy has become so popular in North America that in New Mexico in the 1990s it was even required as a high school credit. Because kids are so bombarded with media, the argument goes, schools should offer them the tools to see what is happening to our minds and separate the wheat from the chaff.

But wait! You don't have to spend more than ten minutes thinking about media literacy to know that what you think about law, order and good government or even life, liberty and the pursuit of happiness will significantly affect what you decide to analyze in the media and what you see when you get there. Are you to stop at camera angles, or are you to ask who sponsors what programs? The Barry Duncan school of media analysis *does* get into the effect of sponsors.

But let us say that your approach to the subject is broad enough to allow some pretty searching criticism of television and radio. Is the standpoint from which you make your observations — and maybe criticisms — to be made explicit and given proper discussion in high schools? To me the best media critic in journalistic circles these days is Rick Salutin, who writes a weekly column for Canada's national daily, *The Globe and Mail*. But can we imagine Salutin's imaginative probing without his commitment to ordinary people and to Canada? His insights about media are anchored in a few strong moral and political commitments.

Students in elementary and high school are much younger than Salutin and are often floundering — and why wouldn't they be? — with what they think life is all about. One key issue in this skills debate is whether the school still has a major role in helping students to clarify what the world is like, what their own personalities reflect, where we came from, what is worthy of allegiance, and what things need changing, before we plunge into a lot of analyzing of how the media *reflect* that world.

After years of lobbying at my school, I finally got thirty copies of *The Toronto Star* (half price) delivered each weekday morning. Each of my classes began, for at least ten minutes, with the students reading either articles of their choice or of my choice. Most days they also "wrote up" at least one article, i.e., three or four sentences describing the content of what they had read followed by three or four sentences of their opinion on the topic. If it was their own choice, it could be anything, including an ad, a cartoon or the horoscope, so long as they developed the opinion part of the answer. (For the horoscope, for example, after giving the prediction for that day for themselves, they could write about what they think of horoscopes in general.) The newspaper write-ups often formed the basis of a class discussion.

Using the newspaper daily for the entire course allowed us to follow stories that went on for many days, as well as doing what media people do, asking questions — what is an editorial, a column, a news story? what is bias? — but with the *prime purpose* being to get through to the news itself and to focus on what happens out there. We used the papers as windows on reality. Yes, we analyze the window, but not ad nauseam. Partly I solved the need for endless teaching about "detecting bias" by saying they should be suspicious of *everything* they read from large newspapers — what we on the left used to call the "boss press." (In any case, since most of my students were black, I didn't have to teach most of them to be suspicious of the official press!)

I've already suggested what the typical media skills teacher would do, often in an English class. The papers are ordered for only two to three weeks and the idea is to teach what different types of writing are found in that paper, how the business side of the paper works, how to detect bias and how two different newspapers can see the same story differently. The students then do a few practical assignments to show what they've learned.

There's no harm in this, except that even when armed with newspaper reading skills most students in our school will never read a newspaper again. Indeed, while they read that paper for three weeks and were supposedly "reading critically," they were merely acquiring mental techniques with very little use of those techniques on the stuff of existence, and with little use of that media itself to deepen their understanding of the world. I would even suggest that someone of my persuasion may have more respect for the medium than many media skills teachers, since I consider that particular non-tabloid paper, *The Toronto Star*, even with its overfocus on crime and its corporate liberal perspective, to be a gold mine for examining the stuff of existence.

I reiterate: is our emphasis to be on looking through the window of that particular piece of the media to life itself or is it to focus almost exclusively on the window? The effect of looking almost exclusively at the window is to see through everything and owe allegiance to nothing. At its most cynical, it is armchair analysis of how we're being screwed without any vision of what we might do about it. Your media analysis skills (separated from any belief in justice or equality) can lead you to suppose that you might as well stay with the bad that you know instead of risking the worse that you don't know. You have then become the very kind of cynical conservative on whom governments count for reelection. And this from a method that is supposedly meant to make you a thinking citizen!

It is the result of a piece of skills mania which is built on too little respect for helping sort out your root beliefs and too much respect for the mechanics of floating "critical thinking skills."

Rodin's *The Thinker*, renamed in the year 2000: *The Portable Generic Thinking Skills Worker.*

Media Literacy: A Form of Spirituality?

Floating is the word, but some people see more hope for rootless float-ing than I do; they also see more hope for rootlessness. One such person is Douglas Rushkoff, who wrote *Playing the Future: How Kids' Culture Can Teach Us to Thrive in an Age of Chaos*.[8] "People who are teaching media literacy today," said Rushkoff in a public speech in Toronto in February 1997, "whether we like it or not and whether we realize it or not, are teaching a form of spirituality." Rushkoff reassures us that snowboarding and raves are not tools of the devil. But neither for me are they the great sacraments of liberation and community that Rushkoff thinks they are.

Surfing the Internet or channel flipping on TV may help you find something you want to see, but let's remember that this surfing is need-ed mostly because of the inordinate amount of crap floating around these media. Our kids have invented marvellous "coping skills" to deal with the chaos and crap of the 1990s, but let's not elevate such things to the level of spirituality. It's only because Rushkoff finds the state of floating something very special that he can imagine media literacy as a religion. (One media literacy teacher in Toronto actually called his field "inherently left wing!")

I had these romantic ideas in the 1960s too, seeing every fad of youth as another example of communalism, mental health, openness and ecstacy — but even back then I didn't romanticize the dropout strategy the way Rushkoff does.[9] I didn't say, "some day there'll be a war and nobody will show up." McLuhan had the same problem as Rushkoff. They're both right that in the past we downplayed the place of media in historical change and we also downplayed the place of youth. But sorry, economics and political power are still deeper causes of such change, and we do a dis-service to youth's coping skills to call them revolutions.

I don't see theories like Rushkoff's being realistic about how youth can find a regular source of funds, a protective community (especially if their families aren't providing this) and, finally, some connection with one of the many political struggles to extend the power and the where-withal of ordinary people. The young people I saw in my high school classes are hurting a lot. Raves, skateboarding and channel-switching aren't curing that pain.

To complete our glance at new fields outside traditional subject areas, chapters 2 and 3 will cover the topic of the collaboration method, as seen by skills proponents.

CHAPTER 2

Collaboration and Collaborators

The Cooperative Way to Compete: The Case of Collaborative Skills

In these next two chapters I will examine another of the Information Age's favourite new fields: teamwork, as it's usually called in business, and collaboration, as it's usually called in schools.

Why an Old Method Is Getting a New Twist

Group work was around in education well before the restructuring revolution in business, but the large changes in corporations have given the method a new lease on life — with a different meaning than I was used to. How people get along in groups is not a new interest in education, but the skills experts claim they have a completely new approach to it. It is obviously not an old "subject of study" like history or science, but a method.

The practical format of the method is familiar to most people: for a topic like "multiculturalism and its affect on national unity," the teacher divides the class into five groups with six people in each, and the point is to discuss an aspect of the topic in each group and then report back to the class. It is a familiar format for adult groups, too. Except for the most traditional, for whom "teacher-centred education" is a proud badge, this method, responsibly carried out, is generally thought useful to air and debate certain topics. I happen to agree and I have used the cooperative method often.

Kids don't always agree with it. Many sharp kids hate group work because most people in the group are lazy, they say, and most of the work falls on one or two people. Sometimes everyone gets the same mark, and those students who have worked harder have to complain and create hard feelings to get their proper credit. Group people are aware of this complaint, but they say the situation is avoidable if teachers consciously make groups work properly.

I agree. Groups have worked very well for me, and I have considered group work a cornerstone of my opposition to the pervasive individual competition and rating system that dominates our schools. For me, this method has not only included the well-known technique of breaking up a class into groups of four to six people to discuss a topic but has often been a project involving a whole class or several classes and has sometimes included parents.

For years, for example, after two grade 9 classes had finished reading Bill Freeman's book *Shantymen of Cache Lake*, a historical novel about lumberjacks in the 1870s, I had them stay overnight at the school and cook the lumberjacks' staple meal of pork and beans for eighteen hours in three huge iron kettles over a wood fire to feed the whole school, 1300 students, the next day. We're talking two hundred pounds of white beans, fifty pounds of salt pork, fifty pounds of brown sugar, twenty cups of molasses, twelve cups of hot dry mustard and twelve large bags of onions. We're also talking about them baking 1500 rolls of homemade bread the previous day. Everyone had to take part and no marks were awarded. The proof of success was that 1300 fussy fellow students liked the meal.

When the second-semester grade 9 classes complained that they missed the bean bake, we invented another large class project based on the same lumberjack book and a companion in the same historical series, *The Last Voyage of the Scotian*, also by Bill Freeman.[1] It involved the class dividing into groups and building large model sailing ships, lumberjack cabins, log shutes, rivers and docks; and all of this was displayed in front of an enormous thirty-foot oil painting on three pieces of 8ft. x 4ft. plywood laid on three long tables in a row. The creation took up the entire length of a classroom. This work, taking over four weeks to complete, culminated in a huge parents' night (I knocked on fifty doors so every student's family was represented by at least one family member) in which every student in the class had to take part, telling what she or he did for the project and what part of the two books it told about.

These classes were G level students who in Ontario's system were (and still are, under a different name) the ones who were streamed or tracked as the dummies. Everyone speaking to the assembled parents and brothers and sisters and grandmothers and grandfathers was an example of how "the dumb could speak."

In chapter 6, I present a group project that emerged from a huge demographic change in our school district in the early 1980s, when Chinese students gradually replaced Anglo-Saxons as the largest ethnic group in our high school. This project involved one class organizing a day to discuss China in world history and the Chinese language and culture in our district, and presenting it to the entire senior section of our high school. Experts came to the school to debate various related topics, student debaters joined them, and the group of four hundred voted on who won the debate. Every student in the audience turned in an anonymous reaction to how the day went, and feedback discussions were held in each separate classroom. We had organized the same sort of morning a few years earlier on the topic of the mercury poisoning of Aboriginal people in Northern Ontario, where native speakers, company speakers and students presented a debate to the four hundred senior students.

I'm talking about classes of students producing movies together, publishing books together, putting on specially focused song and variety shows, doing plays together and often getting these productions and shows out to other students in the school. Often many teachers besides myself were seriously involved, particularly in elaborate group efforts like the bean bake. And I'm not referring here to a small handful of keeno students doing these things. In all projects everyone in a class must take part, and non-marked cooperation is a key feature of the endeavour.

Enter the New Version of Collaboration

Imagine my surprise, then, when collaboration, as it was now to be renamed, became a much-promoted method of the new skills folk! We were to encourage collaboration because teamwork was apparently the way of modern business. We were told that the old group method that some of us had used for years was not the same thing at all. For one thing it wasn't scientifically nailed down and analyzed.

Elaborate charts and reporting techniques accompanied the new version of collaboration. But when you got beyond the window dressing of charts, lists and jargon, you came to the real difference: the new collaboration put virtually all the emphasis in the cooperative group on learning, not about an important topic, but about *how to work in a group*. For many of the most zealous cooperative learning people, what anyone learned about "multiculturalism and its affect on national unity" was strictly secondary. This was teaching "collaborative skills." Collaboration is one of education's top buzzwords these days, right up there with "outcomes," "learning styles" and "empowerment."

I have in front of me a form that one group approach recommends handing out to students involved in a group exercise. Filling in the form is meant to help students and their teacher become more conscious of how they are conducting their group — especially what their "collaboration" rating might be. (See Figure 2-1.)

Figure 2-1

Collaboration skills

STUDENT: _____   _____ DATE: _____

FORMING:
- move without noise
- stay with the group
- use quiet voices
- encourage participation by all
- use names
- look at the speaker
- use no put-downs

FUNCTIONING:
- direct group's work
- express support
- ask for help or clarification
- offer to explain or clarify
- paraphrase others' work
- energize the group
- describe feelings when appropriate

FORMULATING:
- summarize out loud
- seek accuracy by correcting and/or adding to summarize
- seek elaboration
- seek clever ways or remembering ideas and facts
- demand vocalization
- ask other members to plan out loud

FERMENTING:
- criticize ideas not people
- differentiate when there is disagreement
- integrate ideas into single positions
- ask for justification
- extend other members answers
- probe by asking in-depth questions
- generate further answers
- test reality by checking the groups work

Johnson & Johnson 1984

This entire chart under the term, "Collaboration skills," is a sub-heading of just one item on the chart below, i.e., "Collaboration," in the third column.

CRITICAL SKILLS

PROBLEM SOLVING	COMMUNICATION	PERSONAL
Focus	Speaking	Intra/Interpersonal
Organize	Reading	Organization/Time
Locate	Writing	Self-evaluation
Manage	Recording	Listening
Evaluate/Assess	Visualizing	Collaboration
Synthesize/Conclude		
Apply/Transfer		
Communicate		

One thing that fascinates me is the tendency of the skills people to get bigger and bigger lists and charts of all the skills you are supposed to acquire. In Figure 2-1 you'll see the first sub-heading "forming," and under it is a list as follows: "move without noise," "stay with the group," "use quiet voices," "encourage participation by all," "use names," "look at the speaker," "use no put downs." "Functioning," "formulating," "fermenting," all adds up to a cool, clinical message about how a group is supposed to work.

Now remember, something never mentioned on this assessment form is the TOPIC! There *is* presumably a topic, you see, but by the end you realize that, with this approach, what you're trying to find out about a topic is not the most significant thing. How you're working as a group is more important.

So what's wrong with that? you may say. Isn't that a good aim? Aren't we trying to encourage cooperation in our society? The American educator Herb Kohl, looking at this group cooperation emphasis rather carefully, calls it the "cooperative way to compete." He asked, Are people given report cards in groups? No, they're given to individuals. The bottom line for evaluation is still individual. You get a good *individual* mark in your group project for being a good cooperative person.

Furthermore, you are not marked primarily on how wise your ideas are on key topics or whether you can defend well ideas you have been discussing. (For this method, "wisdom," prioritizing content topics and defending ideas that might get you nearer to "the truth" are all part of the bad old conservative — and paradoxically bad old radical — aims of education. All talk of wisdom and idea priorities sounds like propaganda to exponents of skills mania.)

Figure 2-2

High-Performance, High-Skill Work Organization

Work Reorganization

Old Style	New Style
• Specific tasks, performed by specialists	• Tasks delegated to front-line workers
• Small group responsible for thinking, motivation, implementation and discipline	• Less indirect labour, fewer mistakes
• Standards and regulations	• Quicker response time
• Control by supervisors	• Requires workers with flexibility, problem-solving ability, ability to learn and communications skills
• Needs workers who follow instructions and perform rote tasks	• Emphasizes teamwork

The Conference Board of Canada

Source: National Center on Education and the Economy, 1990.

Note that in stressing the teaching of ideas and how to defend them, I am not supporting ramming views down students' throats. Of course we don't want teachers to lay on an imposed ideology, whether the teacher is a conservative fundamentalist, a marxist or even a cooled-out skills proponent. But assuming we are seriously guarding against this kind of oppression and propaganda, surely there is still a place, even while using the group technique, for teaching and debating how the world works, not just how the school thinks you should act in groups.

The Business Origin of the New Collaboration

Turning now to the corporate sector, there's a remarkable similarity between this emphasis on groups in school and the new emphasis on teams in business. Figure 2-2 shows how the Conference Board of Canada, in lectures they give to school administrators, illustrates how teams fit in with the new business and industry.

These charts can become quite extravagant. Figure 2-3 is a version by Stanley A. Brown.[2] Corporations that consider themselves trailblazers like Nortel and General Electric use similar ones for management seminars.

Sounds like a veritable love-in of togetherness and cooperation. The trends these charts refer to are real, and deeply imbedded in major technological and organizational changes. But for workers it's not quite as cozy as it sounds, as the work of Nancy Jackson, David Robertson and Doug Noble has shown. The whole scheme sounds great until you start asking whether a "secretary" in a team gets the same pay as her other teammates, like the manager; whether the teams on the shop floor are ever given substantial decisions to make; and whether many of these "empowered," flexible, multiskilled workers are doing anything more substantial than monitoring a bunch of machines.[3]

Even people as extravagant in their praise of restructuring industry as Tom Peters and Robert Waterman admit that we're usually talking about the *appearance* of empowerment, not the real thing. They have nothing against *appearances* from a business point of view, but they do keep the distinction before their readers. In their bestseller *In Search of Excellence*, they comment about customers who are asked to sample four unmarked cans of soft drinks instead of two: "The fact that we *think* we have a *bit* more discretion leads to *much* greater commitment." (Italics are theirs.) Although it's consumers in this example, Peters and Waterman are careful to make the same distinction when talking about increased *worker* participation.[4]

A later book by Tom Peters, with the swinging title *Liberation Management: Necessary Disorganization For the Nanosecond Nineties*, has lost much of the earlier book's distinction between the reality and the appearance of power. The newer book has over eight hundred pages, mostly profiles of business trailblazers. It's written in adoring, upbeat language.

Peters's models of educators most in tune with the needs of restructuring corporations are Ted Sizer and Dennis Littky.[5] Sizer began the Coalition of Essential Schools and wrote two books about this "essential schools" approach. Littky's school, when *Liberation Management*

Figure 2-3

Management Paradigm

Old	New
Authoritarian	Coach/Mediator
Rigid	Flexible
Clear lines of authority	Blurred/ambiguity
"Do"	Delegate
Decision maker	Empower others to make decisions
Narrow Focus	Broad Focus
"Own" the program	Employee ownership/manager/ eliminates obstacles
Stifles ideas	Promotes creativity
Keeps information	Shares information
Manages defined tasks	Manages complexity
Train	Develop competencies
Specialist	Generalist
Administrator	Manager
Linear thinking	Intuitive thinking
Manager by control	"Pathfinding"
Top Down	Bottom Up

Employee — Self Determination Paradigm

Old	New
Master/Servant relationship	Employee/Manager partnership
Goals imposed	Control over one's work
Standard hours	Variable hours; alternate work arrangements
Individualism	Team; working with others
Promotion	Job satisfaction
Pay	Personal growth also important
Accept unilateral direction	Leadership/ownership of work
Rigid	Flexible
Hierarchy	Participation/democracy
Differentiation work and personal	Link work and personal
Relocate where required	Two careers — unwilling to relocate
Follow company line	Right to speak out/challenge
Rewarded from above	Rewarded from within/through peers
Loyalty to Company	Loyalty to self/ethics

came out, was Thayer High School in Winchester, New Hampshire; it was the first school Sizer chose for his coalition. Both educators place the teaching of thinking skills at the very top of their agenda and both are fascinated by the kind of free-floating, lithe minds that Peters believes are best for modern business. Littky also continues to be a principal who encourages inventive team projects and long-term field placements. Both Littky and Sizer recommend and have put into practice extensive structural changes in schooling along individualized curriculum lines. Even though I have chosen to focus on curriculum aims within current school structures, I still consider these two thinkers to be giants of the modern education debate.[6]

The Downplaying of Topics

To return to the question of "teams": what should the school's response be to this new stress on teams in business? *People and Skills in the New Global Economy*, a skills schooling bible I quoted in the Introduction, believes the direction should be obvious:

> Team work in the workplace is also increasing in importance. And yet our schools too often set students to work alone and competitively on isolated tasks, as though the assembly line and the traditional division of labour were still the models of production or office work we are preparing our students to enter. Work in this cooperative climate will place increasing emphasis on small group projects that combine skills, that require the organization of multiple tasks, that tie the groups own evaluation of work accomplished to the improvement of processes and skills at the group level. Group responsibility for the contribution of each of its members is a far surer buttress against individual failure than assigning individuals to groups pursuing simpler skills (by placing them in lower streams) or increasing the value accorded to lesser achievements (by lowering standards).[7]

To pursue this connection between business and education further, compare the business charts above with this school method summation of "How Co-operative Small Group Learning Works," from a book called *Together We Learn: Co-operative Small Group Learning*.[8]

> Co-operative small group learning is based on five common principles. Teachers whose group work is successful will generally find that they are applying these principles intuitively. Using the five principles intentionally to structure classroom activity enables teachers to improve the effectiveness of their small group activities. The five principles are:

1. Students work in positive interdependence;
2. Students work in small heterogeneous groups;
3. Students are accountable both as individuals and as a group;
4. Students learn through ample opportunity for purposeful talk;
5. Students learn and practice co-operative skills as they study and explore the subject matter together.

Same tone, same feeling and some of the very same concepts. The big difference, of course, is this: in the school setting this method encourages teachers to say that the topic the students are discussing is not that important (a suggestion that many teachers resist, since they thankfully still support the stress on topics), or that what you arrive at in the end is not that important; in business it's very clear what the aim is for the teams. The teams are meant to come up with better ways of making a profit for the firms they're working for. In a broader sense, however, this profit perspective turns out to be the perspective of the leading skills educators as well — even though such educators often get added moral authority for their methods by not mentioning the motto of business, *how do we stay on top?* as the business strategy EDGE puts it.[9]

At its worst, then, collaboration in group learning may produce "collaborators" with business who operate like collaborators did in World War II: the tune is called entirely by the big piper you're collaborating with. In 1964, Hannah Arendt remarked that the intention of totalitarian education was to destroy the capacity to form convictions, not to instill them. Liberal technocratic education may increasingly do the same thing by keeping students busy with skills and thereby preempting all struggle with content, topics and convictions — except as soft commodity "discussion skills" or "values ed." Teamwork, after all, can be skillfully managed.

We might ask, in this regard, whether "teams" of the "empowered" workforce of, say, Nortel, were asked whether they supported Nortel's plan to move work out of Canada. Or is it that the teams were called in and told: once we've decided to move work out of Canada, *you* can then decide how to break the news to the workers.

Similarly in school-based budgeting: "Here's the reduced amount of money your school can have. Now *you're* empowered to decide what programs and people to cut." You notice, getting back to the school context, how the "Collaboration Skills" chart says: "Use no putdowns," cool out the discussion, play down emotion. Don't imagine there's any kind of insight or understanding to get worked up about. After all, who will be able to get that worked up after graduating about producing better cellular telephones or better TV parts? And as for cutting staff or moving work out of the country, we'd *prefer* people who don't get worked up. It is as if the leading skills advocates are saying: When you leave school, somebody else will be assigning "aims" for you, just as they do at school. The important thing is primarily *how* you go about your assignment — or your non-assignment. I say non-assignment because often very trivial things are debated using this group education method. Some serious group exponents sometimes even take pride in that fact, because downplaying the topic puts even greater emphasis on the fact that students are learning how to work together, not how to iron out an important topic together.

Fighting and Rolling with a Deep Trend

Time will be needed for the skills mania to be proven wanting. For now, there's a sense in which we have to go into the middle of it and, when we see through some of the problems, blow a whistle or two and roll with what emerges. It's guerrilla action time. So, for example, as you saw earlier in the chapter, I have used teams — excuse me, groups! — but have emphasized to my students that we were looking for the truth about what we were studying together. Imagine an old pursuit like that in a modern classroom! Also we tried to work out what needs changing in the world and what can be changed. Imagine a political pursuit like that in a classroom! We tried to explore and debate serious topics. This was never an armchair debate, where ideas could be tossed around as if they were as insignificant and formless as trivial facts. That entire enterprise is without commitment and without a sense that certain ideas, if sincerely believed, have serious consequences in action.

This tendency to downplay topics, issues and beliefs runs throughout current education. Note, for example, how a London, Ontario, high school teacher, Brian Kellow, says he develops "a topic" in his student writing program:

> In my senior English classes (Grades 11, 12 and OAC) we first develop a topic, based upon the literature at hand. It may involve the tragic flaw in the character of Hamlet. It may involve the speculations about language and consciousness examined in a splendid essay by William H. Gass entitled, "The Unspeakable State of Soliloquy." *The actual subject of the piece possesses much less importance than the student's attempt to confront and express difficult ideas.*[10] (Italics are mine.)

* * *

With this next chart I will show the extremes to which some coopera-tive educators can go. If there's a big group of twelve people, here's the role for each student that one expert recommends: one student would be the recorder (take down the main things said), one would be the time-keeper, another person the reporter, another person the materials collec-tor, another the encourager, another the summarizer, another the prober, another the energizer, another the clarifier, another the questioner, another the initiator and finally the last, the checker. This is a real list. It was given out at a conference for teachers in 1990 in the Toronto area. Each task has a phrase or two explaining it. Here it is:

Group Roles

1. Recorder — records the ideas, thoughts and suggestions of the group
2. Timekeeper — keeps the group on task within the specified time
3. Reporter — reports the group's findings to the class or teacher
4. Materials collector — gathers all the materials to conduct the assignment
5. Encourager — stimulates the participation of all group mem-bers by inviting reluctant or silent group members to partici-pate
6. Summarizer — summarizes the material at appropriate inter-vals allowing group members to check their understanding
7. Prober — in a pleasant way, keeps the group from superficial answers — encourages group to explore all possibilities
8. Energizer — stimulates and enlivens the group when it starts lagging
9. Clarifier — attempts to get members to remove any ideas which are unclear (ambiguities)
10. Questioner — asks questions to help get more information
11. Initiator — gets group started
12. Checker — asks questions to ensure that everyone under-stands

(Source: handout at a Metro Toronto teachers' conference in 1990.)

One joker, when I showed him this list, asked: "Where's the boss? Is there no chairperson?" There are lots of other questions we could ask about words like "information" and "on task" and "in a pleasant way." There's also a whole other issue about the value of teaching sophisti-cated political techniques to small elementary children or even students in grade 10 — although I am aware of Jerome Bruner's old point about how capable children are of learning many such things. But I'm going to limit my focus to one big question. The question jumps out at me above all others as soon as I've finished reading the list. With all these discrete tasks to concentrate on, how is there any time left to discuss an issue? People are so weighed down with tasks! People who take part in these groups a lot say that when a group gets excited about the topic itself, people forget about all these tasks. People who have this experience are, thankfully, challenging the main purpose of this method — to learn tasks. They are on a general *quest* or *search* that tasks like these should be anchored in, not something that overwhelms it.

Furthermore, I am suggesting that people who emerge from this method with lithe, open and anchorless minds are the very kind of employees who are most useful for teams and thinking skills at places like Nortel. Never mind that they are not too anchored, that they're weak in their understanding of life, of themselves or of what needs changing in the world. The corporations are happy to supply their own versions of these missing ingredients.

In the next chapter I offer classroom examples, positive and negative, of the collaboration method in practice.

CHAPTER 3

Collaboration Part II

Curriculum Examples, Weak and Strong

Beautiful Covers and Good Visuals

A teacher said to me, "I don't make students memorize textbooks. They forget all that. I give them projects." Which reminded me that once, when I raised the role of Métis leader Louis Riel in Canadian history in a grade 12 class, one student said: "Me and two friends did a co-operative project in grade 9 on Louis Riel and I got an A plus." I asked her if she still had the project. She did, so I said I'd love to see it. It turned out to have the familiar ingredients: a beautiful cover, a little play where a modern-day reporter asked Riel questions about leading the Rebellion, a map of parts of Western Canada where Riel and the Métis lived and fought, and some encyclopedia information. My student, though, remembered nothing, absolutely nothing, about why Louis Riel is important, when he lived and died, who the Métis were, and their past and present place in Canadian history. And this is the method this student's teacher probably thought was the answer to old-fashioned rote learning where you forgot it all after the exam!

Projects with attractive covers, essays with clearly stated (but trivial) theses, class presentations with good visuals. Where's the substance? What has been learned? What insight has been gained? My point is that we cannot just blame this lack of substance on bad teaching. Bad government curriculum aims are often the cause.

An Example from a Family Studies Class

Another example: A friend of mine who teaches Family Studies is struggling with these same questions about collaborative learning. Here she describes her criticisms as they emerged doing a unit on prenatal education. The unit concluded with a group exercise and a teaching game. My friend introduced me to the exercise:

> Let's look first at this evaluation sheet entitled "Group Presentations — Peer and Self Evaluation." [See Figure 3-1.] I know you hate charts but they're a big deal in education these days — also in business, by the way.

What was the context in which you used this sheet? I asked.

> You should assume that the separate group research period was finished and each group was now presenting to the class in turn. This sheet was given to the students who were the audience while other people in the class were presenting information on prenatal care of women and influences on the prenatal period.
>
> The topics of different groups were things like the effects of drugs on the fetus and on the mother. Caffeine effects. Also alcohol, the whole problem of fetal alcohol syndrome. Also fitness in pregnancy. What people could do in the way of exercise. So it was looking at that period between conception and birth and what things could go on there that would result in a healthy child and mother and what things might not.
>
> The students were mostly in groups of three. Some of them worked in twos and there was only one person who did it by herself because she skipped classes and came late a lot. Anyway, the whole class had this evaluation form which we seem to have in the department. I don't know who made it up or where it came from. As you can see from the sheet, each column is worth five marks and they total fifteen.

For you, I ask, what is weak in the way this sheet awards marks?

You'll notice that it does say at the bottom "do not give over 10

Figure 3-1

GROUP PRESENTATIONS—PEER AND SELF EVALUATION

TOPIC:_____

GROUP MEMBERS:_____   _____

_____   _____

_____   _____

_____   _____

CONTENT/ INFORMATION	ORGANIZATION	OVERALL PRESENTATION
___clear	___group prepared and ready to teach	___variety of methods used/ did not just talk
___organized well	___each member knew what they were to do	___generally group members spoke clearly
___gave enough information so the topic was understandable	___time was used wisely	___was interesting
___remained on topic	___moved smoothly from one person to the next	
	___an introduction and conclusion were given	___ able to answer questions
___appeared to know and understand the information presented		___involved the other class members
/5	/5	/5
		TOTAL /15

NOTE: 10/15 is an average mark. Do not give high marks for mediocre work.

for a mediocre presentation." But what is mediocre? To me a mediocre presentation is one where the substance of the presentation is not great. Where students don't understand what they're talking about, where they haven't really gotten the gist of what this is all about. But when you examine the subheadings of this sheet, you notice that they don't really get at "mediocre" in this sense.

One comment says "gave enough information." Nothing about the quality. The last item in the first column is "appeared to know and understand the information presented." That's the only place where there's anything about the quality of work. Notice, though, in the marking scheme that this counts for only one mark out of fifteen! People tick off items then they say, well, I've got five ticks so this person gets five in column one.

The second column, ORGANIZATION, has items like "does each person know what they're to do?" "Were they ready?" — all that kind of thing. "Introducing, concluding." Then in the last column: "Did they use a variety of methods, for example, visuals." "Did they speak clearly?" "Was it interesting and were they able to answer questions?"

That's one other place where you might say the *quality* of their work is recognized as important. But there's nothing that really says to them what's important here is that you have really learned something about this prenatal period. So the other students are more inclined to give high marks if the people are bright and cheery and maybe have a little skit and they do a few novel things. And maybe someone else has really understood this, but their presentation is not skillful. And they might be shy. And a number of English as a Second Language students, for instance, who probably have understood this, if not in English, at least in their own language, can't do a presentation that's spiffy, and so they end up with lower marks.

I'm questioning this. I'm wondering how to revamp this form so it means more.

I question my friend further. What is your answer to the common complaint about group work made by some successful students: "Oh, I did all the work and the other three just goofed off"?

Well, I'll come to that with this second sheet called "Peer & Self Evaluation for Group Presentations." [See Figure 3-2.]

It's filled in by the group itself, evaluating itself. They take this sheet and they write down their own name and whoever else is in the group. Then they write what each person did down to details like who looked up what and who typed what.

The main purpose of this section is to evaluate something the teacher couldn't possibly know — whether one person did everything and the rest goofed off, etc. But once again it doesn't bring out anything about *understanding* or *excitement about the material* or *insight*. It doesn't mark anything like that, it marks things like punctuality, being prepared, this sort of thing.

Figure 3-2

PEER & SELF EVALUATION FOR GROUP PRESENTATIONS

TOPIC:_____

Group Member	Job Done	Presentation	Total
	List, in point form, all the tasks actually done by each group member. Give each group member a mark out of /10 for this work.	Give a mark out of /5 to each group member based only on the following factors: punctuality, contribution, being prepared, participation in the presentation.	Add the two marks to give a total out of /15

So I add all this up as their teacher and I feel I'm not getting at what I think are the central issues for this unit. These forms channel me into giving the highest recognition for how slick everything is, for whether they put on a skit, for whether they type things up neatly. And maybe actually *knowing about what alcohol does to the fetus* is getting lost in the shuffle.

Now here's another exercise called Review Bingo. It's from a Family Studies text, from one of its workbooks, and it comes at the end of three chapters on prenatal development, labour and childbirth. The students first get a list of fifty terms. [See Figure 3-3.]

Then they get the fifty definitions, like this one for amniocentesis: "the process of withdrawing a sample of fluid surrounding an unborn baby with a special needle for testing." The students are supposed to be reviewing the meanings of the words by matching them up with the definitions. When the game itself starts, the teacher reads out a definition. The students have put away their list of definitions. The students have a regular Bingo card on which they have written twenty-five of the fifty words — making every card different. If they think they have the word that fits the definition the teacher reads out, they put a marker (in our class, a dried pea) on that word. Obviously, there's a bit of a test of their knowledge here.

Figure 3-3
Terms

amniocentesis	fetus	pediatrician
amniotic fluid	fixed expenses	placenta
anemia	fontanels	premature
antibodies	forceps	prenatal
birth defects	fraternal twins	prepared childbirth
bonding	genes	recessive
cell division	grasp reflex	reflexes
cervix	identical twins	rooming-in
chromosomes	incision	rubella
colostrum	incubator	Siamese twins
contractions	infertility	sickle cell anemia
dilate	labor	sterile
Down syndrome	miscarriage	ultrasound
episiotomy	nurse-midwife	umbilical cord
fertility analysis	obstetrician	uterus
fetal alcohol syndrome	ovum	variable expenses
fetal position	paternity leave	

Sounds like *this* game emphasizes knowledge, doesn't it, I ask?

So far, yes. But in the midst of playing this game this year, a student said, "Once we call out Bingo, do we have to read off our words and give the definitions?" Having played this game before, I said, "No, you just have to say that you've got the words." But suddenly I said — "Hey, that's a better idea, because that would show whether you really know them." Groans from the class. "Oh, we don't want to do that. That would mean we'd have to know them."

Without the checkup which the student suggested, their knowledge of the definitions can be fuzzy and there's some scope for looking on someone else's card, etc. I admit the game is fun. They like the idea of playing Bingo. They like winning. But from now on, though, I think I'll follow the student's suggestion.

Here's a highly acclaimed Family Studies teacher struggling against the trend being pressed on her to substitute soft "presentation skills" for solid knowledge and conviction about the subject she's teaching. I am not saying that teaching students how to work together or how to speak publicly are not important. But I am saying that we must put first things first. All skills teaching must be anchored in a challenging curriculum.

Why are the students learning to work in groups? What are these collaborative skills *for*? Why, in some of these methods, are the *topics* discussed in groups so downplayed? Or, to put it the way I've been expressing it in this book: What are the skills rooted or anchored in?

Two Projects Where Skills Are Rooted

I now offer a project I conducted with my graduating year Black History class (Canada and the United States since Slavery) as a year-end wrap-up. Like the Family Studies example, it culminated in a presentation. Also like the Family Studies example, it involved cooperation in groups.

The year before, this same class had taken the grade 12 Black History class on Africa and the West Indies, and during their last six weeks they had made a video about the black and Italian district where I live, near the corner of Eglinton and Oakwood in the York section of Toronto. Because my house was in the district, it became the planning centre from which student crews fanned out to do their interviews and their on-location shooting. We are fortunate to have a specialty course at our school in TV production, and a few students in that program were also in our class. They were a valuable resource for camera work, editing and studio insertion of stills and titles. We needed wide cooperation from the school administration and other teachers to assist students to get time off for this filming. The class was in on the planning throughout the project.

In that period (late 1980s and early 1990s) the district we were filming was under fire in the media for a few violent incidents that had occurred over the last several years, and the video investigated this reputation through interviews with the local black councillor, the police, local merchants, *Share* newspaper (a large circulation black weekly) and the principal and some senior students at the local high school. The project was certainly a success of collaboration, and it taught many skills besides cooperation. Its general purpose — for black history students to produce a short documentary analyzing a much-maligned black district — was clearly an anchor beyond the skills.

Unfortunately, the project was marred by running out of time in June. A final edited copy of the video was produced, but the time was not available to shorten it to normal, viewable length. That is why I have decided to pass on in more detail the project this class produced one year later.

An Eagle's-Eye View of Black History

The class had three weeks to prepare the presentation called *An Eagle's Eye View of Black History*. The class and I spent three days plus homework assignments working out the following fourteen sub-topics, each of which was to be handled by two students:
1. The Birthplace of Humanity and the Splendour of Ancient Africa
2. Columbus a Hero? Europe Conquers the World
3. The Scourge of Slavery
4. The Breaking In (or Seasoning) of Slaves
5. The Haitian Revolution and the Maroons
6. The U.S. — 13 Colonies, the War of Independence & the U.S. Constitution
7. Civil War, Jim Crow and the Migrations
8. The Civil Rights Movement
9. The U.S. Today
10. Blacks in Canada
11. Black Women in Canada, the U.S. and the Caribbean
12. Migrations from the West Indies
13. Modern Africa
14. Toronto Today
15. Two students tell the story of "The Eagle Who Thought He Was a Chicken."

For all items except numbers 4 and 15, one of the two people on each team was to give a short speech on their (mostly chosen) topic of no more than four minutes, the other — and here was one of the novel features — was to draw freehand a map from memory, which was projected onto a screen and illustrated simultaneously the speech his or her partner was giving.

Topic 4 was to break with the "speech and map" pattern and be a two-person skit. Should students be role-playing one of the the most vicious aspects of slavery, one that is still left out of most accounts of it? (See, e.g., a much-used modern textbook called *The African American Experience: A History* in Appendix A, number 3, second listed text). It must be clear to a class as it was clear to Malcolm X that one is presenting or portraying a wicked, criminal activity that did not finally work for the oppressors. The atmosphere and attitude to the preparation and presentation of the small drama are crucial. I believe that for my students it worked.

Text of Skit #4: The Breaking In (or Seasoning) of Slaves

It was stressed by the previous speaker under topic 3, "The Scourge of Slavery," that the white plantation owners feared the black slaves unless they captured not only their bodies, but tried to capture their minds as well. This meant trying to remove all the old identities and allegiances of the slaves.

Scene: *White male overseer stands, facing audience, legs astride, with apparent whip in hand. Directly in front of him a black woman kneels facing audience, head to the side and fear in her eyes. To the side, but completely visible and part of the act, are three sound effects people with a real whip, real drum and doll that cries.*

Woman: Now that you've taken me from my land, at least I have my name.

[*Sound of whip and overseer swings his fake whip against woman's back. She flinches with facial sign of great pain.*]

Overseer: We will take your name. You shall no longer be Maya Asante. You shall henceforth be Jean Smith, after your white slave owner.

[*Woman recovers and raises her head again in dignity.*]

Woman: Now that you've taken my land and my name, at least I have my own culture and my religion. [*She acts as if drumming — real drummer is to the side but in plain view.*]

[*Sound of whip and overseer swings his fake whip against woman's back. She flinches with facial sign of great pain.*]

Overseer: We will take your culture and your religion. If you play your own music, and if you pray to any but the Christian god, you will be severely punished.

[*Woman recovers and raises her head in dignity.*]

Woman: Now that you've taken my land, my name, my culture and my religion, at least I can speak my own Yoruban language.

[*Whip again. Woman flinches in pain.*]

Overseer: You shall no longer speak your native language from Africa. You shall henceforth speak English only, like your owner.

Woman: [*gradually recovers*] Now that you've taken my land, my name, my culture, my religion and my language, at least I still have my family. [*Woman mimes rocking her baby in her arms. Sound of baby offstage.*]

[*Whip, flinching and painful reaction.*]

Overseer: You shall no longer have your family. Your husband will be sold to a different landlord. And as for that baby, its head will be severed from its body. [*Grabs the baby. Takes a pretend sword and slices off its head. Woman has a look of horror. Then the overseer whips her again (sound of whip) and the scene ends with a freeze. Woman has a look of horror but determination on her face.*]

At the conclusion of many run-throughs in many classes, two initially very shy actors had blossomed and given very powerful performances. In fact what we all knew by the end was that this whole show was potentially powerful enough, if we chose, to be put on later for a full auditorium of students and adults.

Readers should remember that the *revolt* against slavery, the escape from slavery, even the attempts at enslaving the *minds* of a whole people did not finally work: these are finally the most emphasized part of this course. Many weeks are spent on the Haitian Revolution, on the Maroons and on all strategies to resist and overthrow slavery. In this light it seemed important to heed Malcolm X's urging that the wicked details of slavery, and the lengths to which the oppressors went, be taught in all their horror. The triumphs of freedom and revolution stand the taller for knowing how dastardly was the oppression.

The Eagle Who Thought He Was a Chicken

The wrap-up, topic 15, was a Jamaican folktale "The Eagle Who Thought He Was a Chicken." It was told by two students in back-and-forth style who learned how to recite it by hearing former Jamaican teacher and teacher union leader, Pat Wright, tell the story in patois in our class. Here is a summary of this version of the tale — another version of which was made into a book by Michal Wynn under the title *The Eagles Who Thought They Were Chickens*:[1]

A farmer tries to capture an eagle alive hoping to display her in a cage for paying customers. The eagle fights back to the point that the farmer shoots her dead, but not before she lays two eagle eggs which the farmer takes and puts under a hen. He is hoping the baby eagles will survive and he can then display the offsprings for profit. One eagle, who gets dubbed Tom by his brother, grows up thinking he's just a weird-looking chicken; he straightens his head feathers with geri-curl. His brother, whom the farmer calls Turk, listens to a wise old eagle who flies by. The old eagle tells Turk those head feathers are a crown because

Turk is really a king. Turk then learns to fly like an eagle and goes on a long trip to learn his history. The old bird tells Turk that Tom (who is now called Uncle Tom) is too brainwashed to care about his history.

They first fly over a deep valley called the Valley of Oppression. Turk is told he will survive the Valley of Oppression because he has the strength of kings in his wings. They then fly over the Desert of Mediocrity, the Desert of Don't Care, the Desert of only a C-average. Turk asks where he will rest but the old eagle says he will survive because he's got the strength of kings in his wings.

Finally they approach a high Mountain and Turk is afraid he'll crash into it. The old eagle says he'll fly over the Mountain of Injustice because he has the strength of kings in his wings. He succeeds and this version of the folktale ends.

Two Screens Share Attention without Competing

Eventually the two students told this powerful tale with a liberal dose of Jamaican patois.

Also facing the audience was a large video screen on which the final team of four students projected each topic title followed by film clips, appropriately chosen, from movies such as *Roots, Burn, The Autobiography of Malcolm X, Boyz in the Hood, The Million Man March, The Conquest of Paradise* (about Columbus), *Glory, Eyes on the Prize* and *Cry Freedom*, most of which the students had studied during their two years of Black History. As I expected, most of the students did not find having two visual centres of attention off-putting. They gave their attention mostly to the speech and map because of the novelty of the live, "from-memory" map drawing, which also synchronized well with the speech. They would also give quick glances to see appropriate silent images — which, incidentally were not so well synchronized with the presentations!

Audience of 125 People

The audience for this show was my own class augmented by three extra senior classes (total audience: 125). The students in one of the three classes were studying TV; they were asked by their teacher to turn in anonymous evaluation sheets that stressed presentation techniques. The ratings had no bearing on marks, but the students showed a lot of respect for the presentation, even though their teacher had warned me to expect critical reactions. Here is a sample of written comments from students who chose to go beyond circling numbers 1-5 to indicate general quality:

> This presentation was very good and I enjoyed everything the speakers spoke about. It was educational.
>
> I thought that the kids did a great job. One problem was that the video segments and the presenters were not in synch.
>
> I think you should have had some soft music in the background as the presentation was going on. That would have made a better impact on your audience.
>
> It was excellent.
>
> The presentation was very informational. The speakers showed they spent a lot of time with their work.
>
> There was not much on Canada. I didn't see the reason for the videos — they didn't introduce them or say what they were about or even where the scenes were from. Overall it was good, though. I liked the plays.

Skills Training in This Project

Skills teaching was very prominent in this project. To begin with, teaching students how to do an effective four-minute speech that catches the highlights in a concrete and vivid fashion is a demanding task. This was also a four-minute speech to be heard by 125 people. This was far from being a little homework assignment that the teacher could hand back with a few comments — and where the stakes are often all too low. (I've certainly done this myself.)

The four minutes also had to be coordinated, with the pacing of the speaker matching the pacing of the mapmaker — and all this worked out so that the audience heard and saw a unified piece.

At first this map drawing from memory induced a lot of fear: "I'll freeze up and forget the shape of Africa." "My map of the Caribbean will look so different from the original they'll laugh me off the stage." Lots of practice time in class helped dispel these fears.

Once they had "bought in," I knew the map drawers could count on the audience to be knocked out by this unusual skill. The student who drew the whole world (minus bits of Asia!) to tell the story "Columbus a Hero? Europe Conquers the World" was very proud of himself. Several teachers told me he had said "Hey, Ms. ___, how dja like my map?"

Was that my only reason for teaching a skill that has always been thought unnecessary when outline maps are easily available? No, impressing people was not my only reason. The maps are one small example of a skill that is *rooted or anchored* in a deeper purpose. Each of the thirteen maps in this project *teaches a concrete lesson*. It could be the triangular slave trade of the fifteenth to the nineteenth centuries; the migrations of blacks north and west in the U.S. after the Civil War; or why certain concentrations of black population came to Nova Scotia, in Canada, after the American War of Independence, why certain slaves came here before the Civil War (to southern Ontario) or why many West Indian blacks came to Toronto and Montreal after 1960. The students were drawing these maps to make public points about the history of their own people.

Skills Anchored in Telling Your Own History

Which brings me to my main point about this project. The main purpose of the project was for students of African Canadian and American history to present an interesting summary of their history to 125 fellow students. The main purpose was not to show their facility at map drawing, speaking and choosing film clips. It was not to show how to put together a multimedia presentation. It was to teach African and diasporan history.

It was not to "teach cooperation," although it did that for most of the students. Learning cooperation came mostly in the many class periods when different acts tried out their piece on the rest of the class. The class had non-stop recommendations for changes. The general desire in the class to make a good "whole presentation" was such that recommended changes were not resented.

I think the good cooperation had a lot to do with this not being a project for marks. I do not downplay marks. I give lots of marked tests and regular exams. By and large it is knowledge and the ability to debate ideas (as expressed in writing and speaking) that I test. This project would work if individual marks were awarded, but I think it teaches a better lesson about the differentness of cooperation without marks. I noticed that some of my students would occasionally say, "I really like this class" when it was clear that they mean they like *the people in the class*. I very consciously tried to build this feeling by what one student called a "talk show" technique (it was pre-Jerry Springer days!) of drawing people out and personalizing questions when they didn't embarrass a student. "Remember you said on your last test that you didn't like how Spike Lee turned the zoot suits and walks into a stage show. How do you think they're shown in the *Autobiography* itself?"

I was eager to build a group that searched for truth together. If members of the class were also encouraged to offer their own special contributions, they ended up appreciating each other more. This is a long way from what Kohl called "the cooperative way to compete." Is this teaching cooperation? If so, I'm for it.

CHAPTER 4

English

Literature and Film Shrink, Language Grows

We come now to the first of seven chapters that will examine how the skills philosophy has responded to traditional subjects. Since the doctrinaire skills enthusiasts do not believe in traditional subjects (see Bill Spady's revamping of education disciplines at the beginning of chapter 1), it is often an unreal, or even surreal business to examine a skills approach in a traditional discipline. Nevertheless, there is a relatively clear skills premise that gets imposed on each traditional discipline by those who are reconciled for the moment with keeping traditional disciplines; keep 'em but transform 'em, is their motto. The premise running through all serious skills revamping is: What are the principles by which this traditional subject is done or constructed? Learning *how to* do something rather than spending a long time actually doing it. Skills people readily admit you need at least some content to learn the skills of "doing" a subject. But you don't need much.

And so we turn to our first traditional subject, English.

At one time — roughly from 1900 to 1960 — the "queens of the sciences" in North American high schools were English and history, magisterial subjects, as I said in the Introduction, that made sense of all the other subjects. Traditional exponents of this idea said that English taught *character* through its choice of poetry, novels, essays and plays. History taught *citizenship*. Mathematics was important, but English and history set out life's human meaning.

Older Ideas of English Teaching

In the Introduction I mentioned that my first teaching job was in an American military academy in Tennessee. I ended up there because I was at loose ends in England in 1958 after getting my Cambridge degree. An American colleague at Cambridge had been offered a job at this academy by the headmaster who knew him and, since my friend wasn't interested, he recommended me for the job. I went there for an adventure, not thinking I would teach for more than two years, and not expecting to find a mentor who would set my sights on teaching for the rest of my life. And so, at my first school, wearing the green uniform of an American army teaching captain, I got started in English and history.

Soon after I arrived I came under the sway of a remarkable man called Bill Goldfinch. Goldfinch was a very unlikely person to be teaching at a military academy. He was a wrestler who had made his two aims in the army during World War II to have the biggest chest on the base and to read all of Shakespeare five times. To me he seemed to know the Bible by heart, but he was a very unusual, existentialist kind of believer who was well acquainted with Kierkegaard, Dostoievsky, Joyce and Buber. He was as handsome as a movie star, he walked on the wild side and was constantly close to being fired for saying outrageous things to students. Yet here is what one of his old students wrote about him in 1994:

> I was a student at the Sewanee Military Academy 1957-59 during the time that Bill Goldfinch was there as a teacher. He was not only my junior English teacher, but my wrestling coach, friend and mentor. I had wondered over the years what had become of him and I hoped that one day I would have a chance to tell him what an influence he had been on my life and how fondly I had thought of him for the past 35 years. In spite of the fact that I have had about ten years of school since graduating from SMA in 1959, he still gets my vote for the best and most inspirational teacher that I have ever had.
>
> I thought of him often during the time that I was a POW in

North Vietnam as I tried to recall the bits and pieces of my life and education. However, it was not difficult at all to remember sitting in his classroom and listening for the first time to a recording of Browning's "The Bishop Orders His Tomb at St. Praxed's Church," or discussing *For Whom the Bell Tolls*, *The Brothers Karamazov*, lectures by Lionel Trilling and the poetry of Dylan Thomas; all wonderful stuff that he brought to life for me and set me on a new path. (Porter Halyburton)

Goldfinch *was* fired in 1967, ostensibly for disobeying the headmaster and giving out what Bill called "agape candy" to students. (Bill was obsessed with the many meanings of the word "love" and "agape candy" was to be given out at the moments of high inspiration in the class.) In the headmaster's view it was the last straw of many disobeyed rules. For the alumni and some later school authorities, Goldfinch became a folk hero, and in 1999 a wrestling gymnasium was dedicated in his honour. Back in 1967 when he was fired, a friend of his, who was a poet and a professor of French and film at the University of the South next door to the military academy, wrote this poem to Bill:

The Turkey Vulture Who Lived His Literature

Dear Bill
I am lying in the grass by the farm pond
In the noonday sun
Writing this
With Guinevere nibbling the end of my pencil
And attacking me
A Cardinal is singing in the blackberry bush right next to me
A Turkey Vulture sails by
Bill Faulkner
I say to myself
(He wanted to turn into a buzzard when he died)
Finally living his literature
There aren't many who live their literature
Like Villon say and Emily Dickinson and Sylvia Plath
And Socrates and Mme de Sévigné and Virginia Woolf and your
     alter ego Bill Shakespeare
And Bill Blake and James Joyce and Alfred Jarry whose favorite
     expression was "beau comme la littérature"
And you
Who have just been kicked out of the Sewanee Military Acade-
     my for
living your literature

And taking too seriously your old friend Holden Caulfield
And his old friends Huckleberry Finn Ivan Karamazov and
　　Meursault
And their serious doubts about the higher advantages of
civilization
Also for serving candy in class against the rules
You old buzzard
You were corrupting the youth
Like Socrates no kidding
They were all very upset
"They"
The Guardians of Civilization
Those who don't live their literature
Those who live *off* their literature
Those who make up Curriculums
Those who enforce Discipline
Those who kill it for the kids
Those who think they're teaching them What Every Well-Edu-
　　cated Person Should Know
When they're really teaching What Every Intelligent Person Can
　　Readily Do Without
And you know what "they" do to people who take their litera-
　　ture too seriously
They don't serve them candy
They serve them hemlock
They kick them out of Secondary Schools
Well I could go on
You don't meet many Socrates
A person is lucky to meet one Socrates in the space of a lifetime
I consider myself lucky
Bill

— Scott Bates, 1967[1]

Eventually, after I had taught nearly forty years, I produced a book of Bill's own writings with extensive interviews about his life; I called it *The Prodigal Teacher*.[2] So fruitful was this early mentorship that when I puzzled about the best way to begin this chapter, some details about Bill's English teaching came flooding back to me from those years.

Bill's student mentions lectures by Lionel Trilling. In the autumn of 1957, Trilling gave a lecture at the University of the South called "Reflections on a Lost Cause: English Literature and American Education."[3] Bill took his junior English class and a reel-to-reel tape recorder to the lecture. The class then studied a transcript of the lecture and debated its ideas in class; afterwards, Bill and each of his students wrote letters to Trilling with their comments and questions.

The "lost cause" Trilling was talking about was a course familiar up to the 1950s in both American and Canadian high schools and universities: a survey of English Literature that tied the English literature of different periods to periods in English history. It was disappearing from American schools, said Trilling, because of competition from American literature, Great Books of the Western World, World Literature and Modern Literature. It would not come back, said Trilling, mostly because of the decline in the power of Great Britain.

To suggest what had been lost, however, Trilling borrowed a point he had made earlier about Freud. For Freud, the history and literature of Greece was "the other culture": an alternative way of life by which Freud could measure his own. That "other culture" for millions of literate white North Americans had been England — a thoroughly idealized England, of course, and not a favourite with Aboriginals, or the descendants of slaves, French Canadians and millions of third-world peoples. (For some black students today, that "other culture" is starting to be Africa; for some of us, it is the 1960s.) But many white, middle-class people in the 1950s would have identified with a sentence by J.B. Priestley found in the introduction to one of the favourite texts for the English literature survey course in both American and Canadian schools — *Adventures in English Literature*.[4] "Only twenty-one miles of water separate Dover from Calais, but these are perhaps the most significant twenty-one miles in the world. Time after time they have saved Britain from invasion and so have helped to preserve the liberties of Western Man."

You can also see Priestley's emphasis on "character formation" when he says that "it is not the calm, practical, outer man but the inner, secret, imaginative man, the Celt within, who really keeps us [Brits] going. What we are best at are precisely those tasks which demand imagination and inventiveness." Remember that this is an introduction to a book of English literature for high school students. Remember also that most of us middle-class whites didn't notice back in 1958 that the biggest bully empire in world history was not exactly a small beleaguered island defending the liberties of "Western Man."

I should point out here that I'm well aware that not everyone — not even all white, middle-class students — had so rosy an experience of the historical English literature approach as I did! My younger brother remembers going to high school in Nova Scotia in the 1950s and having to memorize quotes like "Carlyle was stumblingly great" from a textbook called *The Story of English Literature* by Edmund Kemper Broadus.[5] Students had to rhyme off these sentences spelling-bee-style when the teacher would call out authors' names: Donne! Carlyle! Anon! When I dug this book out of a library recently I was amazed to find that my brother had the phrase about Carlyle dead on, and he'd never been given a word of Carlyle's own writing.

Actually, Arthur said it was usually much more boring than that — the old "down each row, one desk at a time, each student taking one paragraph" method. With a lenient teacher you tried to go to the washroom in order to miss your turn.

My brother got nothing out of high school except football. One day in class he was reading a book his university brother gave him, André Gide's *The Immoralist*. The teacher, thinking he had caught someone reading torrid pornography, marched him down to the principal's office. Fortunately for my brother, the principal knew that Gide was accepted as famous and, when the teacher left, he gave the book to my brother and told him to go back to class. Art remembers memory work never having to be recited out loud, just written out. He and his friends always remember memorizing the punctuation at the end of each line separate from the poem: period, comma, nothing, nothing, semi-colon, comma, period, etc. In one history class the students had been given PERMS as the tag word to remember so that, for example, when describing the Fall of the Roman Empire, the headings to be used were Political, Economic, Religious, Military and Scientific. My brother and his friends changed the word to SPERM and found it easier to remember.

He remembers best when he finally turned off high school completely, after putting unusual effort into writing a short story. Students were told to take these words: "There was a screaming of brakes and then I lost consciousness. When I came to . . . " as the opening of the last paragraph of their story. My brother had decided to write about a man whose life was so bad that he considered death a boon. In Arthur's story the "hero" had a mindless job moving widgets on an assembly line, and his personal life was no better. Art's story concluded: "When I came to, I was devastated. I wasn't dead after all. I would have to go on living." The teacher stuck a B grade on the story with no comment, written or verbal. My brother says he remembers how much he was hoping for a reaction to this one. This was not parroting back "Carlyle was stumblingly great."

That was it. The big turn off. So much for the good old days.

Bill Goldfinch was also an early user of poetry records. He said this was better than being laughed at for reading English poetry with a Southern drawl. A two-record set called *Hearing Poetry,* with the English poetry arranged chronologically and edited by Mark van Doren, brought outstanding readers to Bill's students and to his not-so-secret teacher-in-training.[6]

Goldfinch's own letter to Trilling said that the Bible had been "the other culture" for him. (All Bill's wrestlers, to be on the team, had to memorize the Old Testament story of Jacob wrestling with an unknown man. They were also encouraged to write an essay about what they thought the story meant.)

The student letters to Trilling were honest and practical. One of his students told Trilling that since he, the student, had taken three different English literature classes patterned on English history in three different schools, Trilling was wrong about English literature disappearing. Another student said if Trilling would just talk in plain English, maybe he, the student, would understand him.

Goldfinch loved to start a semester with a kickoff reading that challenged the students to think about what they might get out of the literature in the course. Later in the 1980s, when he taught at a community college in Canada — the Doon Campus of Conestoga Community College in Kitchener, Ontario — he made frequent use of "An Imperial Message" by Franz Kafka. The Emperor on his deathbed sends a message just for you. The message never gets through, however, since the messenger encounters too many obstacles. Here was one student's reply:

> Think of the Emperor as yourself. You are dying from the day you are born. The message is to be delivered to yourself also. The messenger is part of you too. In fact the whole story never leaves your own mind. The messenger is a thought racing through your mind: endlessly searching for that innermost being, the messenger must break down all barriers which block his way. . . .
>
> The deeper within you run, the more fragmented you become. You can never find your true self by tearing out your insides.

Obviously you were to ponder, discuss and write about some pretty deep things in Goldfinch's classes. The core of his own philosophy always drove the aesthetics people, the ones who limited themselves to explaining metaphors and similes, round the bend. About every piece of literature he asked students, "What did you learn about yourself from reading this?" "The more the self knows, the more it knows itself," was one of his favourite quotes from Kierkegaard.

In Toronto a few years later, the teachers' college I was then required to attend gave me another aim for English. The historical method was verboten. So was Goldfinch's "know thyself." The Ontario philosophy was nearest to LitCrit, but our own Ontario version of it. You were to take students through a series of "Socratic questions" on short poems, short stories and short scenes from plays. The architect of the method, Bert Diltz — who, as the only English methods professor in the only faculty of education, had a monopoly on teaching all of Ontario's new English teachers from 1931 to 1958 — had this to say about his method:

> Like an artist, the teacher of poetry begins with his own subjective experience of the object he contemplates, namely the poem. Like an art, his achievement produces its ultimate effect in the very personal, subjective experience of the observer, namely the pupil. . . .
>
> If the poetry in our school anthologies is selected to illustrate a chronological order, literary movements, artistic forms, exotic symbols, beautiful images, competent craftsmanship, or to set a new standard in amusement value, how small is our hope of perceiving the attitudes of the great experiences of love, hope, despair, loneliness, friendship, courage, misery, sacrifice, serenity, honour, hypocrisy, gratitude, liberty, generosity, etc.![7]

"Without going into a lot of fine detail," says novelist, education writer and historian Donald Gutteridge, "it is evident here [author's note: the passage is much longer than the portion I quote] that Diltz was principally concerned with the aesthetic and moral dimensions, not of the body of literature per se but somehow of the experience of particular texts by individual readers."[8]

I didn't warm to the method myself, possibly because I usually saw it practised so stiffly and pedantically, with the underlying assumption being that every student must accept that whatever poem you were treading through was a perfect gem. "Why does the metaphor in line three move us?" is what sticks in my mind and my craw.

I gravitated more to Herb Kohl's *36 Children,*[9] a book about teaching in Harlem or, a decade later, to the British teacher Chris Searle, who in 1975 published *Classrooms of Resistance,* in which his London inner-city kids wrote about housing battles in their own neighbourhood, about Chile, about the British miners' strike of 1974, about the Irish "troubles." Photos of kids demonstrating with their parents were sprinkled throughout the book.[10]

What's Missing with Skills Mania?

Can one really say that aims as far apart as those of the Survey of English Literature course and *Classrooms of Resistance* had anything in common? Back in the 1960s we might have thought not, but once skills mania arrived we most certainly can. Listen to a quotation from another poetry record, which Bill Goldfinch's students and I heard in Sewanee, Tennessee, back in 1958. It is called *The Nature of Poetry* and the speaker is Professor Frank C. Baxter: "This record is for those who find poetry somehow curious and strange and rather difficult. . . . Believe me, poetry is not a pretty little business, an adornment on life. I'll try to show you that it is the poets above all others who seem in their hearts and in their determination most eager *to understand reality, to dive into the very depths of things that are important in human living*. It is a way as truly as that of science, philosophy or theology of *searching out human truth.*"[11] (Italics are mine.)

This is what all these very different English aims have in common. They are all meant to help students to understand reality, to search out human truth. None of them stops at "how writers get their effects," at endless talk about climaxes and dénouements — which sounds so sexy but is actually so neutered. And especially, they don't marginalize literature or film to the point where the language part of English becomes more important than the literature or movie part.

One of the high points of this "lecture on record" was the quote that introduced me to one of my favourite historians, Johan Huizinga. Baxter culls out this passage from *The Waning of the Middle Ages*: "The contrast between silence and sound, darkness and light, like that between summer and winter, was more strongly marked than it is in our lives. *The modern town hardly knows silence or darkness in their purity, nor the effect of a solitary light or a single distant cry.*"[12] (Italics are mine.)

Baxter chose the passage to show how a prose writer of sensitivity can flip into poetry every so often and give our hearts a special stir. *My* reason to include it here, in two chapters about the decline of English and history, is to show the poet and the historian combining to give us a deep glimpse into the past, the kind of glimpse that skills mania is gradually shutting the door on.

Turning down literature and turning up language is precisely what is happening in my own province of Ontario. The graduation year in English for university entrance is weighted heavily in favour of language rather than literature. Any aim for literature or film study, such as the deepening of a student's understanding of life, is utterly subordinated to mastering the techniques of reading, writing, researching and speaking. This emphasis on mastering techniques is well-illustrated, even in the title of a popular book of essays for high school use called *Thinking Through the Essay*(1986).[13] Contrast an older title, *Man and His World*, and its companion volume, *In Search of Ourselves*,[14] a bestselling essay collection since its publication in 1961. The table of contents of each book, like their titles, show the very different emphases: the newer book on technique, the older pair on human experience. In the light of this contrast, it is noteworthy that the Orwell essay chosen for the newer book is "Politics and the English Language" whereas for *Man and His World*" it is "Down the Mine." Of course if the new prophets of technique treated skills as Orwell does, i.e., as servants of reality ("prose like a window pane" was the way Orwell put it), we would have no quarrel with them. Unfortunately this spirit is almost completely missing in *Thinking Through the Essay*. The newer book has more writings by woman and immigrant groups beyond northern Europe, but what it gains here it cancels out with its overbearing emphasis on the recurring analytical categories of purpose, audience, tone, voice, response, language and structure.

We need vast improvement in the standards of reading, writing and speaking of our high school students. Some of this improvement will come from better techniques which focus specifically on these things. But let us get first things first. Let us start at the right place and get skills properly anchored. Why does this matter? For many reasons, as this book is trying to show, but the most practical is that without a deeper motivation for education than technical skill, that great company of frenetic or numbed students that we're not reaching at the moment will continue to be out of reach.

World War I First, Writing Skills Second

If I may leap now to recent history to bring these ideas up-to-date, I would now like to examine a unit from my own teaching, this one from a mainstream, compulsory advanced level grade 11 English class. For the month of July 1996, I taught two classes daily, one for three hours in the morning and one for three hours in the afternoon. They were all students who had failed advanced level grade 11 English, and they were hoping to make up the credit in this one-month intensive summer course. I was fairly tightly supervised about the content of these courses, about the wording of the exams and about the components of the final 100 marks. I did manage to get my own choice of novel and film, however, even though my supervisor had not heard of either of my suggestions.

Both my choices were about World War I, one a great old fifties Hollywood feature, *Paths of Glory*, starring Kirk Douglas,[15] the other a neglected but brilliant, world-class Canadian novel, *Generals Die in Bed* by Charles Yale Harrison ("It makes *All Quiet on the Western Front* read like a child's story book." *London Bystander*).[16] Both works paint a bleak and cynical picture of World War I, and both stress first and foremost the chasm in the army (Canadian in the book, French in the movie) between officers and men — as reflected by the title *Generals Die in Bed*.

These are two works for an entire class to read and view, ponder and write about *together*. Students are not on some lonely, individual-testing-when-you're-ready outcomes path. They are to focus on challenging curriculum taken in common. A huge pedagogical issue for me is, therefore, to get the right curriculum in the first place. This means that I thrive best in a situation where departments thrash out curriculum choices together, but agree with the notion of literacy levels assigned across larger geographical areas. I think that within this literacy context you then can get most out of individual teachers and individual districts which differ ethnically, etc., when there's a large measure of freedom to choose the actual books, films and tapes that will be studied together.

Although I lean towards curriculum that packs a punch, I still prefer deeper works rather than the easy vocabulary stuff. When you are obsessive about digging hard for good curriculum, you can usually find non-forbidding, high-quality books and films that express more gutsy thoughts than most school books usually do. The unusual side of *Paths of Glory* and *Generals Die in Bed* is their class content and their refusal to settle for easy patriotism in a war setting. Everyone should have this challenge, in my opinion, but working-class students are especially deprived when they don't get it, since they get little reinforcment for what they experience daily as the way the world really works. In fact, because this class of "failures" was mostly made up of working-class students, they were perfect candidates for these books.

Learning Novels and Films Thoroughly

I had a very traditional way of taking students through novels and films. Students read novels in installments — the same length for everyone and we kept going till everyone was done — with very few breaks. Every day, students summarized essay-style, or answered three or four questions based on the chapter or chapters they had read. These summaries or answers were marked and counted for their term marks. Learning to summarize and answer four or five factual questions is definitely a skill to be taught. I would use the same technique with the movie, stopping often to clarify what's happening, and assigning the students the same summaries or questions.

When this know-the-works stage was complete, I gave the students an additional assignment. It's familiar to many teachers: ten quotations from the novel and twenty-five quotations from the movie. What I asked them to do with the quotations are the old chestnut questions: (a) Who said this? (one mark) (b) To whom? (one mark) (c) In what situation? (two marks) (d) What is the significance of the quotation in the film or novel? (three marks) (e) If you have a personal feeling or thought about the quotation, include it in your answer (three marks).

Sometimes a quotation is mostly a link with the plot, as with this one from *Generals Die in Bed*:

> The rusty spoon for dishing out sugar and such things is stuck between two sandbags in the parapet over his head. Glad to straighten himself up for a second, Brown stands up to reach for it. He turns to look in the direction of the woods to his left. . . .

At this point, I hope students would recall that Brown, a major character in the book, is killed by a sniper for making the mistake of straightening up in the trench. Other quotations have a heraldic, summing up tone to them:

> We have learned who our enemies are — the lice, some of our officers and Death.

Other quotation are old sayings, as with this back-to-back set of sayings in *Paths of Glory*:

> Show me a patriot and I'll show you an honest man.
> Patriotism is the last refuge of a scoundrel.

The trickiest part of learning the skill of answering these questions is to distinguish mere factual identification from the more elaborate description of the "situation" in which the statement was made, and then the even more complex task of showing the *significance* of a quotation in the story — to say nothing about expressing a personal opinion without merely saying "I liked it" or "I hated it."

Let me make the pretty obvious point with educational psychologist Frank Smith that you can't learn the skill of answering questions about quotations if you haven't seen the movie or if it went in one eye and out the other because you were so bored. Smith's book *To Think* is a must for anyone interested in this thinking skills debate: "To become conspicuous as creative thinkers, people need experience and encouragement in creative and artistic activities, not special training in general 'creative thinking skills.' Precisely the same considerations apply to *critical* thinking."[17]

Your Response to This Exam Answer?

To make my main point I move now to the final exam, comprising two questions, one based on the novel and the movie and the other based on *Macbeth*. I had to settle with my supervisor for stiffer wording and a more descriptive answer than I would have set. Also, the relative number of marks allocated to "content" and "writing" was hers. But the first question and its answer still serve my purpose here:

Final Grade 11 English Exam

1. *Generals Die in Bed* (novel) and *Paths of Glory* (film).

   In proper essay style, compare the treatment of war in the two works named above. Make your comparison under the following three headings, and present specific evidence from each work to support your points:
   (a) what life was like for the soldiers on the front-line as compared to how it was pictured "back home";
   (b) the attitude of the front-line soldiers to the enemy;
   (c) relations between the officers and the common soldiers.
   (24 marks — content; 6 marks — writing)

I now offer Lisa Schmidt's first three pages of a seven-page answer to this exam question. I am reproducing it exactly as she wrote it. I quote her at some length to pose the question of the relative priority of skill as compared to meaning, memory, conviction and passion:

> There is no fun in war, in both Generals Die in Bed and Paths of Glory, this is evident. The soldiers have it hard — to say the least, they are mentally and physically abused each and everyday. Here are men that pray for their lives every night, they watch the guy who sleeps beside them or even their best friends drop down dead beside them and all they can think is "I'm sure glad that's not me!"
>
> Back home we get a different picture intiarly, the author

from 'Generals Die in Bed' was extemely disturbed when he took a trip 'home' to see a play where they mock the Front line and the war. Here are some well fed people who sleep in cozy beds with clean sheets while the author and the other soldiers lie awake in the mud, because the lice are eating them raw, and here these people are laughing. One ignorant man in an effort to explain the lack of humour on the authors part said "Oh he's suffering from shell shock" clearly these people have no idea of the hell these soldiers indure everyday and night. When it comes to war — killing is ok, right? back home it's accepted without question it's what the soldiers are for, but 'home' they never stop to think how killing another person can effect the killer. When the author was on leave in London and was staying at Gladis's place, they had a discussion which pin-points the difference in the feelings. Gladis was asking him questions of himself and the author said "I once murdered a man," Gladis was shocked. "What, when" the author replise still serious as ever. "I stabbed him with my gun, then shot him." Gladis laughs "Oh silly That's war, I thought you meant you really killed someone." But the soldier knows that the young German boy is dead and he killed him. back 'home' it's accepted and even respected but that's not enough to reconsolle the authors feelings, They are lost at 'home,' living in their dream world! I can understand the lack of knowledge at "home" and it's because of people like the Cheif (Paths of Glory) while the soldiers try to get some rest at the bottom of their muddy trench, the chief is at home in his castle dressed to impress having a dinner party and dance Everyone is chipper and well groomed, they know nothing of the war — as if it wasn't even happening: their at a shin-dig hosted by the chief himself. War? What war? Why just look at the chief's smile, not a concern on his face. Do you think that the million of dead soldiers are smiling, do you know what one of the trench soldiers would do for a small piece of that perfect chicken???

I gave Lisa 22/24 for content and 2/6 for writing, by which my supervisor meant technicalities. I ask you, however, to ignore the issue of marks at this point. I am raising a much more fundamental question. I invite your personal reaction to this fragment as a whole. Can the school build on the passion of this girl's answer (assuming you agree that it *has* passion) or is the poor punctuation, spelling and paragraphing so bad that, instead of all this mysticism about good content, I would have been better to have spent the entire month improving her writing skills?

Of course a scientific answer with such little evidence is not possible. And can you turn around the poor writing skills of thirty-four students in one month even if you'd like to? I'm diligent about the standard of writing technicalities in my regular classes, but with this class of failures I decided to emphasize grabbing them with arresting curriculum and producing a book of their writings and photographs. Lisa told me she failed grade 11 because she never handed anything in.

And should I have spent hours teaching Lisa how the plots of the novel and the film were constructed? Should we have talked and talked about the juxtaposition of the oppressed soldier scenes with scenes of the arrogant and pampered generals? Should I have done all this to show them I'm offering quality works of art — the traditional old-school reason? Or so they can spot when their minds are being twisted — the new media-literacy reason?

I do some of this indirectly, of course. I might ask whether a certain description sounds believable to them. I ask why a scene of soldier misery and terror in a trench was followed quickly by a fancy party in Paris where the military, political and business elites are having what Lisa called a "shindig," where they were all "chipper and well-groomed."

Yes, this has its place, but it pales when compared with the need for deep nourishment of character and citizenship. (I think, for example, how exciting it would have been to discuss the thoughts in a book I'm currently reading: *Blood Rites: Origins and History of the Passions of War* by Barbara Ehrenreich.[18]) If you're trying to grapple with the meaning of war itself and specifically of World War I (and I am *not* a pacifist) can you really afford to crowd out these big questions with the techniques of figures of speech and plot construction? I remember later reading with my compulsory final-year English class an essay called "Labour Day Is a Dreaded Bell in the Schoolyard of the Mind." It's a breezy, chatty work telling why the author hated to go back to school every September. Since the students were to be tested on the details of "style and structure" of all the essays in this book, I plodded through a discussion of "tone," "effective use of contrast," "figurative language" and "how three of the author's observations led directly to his final comments" — all this for an essay worth no more than a chuckle or a groan depending on whether you liked it or not. I'm not sure the editors realized this, but their exercise itself showed one big reason why Harry Bruce, the author, hated school!

So I will come back to the message of this book as I leave you to frame your own speculations and conclusions about this exam answer fragment: a major challenge to the schools in North America right now is whether to accept or reject the technocratic education model (even as we teach the important skills diligently and properly rooted in deeper human matters). We must then go on to hammer out what legacies of the past and what enrichment of the present and the future we wish to pass on. Even the liberal arts philosophy was limited and naive about whether such an aim was needed. Dewey thought it was needed to teach democracy. Unfortunately teaching technocracy just isn't the same. Technocracy finds it easier and easier to say that teaching the grim truths in *Generals Die in Bed* and *Paths of Glory* is unnecessary for the average student. Who needs them to get a job?

What I think is actually happening with the skills-oriented schools is that a small handful of graduates are getting a few specialized jobs and the rest are learning a few technicalities that not only don't get them jobs but also cannot be applied to the basic substance of life since that substance is taught less and less. The really scary part is that a few (in private schools?) are still getting the smarts about the meaning of life and will dominate the rest — those who have learned how to function in teams and write clear memos. We must fight this with all our hearts and minds.

I turn now to the current state of history teaching in our schools.

CHAPTER 5

History

The Fall from Grace

And what of history, the other key subject which has gone from centre stage to the margins of schooling in thirty short years?

By September 1961 I had left Tennessee behind and had moved to Toronto. I began the Ontario part of my teaching career, teaching history in North York, Metro Toronto. History was a compulsory subject for students every year from grades 9 to 12, and most students heading to university took it for a fifth year in grade 13. This history program was held together by a tight rationale: British history was taken in grade 9; Canada, United States and Great Britain in the twentieth century, in grade 10; ancient history in grade 11; modern Western Europe in grade 12; and Canada and the United States from 1763 in grade 13. Readers will recognize this as the "white Eurocentric" story of Canadian origins, and one might add that it focused almost entirely on males as well — and fairly successful ones at that.

A brilliant American book mapped the same process in the United States. James W. Loewen's *Lies My Teacher Told Me: Everything Your American History Textbook Got Wrong* shows the systematic erasure of the history of ordinary people and their oppression in favour of the history of the rich, white and successful.[1]

Earlier I have told about how some of us worked on changing this narrow emphasis in the 1960s. I have also spoken about how those running schools were not only not on our wave length but were not on our planet. We were trying to expand the spread of the actors in textbook history; the authorities were about to shrink the subject itself till it had almost disappeared by 1971. However conservative the history curriculum was in the 1950s (and it was *very* conservative!) it was at least based on the notion that some coherent picture of your own country's background, its ancient roots and its place in a setting broader than its own boundaries, was a necessity and a right of all students.

When I set out to understand the reason why history was so severely shrunken, I found out early that very large historical changes were the main causes of the decline. There are certainly causes within the field of history teaching itself (bad teaching being one, a factor well described once again by Loewen), but usually they pointed to the larger changes in society itself since 1945.

Five Causes of History's Decline as a Subject

I found five large-scale factors that caused a decline in the teaching of history in this period. The first applies specifically to Canada, but the others apply to all developed countries, including the United States:

1. *The increased erosion of Canadian independence since 1970.* History for Ontario students was conceived in 1960 as the story of an emerging independent Canadian nation, first under British control, followed by a brief moment of independence, then moving towards American control. The features that make Canada distinct have increasingly been undercut with growing U.S. domination from the late 1960s, culminating in the Free Trade Agreement (1988) and the North American Free Trade Agreement (1993) and in the increasing challenge of Quebec separatism. This, in turn, has undermined one of the traditional cornerstones of mass history teaching in Ontario.[2]

2. *The decline of faith in historical progress.* Most of the popular high school history textbooks I used in 1961 had hymns to the future in their prefaces or their conclusions. Sir Wilfrid Laurier calling the twentieth century "the century of Canada" was one sign of this belief. The belief was absent in Ontario history books by the mid-1970s. This collapse was caused by twentieth-century cynicism about war, socialism and the disillusionment with modern science.

"History as Progress" was also challenged by the stubborn flexibility and survival of capitalism. Teaching history to everybody does not seem as important if it is not the story of how things are getting better and better.

3. *The challenge from groups opposing the white, bourgeois, male, Eurocentric view.* The chief actors and winners in the traditional history canon were challenged, but not much shaken, between the 1960s and the 1980s by women, people of colour, Aboriginals, recent immigrants, labour and youth. Jack Granatstein, in his *Who Killed Canadian History?,*[3] blames these critics completely and ignores all the other points I am listing. He believes the poor beleaguered government gave up when lobbied by so many "special interests." It's the old habit of blaming those on the bottom rather than those on top.

4. *Loyalty via TV.* Television now creates a strong measure of loyalty to capitalism and "democracy" directly through its commercials and lifestyle programs. This removes the need of traditional Western governments for history and citizenship education as indirect loyalty techniques: mainlining instead of pills.

   Television also provides its own view of what history is all about. History only goes as far back as television, that is, to the Stone Age of the 1950s, when everyone apparently lived in *Leave It to Beaver* families. This led to the next stage of history, the 1960s, when the kids all had long hair, listened to the Beatles and the Stones, and hated *Leave It to Beaver* families.

5. *The new global restructuring of capitalism.* Behind the defence of democracy in our old history courses was the assumption that free enterprise capitalism was the best of all possible economic systems. But the politics of nationalism and the virtues of certain imperialisms (British and American) were always made more central to the way history was presented than was economics.

   As nationalism has been increasingly challenged by the new global capitalism and as the old favoured empires of Great Britain and the United States have been increasingly challenged by other economies like Japan and Germany, the need for national histories is consequently being challenged. Add to this the daydream of people like Francis Fukuyama that history is largely over,[4] that capitalist democracy has come into its own, and students are now being told that the fine tuning of the new world capitalism is what they're being trained for. Who needs history classes if history itself is over?[5]

The Fragmentation of Canadian History

But let us return to the effect of the decline of nationalism on history as a subject. The fading of our interest in the nation of Canada is shown in the kind of books written in the 1970s and 1980s by Canada's best professional historians. Instead of books about the destiny of the country as a whole — as we had from earlier historians like Donald Creighton, Arthur Lower, W.L. Morton and Peter Waite — we saw books on regions of the country and very specific topics covering very short periods of time. In 1991, in a speech given at the University of Toronto called "Fragmented History, Fragmented Canada," Michael Bliss criticized his own writing as an example of the kind of fragmentation he was complaining about:

> Fresh from the classroom in 1968, I published a fierce attack on an older historian who had dared to urge us that we had an obligation to tell our countrymen "Who they are, whence they came, . . . whither they are going." Then I got on with my work which was to explore the intricacies of Canadian business attitudes between 1883 and 1911. These findings were published in a book read by no one who was not a professor or a student. I then had a lot to say about the economics of pork-packing and shell production in World War I, recounted daily, sometimes hourly events in the discovery of insulin in 1921-22, and this season I am happy to sell you 270 pages of the history of one smallpox epidemic in one Canadian city in one year. This is narrow specialization, not containing much political or constitutional history.[6]

In response, I think I can hear some defenders of history saying: "I don't much like the narrowness of the topics, but at least these books are still about history and not the blatant *abandonment* of history in high schools in favour of the sociology of current social problems. This rise of present-day sociology and social studies and, yes, its squeezing out of much of our history study, is one of the two absolutely key issues I had to deal with in my investigation. The other was the rise of skills mania. When I asked retired University of Western Ontario professor Geoffrey Milburn, the most important editor of Canadian magazines for history teachers, what caused the big decline of high school history, he said, "Sociology and skills — and it was necessary to go down fighting on this one." (Later, you will see that I have more hope for sociology than Professor Milburn, but I agree with him that the rise of sociology and skills were two crucial causes of history's decline. Those who wanted history gone now had something to offer in its place.

Master Narratives — Better New Ones or None at All?

Both these new cousins of history helped to fragment further a subject that had already begun to feel the breakup described by Michael Bliss. In the jargon of academia, the "Eurocentric master narrative" of the old history program, which I was part of in 1961, survived by 1980 only for those students who opted each year to take the old set of courses. It was no longer compulsory for everybody. For the population as a whole we were no longer passing on the master narrative, or any narrative.

Meanwhile, in the 1990s back at Westminster, England, and in Washington at the U. S. Congress, the love of the old master narratives was alive and well. According to the dean of Canadian history and citizenship teaching, Kenneth Osborne, both the British government in 1990 and the American Senate in 1994 "went apoplectic about the lack of traditional textbook patriotism in their respective new documents, the New British Curriculum's history guide and the American History Standards documents." "Thatcher even pontificated," Osborne continued, "that there wasn't enough *English* history in the Curriculum and too much Scottish, Irish and Welsh history! Despite the fact that the American *Standards* documents were not meant as lists of every name teachers should mention to their students, Senators in Congress pounced on the names issue and were asking where was Robert E. Lee, etc. To them it was largely a question of missing names and facts and traditional patriotism. Documents by teachers and professors of education and history were a safe and easy mark."[7] I would add that at sound bite and photo-op time, politicians did not notice an even worse problem than the lack of super-patriotism: history credits themselves had been largely evaporating before their eyes.

But to return to master narratives that attempt to be more substantial than waves of a flag: one complication of this shrinkage has been dealing with thinkers who say good riddance to all master narratives. The new transformed narrative or paradigm we thought we were working out in the 1960s — a rationale that would tell the truth about all peoples — is a futile quest, these people say. Some of them are even feminist or black historians who say that all master narratives are by definition oppressive. The black historian Nathan Huggins knew better when he counselled against tucking black history away in Black Studies departments as yet another part of the fragmentation. The truth historians know about civilizations in Africa before the whites arrived and about slavery in the early period of the United States needed to be forced into the old master narrative of American history, said Huggins.[8] This way, the old story about beleaguered Europeans building the land of the free and the home of the brave would be exploded and transformed by the African American story. Without some new general pictures like this, it is unlikely that a comprehensive history program will ever return to our high schools.

Sociology and Skills: Add a Few More Coffin Nails

And so, for the moment, skills and sociology are firmly in the driver's seat. I find the development of sociology much easier to defend than the spread of skills obsession. I will say more about the spectre of skills when I come to talk about citizenship education. In this section, I will limit myself to invoking Christopher Friedrichs, history professor at the University of British Columbia, on the subject of turning history into primarily a skills subject. Just before making this statement, Friedrichs had commented on the disappearance of Latin in similar terms:

> I would argue that whenever an intellectual discipline ceases to justify itself on its merits and starts to justify itself as the instrumental means to some other goal, it is beginning to undergo a process of self-destruction. . . . If the study of history is seen only as the means of acquiring certain intellectual skills, people will soon find even more efficient ways of teaching and learning those skills.[9]

What Only Proper History Analysis Can Do

Before I comment in the next two chapters on "seizing the moment of sociology," I will present a curriculum example which only a proper history study can solve. For four years in a row towards the end of my grade 12 Black History course (Africa and the West Indies), I took up a major unit on the invasion of Grenada (October 1983). But since most of the course took them back to Africa and then to early West Indies history, the students had the possibility of seeing the invasion in the light of major movements of history over five centuries. To modern sociology, even the year 1983 is considered to be stretching history back a bit far! In Appendix A you will find the major curriculum items the class studied in the first half of this grade 12 course.

I think it's obvious that millions of the problems of this earth cannot be understood without studying history. The invasion of Grenada is surely one. And it is surely daydreaming to imagine, as Bill Spady does, that a course in how history is done, plus a few "detecting bias in history" lessons, will equip each student to dig out the background they need when they need it. (Good luck, for example, to non-academic students who, on their own, try to understand two essential, brilliant but difficult books in this field, C.L.R. James's *Black Jacobins*[10] or Walter Rodney's *How Europe Underdeveloped Africa*[11] In fact, good luck to most high school *teachers* on these books, without the aid of a knowledgeable teacher. Also, good luck without a teacher and a group to brainstorm ideas in even understanding a stirring, deep but demanding *movie* like *Burn*). Yet this is how Ontario justifies requiring less than one year of compulsory history for high school students. How can someone get "a perspective" with such paltry historical content and without the deepening that should come from seeing, in a group, different pieces of the past for three or four years in a row?

Marginal Comments as You Read a Book

Before I continue with our curriculum specifically connected with the invasion of Grenada, I wish to pass on several important examples of complex skills that I have taught in connection with the works listed in Appendix A. I do this partly to make very clear that my position is not that skills should not be taught. The students need to be consciously taught these particular skills over the course of reading an entire book, in this case *A Glorious Age in Africa: The Story of Three Great African Empires — Ghana, Mali and Songhai*. Even though the book is written for young students in straightforward English, the students will need lots of help distinguishing big things from small.

To get rolling, I find best the old-fashioned methods of quizzes on reasonable chunks of reading and class discussion of main points. I also give marks for the way students mark up their sheets (the book was out of print), not with a highlighter which forces them later to reread all the highlighting but from words they write in the margins. It has been said of Ben Franklin's books that they show a running conversation between Franklin and the authors of the books in his library. This can only be asked of students who own their own book or are reading from sheets as mine were since they cannot do this marginal commenting in school-owned texts.

I encourage students to write argumentative comments: Why So? Nonsense! etc. Or positive comments: "Right On!" "Excellent." Or study organizing comments: "Trip to Mecca shows Mali's wealth, power, trade, travel." Or enquiry comments: "Check this out." "Where's the proof?" Sometimes they might be amazed by something they have read and just write "Wow!" in the margin. My approach here is meant to lead to more active and involved student reading.

Early on I realized that this was another skill which, as psychologist Frank Smith stresses, cannot be learned strictly as a list, as a concept. It is much more a question of becoming knowledgeable in a field. This is a point that is often not grasped by those with a shallow view of skills training. Students will not ask "Where's the proof?" who do not know what proof is or who have no conception of what history writing is all about. Students will not write "Why so?" or "Nonsense!" in the margin if they do nor feel they have the right to judge something in cold print given out in school. They will not feel safe writing these comments if they feel it's all a trick where they're going to be pounced on to justify what they've written. The more history students know, the more confident their minds are, the more they become capable of a more helpful conversation with the authors in the margins of their books.

I examined the whole class's reading comments walking around the class after every reading. Then I took home everyone's sheets after they'd been doing this for a while. I pushed for improvement.

Giving Life to a Dead Chart

It is not easy, while going through a solid book with a class, to keep the larger aim in mind. This book about ancient Ghana, Mali and Songhai is obviously written as an answer to the justification for slavery: It's okay to enslave black people because they are sub-human.

In answering this viewpoint, the tradition has been to stress how civilized much of ancient Africa was. Often this emphasis has been summed up as "We were once kings." A smart friend asked me: "Why are you glorifying African kings any more than we would want to glorify *any* kings? We teach our Canadian kids that the Indian tribes considered the least "civilized" had the most equal and most flexible culture, way ahead of the Aztecs, Mayans, Incas or Haida. Check out, for example, scholarly writing on the remarkable culture of the African pygmies."[12] I do raise this important point with my students, but I continue to stress the "we were once kings" theme because many students, depending on their age, situation, race, etc., need to hear the "kings message" before the other message can make sense. They need to understand that their tradition can produce as complicated, beautiful, powerful and intelligent things as that of any white person. Now they're ready to see the good features of "primitive" societies.

In the midst of all this serious purpose another large skill issue did emerge. The straightforward task I was engaged in was assigning the students the reading of the book and asking them to fill in a chart as they were reading:

Civilized Characteristic	Ghana	Examples from Mali	Songhai
1. Cities			
2. Complex Class Setup			
3. Advanced Knowledge			
4. Fine Arts			
5., 6. Etc., etc.			

When the students finished the book and had discussed as a class their reactions and their charts — and had time to study all this — I asked. them to write under test conditions an essay from their knowledge with no notes in front of them. The topic: "The old civilizations of Ghana, Mali and Songhai prove that black people were highly civilized before the whites arrived."

I only realized a year after I started teaching this course that the translation of a chart into an essay posed some key perceptual problems for a significant handful of kids who needed help in developing this *skill*. "Do I write *cities*, then give examples?" asked one student. It was not yet clear to her that converting this chart to a "discursive essay" meant: "A first characteristic of advanced civilization is the presence of cities. Examples of these in the Empire of Mali were Timbuktu, the great university town, and Jenne, which was put under seige by the forces of the Songhai Empire for seven years, seven months and seven days." This is in fact exactly what the student thought should be done, but the introduction of prose style was at first a confusing new factor for her.

So learning this particular skill of turning a chart into prose (a bit like turning mathematics into literature) is partly a skill or technique, like boiling something down into an essence, then mixing it back up again into your sauce, but it is also intimately connected with understanding a context, a story, potentially with passion and conviction behind it.

Explaining the Invasion of Grenada

In Appendix B I list the curriculum for the second half of the semester up to and including the invasion of Grenada. Why would I make a major unit on the invasion of this small island way back in 1983? Wasn't the invasion of Grenada a "blip" in history? a professor of education said to me. I have two responses. My main response is that I present this invasion as a universe in a grain of sand. The United States has always thought it could go in and out of Latin America and the West Indies at will — whether through heavy manipulation of, say, the Michael Manley government of Jamaica in the 1970s, or the outright invasion of many countries during the twentieth century. It was in this light that I took up the invasion of Grenada. (Incidentally, I notice that despite the glories of American democracy available to Grenada since 1983 my morning paper says that on August 2, 1998, "Grenadians Cheer Castro." Looks like the blip is still blipping.)

Second, I disagree with the curriculum approach to recent events, which rules that any event older than five years is "out-of-date." A strange attitude for a history teacher. A detailed study of Ralph Nader's and Phil Edmundston's car safety campaigns, Minamata disease in Japan and Northern Ontario, even the On to Ottawa Trek of workers in the 1930s are not out-of-date topics, especially for high school study. Also, the more detail the better, I say. That way they really get into it.

Before focusing on the invasion of Grenada, I offer a few remarks about my general purpose with this curriculum.

There are many approaches I could take in pondering what students did with this curriculum and what it might mean for the question of skills, content and conviction. What I have chosen to look at is the very large challenge posed by the startlingly new interpretations and knowledge by newly confident groups of minority racial and ethnic groups, women, marginalized socio-economic classes and victims of imperial domination. At this point some readers may say, "Oh, here comes the politically correct line." You're right if you think I'm saying we should give a fair hearing to groups formerly exploited and put down. You're wrong if you think I'm going to defend the finicky details of doctrinaire political correctness.

The challenge to schools that I'm talking about is very serious. When a new view of Christopher Columbus is put forward, are we prepared, after examining it carefully, to allow it to replace our old view? Similarly for a new view of the invasion of Grenada. Or are we prepared only to allow it into a polite debate where the intention is to slip back

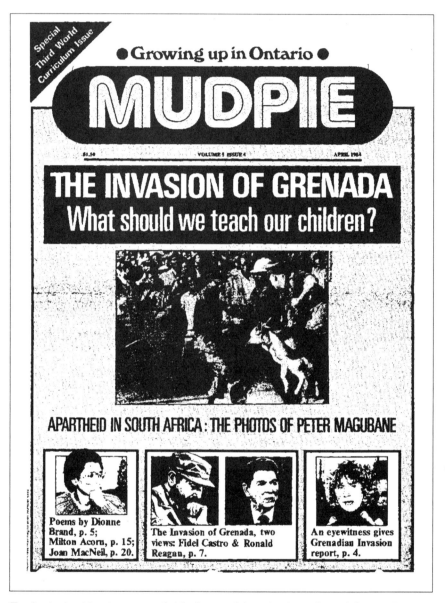

Each student had a copy of this for studying the invasion of Grenada.

to our old view while we affirm that somehow the debate itself was the purpose of the whole enterprise? One of the new things we may learn is why the interests of some people virtually *require* them to believe one view over another. Are we prepared to bring that issue into the open, yet be ready for the battle with the powers that be implied by a general switch of belief by many of our students? Are we — teachers, parents, students, legislators — ready to build in our school departments, in our schools as a whole, and in our boards of education the kind of protection for provocative teaching that some of us have spent years building with others?

"What I saw during the Grenadian invasion - and how the U.S. version of that tragedy must be exposed"

by Barbara Thomas

Is the Domino Theory the only way to understand Caribbean, South & Central American revolutions?

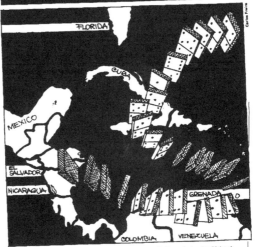

Have the people of Cuba, Chile (under Allende), Grenada (under Bishop), Nicaragua and El Salvador wanted radical changes in government mostly for their own internal reasons (with inspiration and assistance from outside), or are they merely pawns (dominoes) of Russia?

Barbara Thomas was working in Grenada for CUSO (a Canadian non-government development agency) at the time of the U.S. invasion in late October 1983. She also taught in Barbados from 1970-1972. She is a Toronto adult educator and writer. Bob Davis interviewed her late in March 1984.

MUDPIE: When I first heard of the invasion of Grenada, apart from my general shock, I also realised I knew someone there, namely you.

THOMAS: I know, that happened to a lot of my friends.

MUDPIE: I had simple questions, like were you scared?

THOMAS: Yes, I was terrified. I never knew how scared one could be. I think you go through different stages. I think we stopped being so terrified on the second day when we actually decided that there might be no hope of us getting out. At a certain level we had given up hope of getting out, and I think when you give up hope of something, then you deal with the much more immediate moment-by-moment present and that's much easier.

MUDPIE: You had a family back here too, two kids and a husband. Did they try to get in touch with you?

THOMAS: Well yes. The last I had talked with Jim, my husband was at 12:30 on Tuesday, Oct. 25th, which was the first day of the invasion. He had called in the morning. He had had a phone call from a friend in Barbados at 6:30 in the morning who had said the U.S. had invaded at 5:30 in the morning, and he got through to me at 10:30. The lines had been down a week, so we hadn't been able to call out.

So he got through at 10:30 and we were on the floor in the hall, and he could hear the bombs and he could hear the fear in my voice and then he got through again at 12:30 and the situation was the same. The only way he could get to the phone was by crawling on your belly to the other room where the phone was and I of course didn't want him to be any more terrified than he was. But it was difficult to feign that on the phone.

Then the lines closed down and we had no further contact until Friday when he heard our six names read out on the news on Friday at six o'clock. That was the first that he knew that we were OK.

MUDPIE: Was he trying to get in touch with you by other means?

THOMAS: He didn't have any other way. He called External Affairs — they have a Crisis Desk which even during the invasion closed promptly at five o'clock. He didn't have any way of getting through to us. He went on a radio show on Tuesday evening. As It Happens, because he thought that might allow the government to put a little pressure on the U.S. to find us. I don't know whether it did.

MUDPIE: The media in Toronto said that the U.S. was not co-operating with Canada in getting the Canadians out. What's the true story on that?

THOMAS: Well certainly the signals point to that.

MUDPIE: When you say you were on the floor in the house, what was this place?

THOMAS: Well the place that we were living and working—where the CUSO office was—is on a rock. In fact the place is called "The Rock". It's an abutment that hangs out over the city a bit. If you like, and has a very good view, not only of Fort Rupert where Bishop and people were killed. It looks out over half of the entire town and also has a very good view of Point Salines which is where the U.S. landed. This was the place we were and it felt very vulnerable, very exposed there.

So when I say we were on the floor, we found one small corridor where there were no windows. Somehow all your war movies come to your mind in a situation like this and somewhere this wisdom became current that if we just stayed away from shattering windows it might be better. But besides that, there is an instinct to make yourself as small and inconspicuous as possible when things are going on around you. So we huddled on the floor in this corridor. We were at first frightened of the noises, but one wit in the group informed us that it wasn't the noises that we should be frightened of, it was the things that dropped that we never heard. It's wonderful to have somebody who really thinks in the group.

An eyewitness report of the invasion of Grenada. Note another Domino Theory map.

Listen to one of my students after reading selections from *Rethinking Columbus* and seeing the Columbus movie starring Gérard Depardieu (Details in Appendix A, Item 7):

1492 — The Conquest of Paradise by Steve Brown

This film is a docudrama based on the life and ventures of Christopher Columbus. The movie, unfortunately, approaches this subject in the same manner as American History textbooks do, either in part or falsely. The film outlines Columbus' supposed "discovery" of new and uncharted land, when the land was already inhabited by Indians. This film, especially during the scene where we see Christopher Columbus for the first landing, walking slow motion through the water to the shore glorifies Columbus and his journeys, making him out to be a very noble and persevering man.

I did not appreciate being "spoonfed" this image of Columbus, especially in the light of what I've come to learn about him in this course. The fact that Christopher Columbus is a conqueror is undisputed, in fact he was also a pillager and tyrant responsible not only for the deaths of many natives, but also for initiating the trans-Atlantic slave trade. The truth is long overdue and I'm glad sources like *Rethinking Columbus* are available to open the eyes of society. I did not enjoy the film from an entertainment standpoint or an informative standpoint as it tried to shadow Columbus' evil behind another character called Musaka (?), who is unlikely to have existed and took negative pressure off Columbus' character. Inventions of such characters only take away from the film's authenticity and gives us the typical "glamour and glitz" Hollywood version of the story. I give this film about as much credibity as *Star Wars* in the realism or nonfiction department.

Many teachers, especially those with a liberal or left orientation, would regard this piece of student writing as a "critical thinking skills piece," an example of media literacy. It *is* in part. It criticizes a movie from various perspectives. So, is my concern about more and more knowledge being called "skills" merely a word game? Not if, as I believe, we are in an era where we need to establish first getting as near as we can to the truth of an issue, not just to this or that bias, as if all biases are born equal. This emphasis is totally in keeping with sorting out the "natural bias" of the corporate class or of an imperialist European country. Often it is the bias of a certain group that has omitted

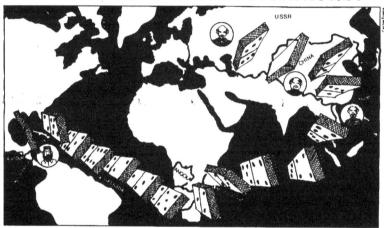

GROWING UP IN ONTARIO

TEACHING ABOUT THE THIRD WORLD IN CANADIAN SCHOOLS

Is the Domino Theory the only way to understand world revolutions?

Do countries have revolutions (like U.S. in 1776) mostly for their own internal reasons (with inspiration and assistance from others), or are they merely pawns (dominoes) in the hands of big powers?

In the interests of developing curriculum as an alternative to the domino theory of world revolutions, MUDPIE presents a special curriculum issue in the form of a feature interview about Grenada by educator, Barbara Thomas; two speeches about the Grenadian Invasion, one by Ronald Reagan defending it, and one by Fidel Castro decrying it; three poems by Canadian poets Dionne Brand, Milton Acorn and Joan McNeil; some photographs from South Africa by Peter Magubane; many newspaper clippings for study; and a resources list on page six.

Few students or teachers are able to spend much time in the third world living among the people (as distinct from being tourists). Stretching our students' minds on this issue, therefore, seems primarily a two-fold matter: letting them hear stories and seeing pictures and films from third world countries presented by people not totally biased in a domino direction, and giving them other theoretical frameworks to make sense of things — frameworks other than those available from the extreme right. At the same time all information which appears to support the domino

theory must be dealt with head-on. Hopefully these materials give the domino theory its due yet open up other ways of seeing revolution around the world.

We suggest you also obtain copies of MUDPIE's December 1983 issue which contains a personal account of a trip to Nicaragua in the fall of 1983 by Ontario teacher, Brian Kenney ("I went to Nicaragua a sceptic; I came back a troubled man."

As with this current issue, we can offer teachers and readers special deals on copies purchased in bulk.

These Domino Theory maps were a very important teaching tool.

from the history books such awkward facts as Columbus cutting off the hands of thousands of aboriginals who didn't bring what Columbus decided was their regular gold quota, or filling ships with hundreds of aboriginals and shipping them back to Spain as slaves.

Now let us also look at student Steve Brown's point of view in his movie review. This hostility towards Columbus was the perspective of most of my students. Is this because they are captives of Bob Davis's propaganda, or have they been persuaded by the solid historical evidence in *Rethinking Columbus* that the traditional view is wrong? Obviously readers who haven't read *Rethinking Columbus* will not be in a position to answer my rhetorical question, but I raise this to show what momentous changes are possible in student thinking in a serious history course. I am also asking whether we teachers will develop the stomach to do battle for the right to tell these kinds of truths in class or whether we will run and hide the minute the authorities accuse us of propaganda.

Let me remind you that the *debate* in school classrooms about these matters is crucial for me. Any teacher with strong views must prove to students that they do not base marks on how much a student agrees with them. For me, a teacher who has a proven record as a squelcher of debate or as a marker who favours certain views for good marks should be dismissed.

Nonetheless this does not cancel my belief that we are in a period of history when power is shifting, battles have intensified and knowledge and beliefs have therefore become controversial to the point where the old naive notion "let a thousand ideas bloom," if approached in a shallow debating-skills way, hides an obsolete sentimentality. Remember that the original cry was not "let a thousand flower buds be gazed at and critically thought about." The flowers were meant to bloom.

Fidel and Reagan Thrash It Out

I offer next the opening of a three-page debate created as a major assignment by two students working together. When they finished they held this debate in class. Ideally, the students who created this debate between Ronald Reagan and Fidel Castro are not only wrestling with two different views on a major disruption in the Caribbean in the early 1980s but are also learning what real argument is and are trying to decide who is closer to truth and justice for common people. (Their main sources are the speeches of Reagan and Fidel on the eve of the invasion as carried in *Mudpie* magazine. See Appendix B.)

The Opening of a Debate between Ronald Reagan and
Fidel Castro about the Invasion of Grenada

Reagan: A most important reason for invading Grenada was simple: to facilitate the evacuation of any Americans who were trying to escape the country. We were worried. We feared for the lives of the innocent. We had also received many reports of Americans who attempted to escape but had been stopped by Cubans at the airport.

Fidel: You lie, Reagan. The Cubans working at the airport had been instructed not to interfere with any American evacuation. Just days before the invasion you had been guaranteed that every single American was safe. All of them had been offered safe passage out of Grenada but none had wished it. In your country the Chancellor for American medical students in Grenada had publicly stated that all were safe. No, Reagan, there was never any danger to Americans.

Reagan: Then why had my country received a plea from other Caribbean countries such as Jamaica, St. Lucia, St, Vincent and Dominica to enter Grenada and restore democracy? Obviously Grenada was in a desperate state and in need of outside assistance.

There are other reasons for invading: to prevent further chaos and to restore democracy in the region. If we had not been wanted in Grenada, why did the Grenadians welcome us so openly and emotionally? It is on camera, the people, down on their knees, thanking us for coming to their rescue.

Fidel: That's more propaganda. They only thanked you because behind the cameraman stood an America soldier with a gun ready to fire if the truth were told. Your country forcefully kept the people down, throwing them in jail if they disagreed with your overtake.

As for requests from other Caribbean countries to invade, that was probably an American set-up too. Why did you impose a media blackout to the Island?

Reagan: To protect any journalists who might have been injured in the chaos.

Two essay questions for homework—one week to complete
1. "The Invasion of Grenada is part of a long pattern practised by the American Empire all over the world but especially in America's 'backyard.'"

   Do you agree or disagree? Support your view by using

relevant parts of the history you have learned in this class.

2. "The three documentaries, *Americas in Transition, The Future Coming Towards Us* and *Operation Urgent Fury* are anti-American propaganda pure and simple."

   Do you agree or disagree? Support your view by using relevant parts of the history you have learned in this class.

Student Answer — Peter Jackson

1. Yes, I agree that the Invasion of Grenada is a pattern for U.S. government from way back. Slavery was part of the system which exported items like sugar and coffee to Europe. When slavery was abolished in the 1800s, and still when independence was achieved in most of the Islands in the 1960s, the economic dependency remained. We Caribbeans were making other countries rich and the big emigration from the Caribbean to Brixton, England, New York, Toronto and Montreal is there to prove the serious poverty in the Islands. By this time the United States rather than Europe mainly got the benefit of this dependency, or should I say the rich Americans and big American companies got the benefit. It's a bit like South Africa today. Official apartheid is gone but extreme dependency and poverty is still there.

   From my notes about *Americas in Transition* I notice this statement by American general of the 1920s and 1930s, Smedley Butler: "I pacified Mexico for U.S. Oil, I secured Haiti for the National City Bank, I invaded Nicaragua for the Brown Brothers banking interests, I invaded the Dominican Republic to protect U.S. sugar interests, I pacified Honduras for the American Fruit Company."

   That says it all, folks. No such feisty language today, but it's still the same thing.

   Here's another quote made by Prime Minister Bishop to a New York African American audience not long before the invasion. It was in *The Future Coming Towards Us* video. It was a discovered secret document in American State Department files. The document read as follows: "The Grenadan Revolution is in a sense worse than the revolution in Cuba or Niacaragua. People speak English there and therefore they can communicate directly with the U.S. Grenada is 95% black and therefore they have a dangerous appeal to 30,000,000 black people in the U.S."

   What more can I say?

2. I suppose it would have been good to see a documentary
made to justify the Invasion, but my teacher says there didn't
seem to be one. Reagan didn't need one when he could speak
and did speak often on prime time about the "airforce and
navy" build-up on Grenada. On *Operation Instant Fury* Sally
Shelton Colby, former U.S. Ambassador to Grenada during
the Bishop time said the navy part was completely made up
and the airport being built had U.S. medical students jogging
regularly up and down the runways! Who testified in *Americas in Transition* and *Operation Instant Fury* about Latin American countries having problems of their own and not needing
Cuba or the Soviet Union to convince local people of this
fact? Was it Fidel Castro? Was it someone from Moscow?
No, it was a former CIA director, a former U. S. Ambassador
to Grenada and another to El Salvador, plus a Catholic nun.

These two movies also stressed checkable facts: twelve
armed invasions by the U.S. in Latin America since 1900,
removal by the U.S. of democratic leaders in places like Chile
and the Dominican Republic by the American CIA and often
actions like this which were boasted about by the CIA.

As for *The Future Coming Towards Us* which was a movie
about Grenada officially supported by that government, the
U.S. never denied that Grenadans were happy with Bishop's
reforms. The Grenadan people were *too* happy with them, as
far as Reagan was concerned. The economic improvments
were simple fact. Also there were too many mass scenes and
heavy machinery road work, and all sorts of natural life of the
people in that movie for it to be an uptight prettied-up picture.

Of course during the Invasion the Canadian press constantly said that Grenadans were happy to see the American
troops. My own view is that they were freaked by the assassination of Prime Minister Bishop and also they knew how to
"act happy" in case they would be harmed if they acted
unfriendly.

So the challenge my teaching offers to skills mania is not just that
skills teaching must be rooted in an emphasis on good content. It is also
that what students believe, what they are convinced of, and the whole
process of developing such convictions, is more important than any
stress on or exposure to a multitude of ideas that ends up suggesting
that one idea is as good as the next. Weighing ideas is not a game of
Trivial Pursuit.

We have got to rethink all those cool things we learned in university about nothing being provable, about everything being a construction of our own minds, about "critical thinking skills" being the only important thing to learn in the humanities. We've got to realize that it's not only repressive old conservatives who think this view is inadequate. Understanding the world we see through the windowpane is surely more important for a high school history class than an obsessive emphasis on the nature of our eyes, the nature of the window glass and the nature of the Windex we wash it with.

Let us learn through these debates on Columbus and the invasion of Grenada that searching for truth, weighing real evidence and deciding on where these convictions take us in our present and future plans and commitments is what a genuinely useful education should be like. Otherwise we can expect to hand over our general judgements about life and society to other people, people like our employers, our managers and our politicians.

Lament the Passing of History, or Seize the Moment of Sociology?

But these days, situating problems like Columbus or the invasion of Grenada in a chronological history course is only possible for the small handful of students who choose to take courses like this. History is not thought important for everyone. What are those of us — teachers parents and administrators — who love history to make of the vanishing act to which our field has been subjected? We are faced with a most crucial choice. Will we settle for lamenting the passing of our subject as do many of the leading editors and writers of the magazines I have examined? Or will we face up to the fact that this is sociology's moment in the high schools and that the modern fragments of topics like abortion, cults, abuse, racism, sexism, world issues, law, the family and the environment are where the current pulse of life resides in our schools? Either we will be present where the pulse of life resides — where our students are given a chance to think, write and talk about what these pulsations mean — or we will remain lamenters.

This choice does not imply letting up for one minute on our lobbying for a proper history program. Neither does it imply that we stop insisting that students in our sociology classes see *the larger picture*, study the *history* of current issues we are discussing and hear about how the world can be changed. It does imply, however, that we cannot push history beyond that place where deeper economic priorities have currently landed it. The fragments we are faced with are meant to be there. Influential people want them, and, in certain cases, oppressed people need them. A new and larger historical narrative may only return when voices from below feel they can speak clearly their own oppositional stories yet are able to link their struggles with those of others. But such a development implies a period when oppositions have much more political and economic power than they now have. Certainly, dominating neo-conservative groups seem to have decided they don't need history any more as a loyalty tool. So, for now, what we face are fragments.

I have worked with a fragment by teaching Black History. The topic interests me greatly and I admire the fighting spirit of African people. I am proud that my high school still offers two such courses, both traditional, chronological history courses. The school is right to offer these courses because I do not see much significant movement towards transforming mainstream history courses to embrace the African and diaspora story. Consequently, I put top energy into an admittedly fragmented situation. The personal and family histories I encouraged from students (see chapter 8) are fragments too, but oh, what rare and sacred fragments![13]

Similarly, I worked for two decades in the field of sociology in our history department, particularly with general level students, even though I could have asked for — and probably would have gotten — "straight history" with advanced level students. I have preferred to work with "fragmented" working-class classes — though I disagree with streaming — and with fragments of current social problems as my course content. Why work with these students and with this content? Because I have decided to work with oppressed kids, but also because this is sociology's moment in the schools. In some classes sociology is mush, and in others it is the boring, official version of sociology. But in plenty of others it is alive. I feel a special solidarity with that company of sociology teachers who cross department boundaries, meeting in the school photocopy room every morning and exchanging words about favourite newsclippings being photocopied for class discussion.

But what will it take to show the inadequacy of this obsession with the present and with fragmented knowledge? One possible development could parallel what happened with Special Education in our schools. In the early 1970s there was a great fuss about the need for vastly increased Special Education. In the last ten years the abysmal failure of much Special Ed. has been recognized by more and more parents, teachers and students, and now mainstreaming or semi-mainstreaming many of these students is increasingly the new official policy. Similarly with the skills mania and all the paraphernalia surrounding it, like outcomes-based education and the huge increase in standardized testing: time may gradually show to masses of people that such philosophies will not solve modern employment problems. Subjects meant to impart wisdom and political participation may then have openings once again.

The situation is a bit like Heidegger's idea of the gods being absent for a time. History is absent, but not forever. Or, if you prefer a political comparison, history is underground right now. The great narratives were found wanting, and we have to work away at building the new ones. In our high schools, sociology is where the pulse is found, and it is there that we will start learning what the new narratives should say.

> The pulse of life is not absent, but the new narratives are.
> Meanwhile, we must find the pulse in the fragments.[14]

CHAPTER 6

Citizenship Education

Seize the Moment of Sociology, but Fight to Restore History

Such has been the fate of history as a high school subject in much of the West since 1945. Such too are my judgements of what it will take to revive it. Where, then, does the teaching of citizenship fit into all this decline? Traditional citizenship education tried to teach the details of parliamentary or congressional democracy and pass on, in particular, how the election system worked with the strong recommendation to students to get out and vote as soon as they came of age. It was overly factual and very conservative in that it suggested that the system functioned well and produced the best of all possible worlds. It linked with the patriotism of the history program and it often had its own little textbook.

We've moved on a long way since this system of the 1950s and early 1960s. Sociology has now arrived on the scene. The switch to what might be called "sociology across the curriculum"[1] sometimes looks like a switch to full-time citizenship education. I don't mean the boring government version of sociology, although that, too, is citizenship training of the conservative Talcott Parsons variety, where every part of our social system supposedly fits cozily with every other part, and where we discuss endlessly the difference between social science methods and natural science methods; where we have the longest unit on the comparative influence of heredity and environment, and, of course, where we endlessly discuss the socialization process.

I mean the livelier version where teachers and students analyze and discuss modern social issues like the family, abortion, racism, wife and child abuse, cults, prisons, sexism, militia, political correctness, gun control and the environment. This is what's happening in North America right now in so many courses from Family Studies to Business. I'm thinking in my own bailiwick of courses like Canadian Family in family studies; World Issues in geography; Law in business; Science and Society in science; World Religions, World Politics and Society, Challenge and Change in history; and Canadian Literature and Women's Literature in some English departments.

Sociology across the Curriculum

Here is a list of debate topics (not my own) where the Society, Challenge and Change teacher asked students both to write a newspaper column on one issue and present the issue to the class. I include the complete list so that readers can see the real sweep of this conception:

1. Victims of crime should be compensated.
2. Drunk driving sentences should be more severe.
3. Marijuana should be legalized.
4. AIDS carriers should live in separate communities.
5. Food drives no longer provide properly for the poor.
6. Grey power! The rights of the elderly cannot be ignored.
7. The government is wasting money on daycare.
8. Industry must be forced to clean up its pollution.
9. Smokers have rights too.
10. Greenpeace! Environmental Saviour or Lunatic Fringe?
11. Animal Rights are being ignored in the name of progress.
12. The Toronto Humane Society has forsaken the animals it has sworn to protect.
13. The demands of Amnesty International cannot be ignored.
14. Abortion on demand should be legalized.
15. The unborn fetus has a right to life.
16. Alcoholics Anonymous is fighting a losing battle.
17. Prostitution should be legalized.
18. Homosexuality: Born or Bred?

19. The government must increase funding for battered women.
20. Halfway houses are a joke.
21. What do women want now! ?
22. Street gangs! Do we have anything to fear?
23. Canada is ignoring the plight of aboriginal Canadians.
24. Very little is being done for the drug addict.
25. Bring back capital punishment.
26. Suicide. Is anyone listening?
27. Society expects too much from the police.
28. Euthanasia should be legalized.
29. Advertising has a responsibility to portray people in a realistic way.
30. Any local issue.

It's not *my* list, but it will give you an impression of the kind of social issues one teacher in a Society, Challenge and Change class thought worth debating in class. Christopher Lasch, commenting in his last book on the pile-up of information these days — coupled with the decline of public debate — says this about "ordinary citizens" :

> Having been effectively excluded from public debate on the grounds of their incompetence, most Americans no longer have any use for the information inflicted on them in such large amounts. They have become almost as incompetent as their critics have always claimed — a reminder that it is debate itself, and debate alone, that gives rise to the desire for usable information. In the absence of democratic exchange, most people have no incentive to master the knowledge that would make them capable citizens.[2]

This point applies to us in Canada as well. As for teachers who demand prepared and serious debate rather than mush and "shooting the breeze," they are surely helping to build the kind of "civil society" that Lasch found lacking. By contrast the government version of this course should be Society, Not Much Challenge, Not Much Change.

Citizenship in "The Country of Everyday"

Of course, to citizenship purists, debating this list of topics doesn't seem like citizenship education at all. Where, they ask, is the thread of political economy that should connect the issues above? And where is the historical background of the issues? I share these criticisms, but remember that important forces have brought this emphasis to us and we can either choose to deal with it strategically or, as I suggested concerning the disappearance of yearly compulsory history courses, we can settle for lamenting the passing of what we miss.

And sometimes teacher criticism of this kind of sociology is downright snobbery. Notice that student interest in topics like those listed above is the same phenomenon as the adult habit, when reading a daily newspaper, of bypassing the latest story on Quebec separatism or on congressional or parliamentary debates in favour of stories about incest, murder, rape and multiple-injury accidents.

We don't have to go all the way with yellow journalism to acknowledge that issues like family, sex and violence cut close to home. The British educator A. S. Neill used to say that tabloid newspapers could teach us a lot about what the misery of modern life does to the average person. The down-and-dirty lives of the great mass of the population might surely be allowed to enter our school halls for a little more examining and weighing. More of what we might call "people's curriculum" might even help us discover — where so many churches have failed — some of the sacred in the muck and mire of daily life.

One perennial difficulty of traditional citizenship education which the sociology of specific problem issues has overcome is a difficulty Isaiah Berlin identified back in 1959. Democracy, he said, wasn't about "issues" and certainly wasn't about "taking a stand on issues." It did not "mandate ends, only means."[3] There was always something unreal with young students about discussing the "method of democracy" without getting into what issues the method was to be applied to. For example, the capitalist content of democracy has been deliberately masked since World War II (until the Thatcher/Reagan/Mulroney era). So has the humanizing of it by left-wing parties and the left-wing unions whose pioneering of issues like medicare then became the issues of traditional parties.

Remember the straightforward way of talking of U.S. General Smedley Butler quoted by a student in chapter 5: "I pacified Mexico for U.S. Oil, I secured Haiti for the National City Bank, I invaded Nicaragua for Brown Brothers banking interests, I invaded the Dominican Republic to protect U.S. Sugar interests, I pacified Honduras for the United Fruit Company."[4] No Canadian or American politician could talk this way today even though they might be *doing* the same oppressive stomping on people.

The sociological attack on history and other subjects has ripped off this mask. We discuss issues directly in these classes; arguments for and against issues and certain political tactics to achieve certain ends have, thereby, a greater concreteness than many of the old discussions about voting at election time. In fact I believe the popularity of conflict-issues sociology courses reflects the disillusionment of our larger population with traditional politics. The percentage of people who vote has plummeted in both Canada and the United States. Those who have returned to politics have often been those single-issue citizens who feel that this is their only way to exert influence. In turn, the most popular issues in the new sociology courses are exactly those issues most popular in single-issue politics.

I am not saying that useful civics and citizenship education of the traditional kind should be stopped or that it has disappeared. Some of it is very helpful. A fairly conservative unit on citizenship and law education is still part of Ontario's compulsory history course. Many students across the country are still taught the number of M.P.s in the House of Commons and the process a bill goes through in that place. And, yes, in the programs that exist there is indeed the distinction Alan Sears and Andrew S. Hughes make between elite and populist citizenship education[5] — with the first presenting a Canadian democracy that is supposedly healthy and viable and with the populists often getting students out to courts and council meetings and doing some real electioneering at election time.

We must salute these teachers and administrators who keep alive and develop these schemes in a time of great confusion and lack of government vision and leadership. Partly, these days we need to support each other and nourish what *does* exist because we are not urged on by a surrounding citizenship education movement as practitioners like J.R. McCarthy and H.C. Newlands were in the 1930s and 1940s. McCarthy, who later became Ontario's deputy minister of Education in the late 1960s, helped design exciting community action programs for Ontario elementary students after 1945, and H.C. Newlands, a leading Alberta educator of the 1930s, even spoke of citizenship education as "the preparation for a new social order."[6] The parallel in the U.S. was the left-wing and liberal tradition in midwestern states like Wisconsin and Minnesota.

Today, surrounded with more political confusion and less political hope, we have substituted The Country of Everyday — as Canadian poet Tom Wayman calls it — for the country of Canada or the United States. Even in the United States, where furious flag-waving can still be in style — especially for brief wars like that in the Persian Gulf — The Country of Everyday, through plebiscites and single issue politics, commands more citizen interest over the long haul than traditional patriotism. Tom Wayman puts it this way:

The Country of Everyday: Beginning

This is what we have, who are not possessed
by Jesus, or any dream
beyond what there is available
to us
also not by Marx
who became a committee
This is our Country: what there is
what we make every day
and live in. For us
there is no country to fight for
but The Country of Everyday.

— Tom Wayman[7]

So the next time we old history teachers lament the passing of our great subject, let us remember how many of our students have named history as their most-hated subject. Wayman's poem shows how few students were convinced that the country we taught about in history classes had anything to do with "what we make daily together."

Serious History Programs Gone throughout Canada, Great Britain and the U.S.

In Canadian provinces that have not embraced sociology or social studies with the gusto Ontario has shown, it is important to note that the trend is still toward studying the present with fragmented bits of social studies. Ken Osborne sums up his 1994 study of history programs in each Canadian province with thirteen observations. Here are the first five:

1. History has been largely subsumed under social studies so that it appears in curricula less as a systematic study of some part of the past, and much more as a source of case-studies, examples and illustrative topics.
2. The study of the present is favoured over the study of the past.
3. There is very little compulsory non-Canadian history.
4. There is virtually no systematic study of the past as a whole.
5. Some provinces do not make Canadian history compulsory.[8]

People concerned about the future of citizenship education agree that this is the real situation we face. But there is strong disagreement about whether, as I maintain, this current emphasis on social problems is a beachhead for new battles about new forms of teaching citizenship, or whether it is a lost island or a no-man's-land with strategic possibilities only for the wrong people.

Many enthusiasts for both the traditional and the progressive versions of citizenship education are deeply hostile to sociology. They see only aimless class discussions about current issues, or they see the conservative, government version of sociology. They need to ponder something said by Noel Annan back in 1959 — a message that fits citizenship education not just in England in 1959, but in Canada and the United States in the year 2000:

> Certainly one reason why political theory in this country is in decline is that, with some notable exceptions, we are still trying to produce ore from mines which for long have been worked out, namely the old concepts of state, society, will, rights, consent, obligation; and we have turned our back on the social studies and methods of analysis which alone would restore some value and new meaning to those concepts. Such rejuvenation can come primarily from the fruit of that revolution in sociology which so curiously passed us by over half a century ago and is still despised and feared by some of the most influential figures in academic life — to their very great discredit.[9]

"Political Literacy," not Citizenship Education

One result of this political confusion with our topic of citizenship education is that, from the very top, a new motive is now being pushed for studying these matters. We are urged to develop "political literacy" in students rather than ask them to become participants in a political process. The word literacy, as I pointed out in chapter 1, is most commonly used these days to mean conversant with the skills of a particular field. This has its good side, of course. It's surely good to help students sharpen their minds, to teach them to discern between gold and garbage. But there is also an ominous side. It has to do, of course, with how you can tell the difference between gold and garbage if you have never studied the *nature* of gold or garbage.

And if a reader rushes to ask me *"whose view* of the nature of things?"* I would suggest I mean the government's view or the teacher's view — but freely offered to the student, who can disagree and debate the issue. But I would also suggest to the questioning reader that this predicament is no different from the media skills approach, which has its own bias. No set of skills comes floating in from Objectivity Land.

It's not a choice between teaching objective skills and biased content. A point of view is firmly in place, no matter which approach you stress.

"Politics" is increasingly what we are asked to teach, not citizenship. To quote Ken Osborne once again: "Citizenship is not . . . a word that generates excitement. Most people seem to put it in the same category as clean underwear: a useful and even a desirable thing to have, but dull and respectable and not worth talking about."[10] When I did a study of magazines for history and social science teachers published in Ontario between 1944 and 1990, I was intrigued that in the *History and Social Science Teacher,* for special topic issues on politics produced between 1976 and 1988, only one out of seven used the already tainted word "citizenship":

Spring 1976	*Teaching Politics*
Winter 1978	*Educating for Citizenship*
Summer 1978	*Global Education*
May 1983	*Political Issues & the Teacher*
Summer 1987	*Teaching with Political Cartoons*
Fall 1987	*Canadian-American Relations*
Fall 1988	*The State of Political Education*

The feeling from these articles was of a profession in search of a new rationale for political instruction. What little consensus there was suggested that memorizing details about the mechanics of the Canadian democratic system was not valuable on its own, and that we should be teaching how the system *really* worked, warts and all.

The positive side of this change is obvious. The negative side is that the connection of the old method with actual participation in a democratic system has been dumped in favour of nurturing "critical thinking" (inquiry skills) with no challenge to participate in this system, do battle with it or actively turn your back on it. It is one step forward and two steps back to replace the naive voter with the armchair critic. You start off with Ricker and Saywell's civics book *How* ARE *We Governed?,* with the ARE in the title emphasized to suggest a more realistic look at how politics actually works.[11] Then you end up in the 1980s and 1990s with the aim not of being a participant in improving the system but of being a cool, detached judge of all versions of the system. Maybe the problem is that when you saw how the system actually worked you got so depressed you lost all interest! There's a little of that going on, but the real source of what I call skills mania in modern education is not this.

Restating the Central Political Point of This Book

As I have been arguing, what we are seeing is a new kind of education being imposed which is thought to fit the new developments of global capitalism, a capitalism highly affected not only by new computer and communication technologies but also by an intensified hostility to national boundaries (recall that we are citizens of nations), trade unions and education systems that stress content, "civil society" networks and blueprints for better societies. Now of course the education part of this is presented in the most glowing and optimistic terms as teaching students *how* to learn rather than teaching some content which they don't remember a month after the test and which, in any case, will be obsolete by the time they graduate. It's also presented as the absence of propaganda.

The trend towards labelling more and more knowledge as skills, and measuring whether you've learned such skills with the notion of "outcomes," is a trend which, for citizenship education, plays down the transmittal of political or moral principles, including traditional, liberal or radical ideas of how the world of government works, has worked or should work. What appears to be an emphasis on probing how things really operate is learning how — you've heard this from me before — to see through all systems while owing allegiance to none. Skills have been unstuck from the anchors they should be attached to. Maude Barlow and Heather-jane Robertson, in their book *Class Warfare: The Assault on Canada's Schools,* quote Neil Postman, who says that this culture "subjugates people to the interests of technology, elevates the pursuit of quantity of information over meaning, and divorces the population from belief systems, as information management has no moral core." Postman goes on to say that high-tech companies want schools restructured to produce "a technocrat's ideal: a person with no commitment and no point of view but with plenty of marketable skills."[12]

Mind you, it is not as if *nobody* thinks of what the anchors should be. Heads of state certainly think a lot about anchors when they talk to potential new investors in corporate high places around the world. I can see one of these CEOs with a Protestant evangelical background, after getting the pitch about tax breaks from the politician, saying — in the words of the old gospel hymn — "OK, friend, will your anchor hold?"

But those places in the older curricula which were meant for discussing the anchors of life (albeit discussing them in a very conservative way) are increasingly thought a waste of time for skilled modern workers. "Leave thinking about commitments and visions and wisdom to those who employ you and govern you," is the implication.

Unfortunately, many forward-thinking teachers think that the new skills emphasis in a subject like citizenship education is liberating when they compare it to the old approach of memorizing the number of M.P.s in the House of Commons and telling students that our democratic system was near perfect. In their own classes today, such teachers see animated student discussions and they credit the "critical thinking skills" method.

Yes, History Is Often Badly Taught, but It's Still Indispensible

But even if citizenship education can be partially approached via the social science of modern society, and even if the citizenship of single issues has possibilities for citizenly action where history failed, how can citizenship be taught properly with the arm of history chopped off? Absurd.

This brings to mind Bob Davis's Axiom #1: "When someone takes away from you a weapon that is essential to better your situation, assume they did it for a very good reason." Is this the conspiratorial theory of history? I plead guilty. The movers and shakers don't want vital and empowering citizenship training for our children. They prefer the shockingly low percentages of people voting at election times because they can carry on their work with less interference. (Incidentally, the statistics from the U.S. are worse than Canada's, but Canada's are heading in the same direction.)

The Chinese Revolution, Norman Bethune and Local Chinese Immigration

In the school year 1986-87, I had a lively class of thirty-four in World History. The change of population in our district was well underway by then, and the fastest-growing group was wealthy Chinese students from Hong Kong. Very few of these Chinese students took my class, preferring maths and sciences where they could do well. In our particular district (split 50 percent upper middle class and 50 percent *very* working class), the Chinese who settled had investment visas, which meant they had money.

The curriculum for the World History class had a major spot for the Russian and Chinese Revolutions. While we were discussing nineteenth- and twentieth-century China (which, of course, included a glance at

Hong Kong's special history), two different students brought to class two hate leaflets, both of which had been widely distributed door-to-door in parts of our district during 1984 and 1885. None of the class or I had bumped into any media coverage of these leaflets. The leaflets developed the points that (a) opening immigration doors to people of Asian, African and Latin American origins was ruining the "solid European stock" of Canada, and that (b) one of the chief ways the Chinese ruined Canada was that they were big-time drug dealers — all controlled by the "Chinese Mafia."

After studying and debating the contents of the leaflets, the class and I checked out what had happened after the passing out of the leaflets. Had the police been called? Had there been community meetings? Any arrests? There seemed to be a real hush about these hate leaflets.

Sensing that this whole issue of racism towards the Chinese was something to run with, I gave out a sheet of racist comments about Chinese heard around the school. Before I present this sheet, let me offer two different approaches to tackling racism when people bump into each other daily in a public institution. The first is favoured by official bureaucratic policy makers: tell your students you're colour-blind, correct all official textbooks and documents and photographs for gender and race, then walk around acting as if racism and sexism are gone. The other approach is more upfront: if you're a white teaching blacks, admit it and expect fallout and deal with it as it comes. Admit that differences do exist between groups and deal with them as openly as possible.

For twenty years, an incident in my teaching has stood out to me as the one that best explains the difference between these two methods. A class of grade 9 general level students had produced a fine magazine of their writings, drawings and cartoons for which we needed a title before it was ready to print. One student suggested a title which the whole class was immediately wild about: *The Dead Beat Bugle.*

When I went with the details to the principal — who put up the money for the publication — he said everything looked great except for the title. *The Dead Beat Bugle* should not be accepted by any teacher or school that promoted self-esteem, etc. I felt he missed the irony in the kids' understanding that around the school they were indeed known as deadbeats, but that they had produced a very undeadbeat magazine. We stuck with the title, which the principal, to his credit, did not force us to change. When the magazine came out, the grade 9 "dummies" fanned out to all the "academic level" middle-class classes in the school and proudly sold out their creation, five hundred copies for twenty-five cents each.

I am not suggesting that the decades of battles establishing laws about employment and school equity are not important. What I am saying is that using legal gains in hiring or school practices are not sufficient for dealing with the same issues between people who bump into each other on a daily basis. The distinction also applies to new issues like "bereavement counselling," where turning the loss of a parent by a grade 1 kid into an issue solely for an out-of-school bereavement counsellor does not answer the human dimension of the child's community of classmates, teacher and their activities together during a school day.[13] The establishment sometimes has difficulty telling the difference between establishing just laws and burying conflict for fear of its potentially dramatic consequences.

With this major aside I return to the handout list of racist comments heard about Chinese in my school in 1987. Obviously I assume the teacher giving out the following list is not a racist and believes in the potentially lively exchange that will probably ensue.

Stephen Leacock Collegiate Institute, 1986

Here are ten comments made by some Leacock students as criticism of the Chinese in Scarborough. Write 3-4 sentences giving your own personal opinion of each statement:

1. "They're so loud."
2. "Why do they always hang around together and stay by themselves?"
3. "They always speak their own language."
4. "Why should street signs be in Chinese? Is this an English-speaking country, or isn't it?"
5. "They're all so rich. They're buying up all our property and turning Agincourt into Asiacourt."
6. Maybe they're smart in school, but their gain is at our expense. They're crowding us out of school honours."
7. "How come their stores have signs in their language only? This country is English."
8. "If they come here, I figure they can learn our ways or go back where they came from."
9. "Why doesn't someone teach them how to drive?"
10. "Chinese males are wimps and nerds."

Conference for Four Hundred Senior Students

It wasn't long before the school (1300 students) was buzzing about this study. I realized because of the interest that it was time to organize something bigger. A student class committee and I went to the history department, whose members were very co-operative in setting up a special-event day for all four hundred senior history students. The administration and other teachers supported the right of students to miss other classes that day. The program was to be as follows:

Senior History Students
"Mini Conference"
Stephen Leacock Collegiate Institute
Canada and China
Wednesday, December 3, 1986

9:00 am	Leacock Auditorium — Debate Session — Be It Resolved That "Communism Has Been Beneficial to China"

Affirmative	Negative
Dr. James Endicott, retired United Church minister, raised in China	Dr. S. Y. Lee, Ph. D. in Economics from Cornell University, now employed with Ontario Hydro
and two Leacock students: Clarence So and Miyoung Byun	and two Leacock students: Sonia Sabir and Glen Yeung

10:15 am	Question Period
10:30 - 10:45 am	Break
10:45 - 11:30 am	Leacock Auditorium — Presentation on Dr. Norman Bethune by Roderick Stewart, one of Canada's leading authorities on the life of Bethune
11:30 - 12:30 pm	Lunch
12:30 - 1:15 pm	Auditorium: The Chinese Community in Scarborough — chaired by two Scarborough Board community workers
1:15 - 1:45 pm	Classroom Seminar and Wrap-up Session

Student Reactions to the Big Day

The plan for the 9 a.m. debate was to invite two experts on "China since 1949" who would share the affirmative and negative sides with two student debaters each. The pro-Communist expert was Dr. James Endicott, eighty-seven-year-old friend of Chou En-lai. Endicott had spent most of his life as a United Church missionary in China. For the negative side we had Dr. S.Y. Lee, an eloquent Taiwanese Canadian economist who worked for Ontario Hydro Corporation. The collaboration of four of our students with these experts was one of the exciting features of the day.

Our famous Canadian doctor Norman Bethune, whose life had mythic and heroic dimensions after surviving tuberculosis and serving as a field doctor in the Spanish Civil War, died of an infection while serving with the Chinese Communist Army in 1939. We asked one of Canada's leading experts on Bethune, Roderick Stewart, to talk about the famous doctor. My own class had already read one of Stewart's books in class. In the all-student question-and-answer sheet, which everyone had to complete and hand in after the three sections of the day, students were asked whether they thought Bethune should be better recognized in Canada and to explain their reasons. Sixty percent said "not," because Bethune was a communist. Stewart had stressed that Bethune was a communist (which he was), and that he personally (Stewart) did not care about how well nations recognize people.

Many interesting writeups came in to us from the four hundred students. A majority said the debate had been won by the affirmative (Communism *had* been beneficial to China). From the reasons given, it appeared that eighty-seven-year-old Endicott, easily the best speaker, and one of his two student colleagues had grabbed hold of the audience. Endicott, partly because he spoke well but also because his age gave him a certain charisma, fascinated many students. "The old boy was great!" and similar comments, popped up in the comment sheets.

But the largest interest was reserved for the "Chinese in Scarborough" topic. Two very articulate members of the Scarborough Board's outreach department led a very lively discussion. Many students present who had not hammered out the topics of Communist China or Dr. Bethune — since they had only a one-period orientation — had clear and pressing things to say on this topic of the arrival of lots of Chinese in "their" district. The two chairpersons did an excellent job fielding debate, and many positive things were said. But this was a real and honest discussion, so many negative things were also said. Except for a positive headline, *The Toronto Star,* the country's largest newspaper, decided to feature the negative: "If you wouldn't park so close to the end of the curb we wouldn't be so mad," said one Stephen Leacock Collegiate student in a question period following the conference.

I took *The Toronto Star* to task for this article and they printed my letter:

I would have hoped that maybe your reporter, knowing that racial hostility is rampant in our society, would therefore have considered that yet another expression of such hostility was not news. But I had hoped that she might consider that it *was* news for a school to be trying to meet this hostility head-on and give two articulate Chinese Canadians a platform to answer frank student questions on the Scarborough scene.

Many students wrote letters, but none were printed. Here is one such letter:

Dear Editor,

I am writing about your story "Students Tackle Open Resentment of Chinese." Yes I think differently about the Chinese in Scarborough now because I used to be against them all living together and only talking to each other, but the Chinese speakers convinced me about the reason they do this. They don't speak a lot of English when they first come. The Chinese in Scarborough are recent immigrants and their culture is different.

I look at these facts, and put myself, *being black,* in their position and realize that I would probably do likewise.

Sylvia George

Our principal also wrote to *The Star* asking why there was no recognition for a school trying to deal head-on with racism. He also pointed out that the Students' Council president, the Parents' Council president and last year's valedictorian were all Chinese Canadians.

I liked the fact that this project had engaged so large a segment of the school community and, because of the newspaper report, it was also beginning to produce a small public debate. Before the issue died out in the papers, *The Toronto Star* had printed ten items that specifically mentioned our conference, and the local *Scarborough Mirror* had printed four, including a column of resounding praise for the conference.

Should Issues of Racism Be Buried or Publicized?

The two Chinese speakers from the Board of Education were annoyed that *The Star* and the *Mirror* had been invited. I had invited the newspapers, not knowing the views of these guests. Their views turned out to be a reflection of the same views that may have been responsible for burying the two pieces of hate literature: Don't publicize racism and it'll go away.

By the mid-1990s the Chinese in our area were no longer

experiencing much blatant, up-front racism. I decided there was a socio-economic class point to all this. Since money talks in this society, people with money who hang in and buy and sell with the best of them get at least grudging respect. I don't see black leaders in Toronto opposing publicity for school conferences to fight racism. Neither was this the attitude of most students and parents from our school. In fact the Chinese chairperson of our Parents' Council had written a letter to *The Star* supporting the one-day program.

Readers who know schools will realize that some features of my program assume a protective administrative structure which allows such work to go on. My school, for the twenty-one years I taught there, usually had strong, liberal principals of the old school, who fought with some of us on many occasions, but stood behind our right to offer a challenging curriculum. For years the history department had also been a tight, supportive unit chaired by a generous, left-leaning conflict healer. These supportive structures had to be constantly worked on and re-inforced; for example, our school staff of eighty was prepared at one time to crash a Board meeting if the Director did not come to a school staff meeting to hear that we wanted the same type of tough liberal to replace the principal who was leaving.

How Can Students Be Engaged in These Issues?

Coming back to our school's Chinese "special event," I stress that engagement by students in citizenship issues cannot be achieved by a few simple "political skills" exercises. It comes by a mixture of challenges, as you see here, where students may be "arrested" by something local, where a teacher helps to capitalize on existing issues and break a discussion out of a too-narrow local context, where a variety of school constituencies cooperate, where solid materials are studied to increase real knowledge, where a bit of drama is tossed into the mix, and where all skills of letter writing, debating, discussing, note taking, listening, psyching-out documents, memorizing, etc., are brought together by a human focus on understanding a piece of society so that we can get more clues on surviving better with each other.

This anchoring of the skills does not make them unimportant. I could tell you of the hours I spent with the debaters. Or perhaps you can imagine the time students spent searching for the kind of outlines or structures best suited to hold together the history of the Chinese Revolution and the life of Norman Bethune.

But that amount of work by students meant more because it was grounded in how they felt about the multicultural mix of their own school and their own district — and to an extent in historical dramas like the Chinese Revolution and the life of Dr. Norman Bethune.

The Hedgehog and the Fox

All this reminds me of an ancient saying which became the title of a book, *The Hedgehog and the Fox*, by the late Isaiah Berlin: "The fox knows many things; the hedgehog knows one big thing."[14]

Both are necessary. Probably the fox knows many skills, but if he never learns the one big thing — for example, the mind of God? what makes the world tick? what can be changed in this world, and what must be accepted? — his skills may be of little use, or, worse still, they may be available only for ill to the devious masters of our unfortunate zombie, the fox.

CHAPTER 7

Sociology

Know the Conflicts, Know Your Own People

It is now time to give some examples of the lively approach to sociology as a genuine political topic. Not all schools call it sociology. It might be social studies, it might be social science or it might have some fancy title like Society, Challenge and Change, as it does in Ontario. Remember too that sociology's influence goes beyond history departments, since courses in family studies, geography, politics, religion and sometimes English are now like sociology courses. I am going to focus here on topics of current conflict in society. I am indebted to Gerald Graff for writing a fine book recommending for universities what some of us have been doing in high schools for years. In his book *Beyond the Cultural Wars: How Teaching the Conflicts Can Revitalize American Education*[1] Graff mostly talks about universities and, first of all, about battles concerning the university curriculum. As I suggested at the beginning of the last chapter, I am thinking about topics battled over in society at large:

- Abortion and Euthanasia
- Greenpeace

- Environmental Protection
- Cults
- Crime and Punishment
- Daycare
- Canada's and Ontario's Social Programs
- Unions and Strikes
- Homosexuality and Lesbianism
- Race in Toronto
- Mental Illness: comparison of the film *Warrendale* with *One Flew over the Cuckoo's Nest*
- Gun Control
- Injuries on the Job
- Industrial Diseases
- Consumer Complaints about Cars
- Rent Control
- U.S. Militia Groups

Know the Conflicts

I have been presenting these lists at various times in this book partly to make it clear that it is not contemporary features of education per se which I am arguing against. The fact that I argue strongly against the contempoary skills emphasis does not mean that I consider contemporary *sociology* to be a waste of time. But is it possible to do a bad job taking up the current social conflicts? It most certainly is if the courses are undemanding "bird" courses.

Take the use of films. Here is an obvious place for wide use of the many good films available. It is not the place, however, for downplaying reading. On the topic of crime and prisons I still use the great film, *Attica*.[2] (My main question: Was Attica a riot or a rebellion?) But that does not preclude the use of *The New York Times*'s editor Tom Wicker's long *Esquire* article on the subject,[3] or handing out sheets containing the Five Demands and Fifteen Practical Proposals and the official Twenty-Eight Points from Wicker's book, *A Time to Die*.[4] It didn't preclude the required reading of Canadian Roger Caron's autobiography of prison life, *Go Boy!*[5] — or following up through clippings of the fate of Caron as a freed and later reincarcerated man. When I took up mercury poisoning in Minamata, Japan, and in Northern Ontario among Aboriginal peoples, the class studied very thoroughly a twenty-eight-page, special-edition newspaper put out by the Ontario Public Interest Research Group, called *Quicksilver and Slow Death*.[6] Showing movies about Waco and the Hare Krishna organization did not preclude reading a 108-page, thoughtful book, *Are Religious Cults Dangerous?* by Carol Coulter.[7] Taking up the issue of abortion did not mean watching a film about Dr. Henry Morgentaler[8] followed by the Right to Life film entitled *The Silent Scream*[9] and then leaving it at that. Among many other things, it also meant studying in detail pamphlets from various sides of the issue including ten sheets of twenty-eight arguments presented in detail by the Toronto Right to Life Association and writing a detailed response as required homework. These readings and writings were required of every student. And seeing the films required compulsory and extensive note taking on each film.

These topics are ideal for class discussion and debate, but vaguely shooting the breeze is not what I mean by discussion and debate. What I expect is that students will confront each other with gradually deepening knowledge and arguments.

The study of contemporary social conflict is also an ideal project for both group field trips and for individual and group research. But this can also be an excuse for skimming the surface of a topic, for research assignments that require one page of scribbling from one interview with someone not much involved in the topic. We must expect better.

Here is a selection from a student report on a class field trip where we visited Seven Places of Protest: a new subway station where disabled people had protested the lack of access for the disabled, City Hall, the U.S. Embassy, the provincial legislature, a labour strike location, Greenpeace headquarters and Dr. Morgentaler's abortion clinic.

> Following our trip to the Provincial Legislature we stopped over at Morgentaler's Clinic, where the Right to Life people had rented the attached building. When we arrived two protesters from Right to Life were walking up and down with signs that read "Is this not a baby?" (With a picture of a healthy baby underneath.) I approached one of the men and began a conversation.
>
> Me: How did you begin to support Right to Life?
> Him: I read a few articles, found I was strongly in support and joined them.
> Me: Are you married?
> Him: No.
> Me: Do you have a girlfriend?
> Him: Yes.
> Me: Is she on a birth control pill?

Him: No.

Me: Well, don't you believe that is the biggest reason for abortions? Do you use a condom?

Him: No.

Me: So what protection do you use?

Him: Nothing.

Me: Nothing! So what if you were going to have intercourse with your girlfriend, what would happen?

Him: I'd marry her first before I'd ever do anything with her.

Me: Are you Roman Catholic?

Him: Yes.

Me: Thank you.

I wondered whether this was plain and simple prejudice against Roman Catholics, so I asked Susan why she stopped the conversation when she did. She replied "I've studied all the Right to Life points, sir, but I still think that Catholics are out to lunch when they lay on this 'Just Say No' crap. They don't know where teenagers are at."

Conflict in Its Raw Form, Not Prettied-Up

I have repeatedly emphasized the importance of setting up an atmosphere that encourages students to work towards getting as near as possible to the truth of an issue — and not having a superficial debate atmosphere where the implication is that debating forever is more important than coming to any conclusions or making any changes. This does not mean that I don't stress the actual differences on each issue; serious debate is essential on conflict topics. I once produced a video interview of seven people who supported six different social programs: daycare subsidies and mothers' allowance, unemployment insurance, injury on the job (carpal tunnel syndrome), medicare and old age pensions. I was doing these interviews for a union that wanted to design a piece of curriculum for high school students. For each interview, I also designed a set of questions for class discussion and written answers.

The first interview was controversial because it was with a high school student who received full subsidy for her two children to be in the school daycare centre while she attended school. She also received mothers' allowance. Some viewers were outraged that this young women was "rewarded" for not being more careful about birth control; others agreed with the young mother's own view that this financial support was keeping her from turning to drugs and prostitution, that she would soon become a working and tax-paying citizen and the government would get back "their investment." The interview itself obviously gave the mother the chance to present her own defense very strongly.

But this wasn't good enough for the union. When I designed the questions raising the conservative "no rewards" view, the union turned down my questions and demanded a nice, so-called "politically correct" set of questions — which completely eliminated the ferocious public debate on the issue.

Students Differ about Warrendale Movie

Sometimes it was a real challenge for me to let students hate a piece of curriculum that I love. I often showed a movie called *Warrendale,* a full-length documentary made about methods used to treat disturbed children in the mid-1960s in a Toronto treatment centre. I even worked there for a year as a teacher of music and drama. The movie was so controversial that even though it won scores of international film awards, it was not shown on the Canadian Broadcasting Corporation until 1995. I am very impressed with the methods used at Warrendale, but at both university and high school I always had about one third of each class who were very disturbed by the film. Here is one university student's reactions:

> At the beginning of the film, for example, we see Tony, our foul-mouthed young friend, being locked in a painful hold because of an insult he had made regarding someone's bad breath. Shortly after this, Carol, a girl of at least thirteen or fourteen, was shown being fed a baby bottle and read a fairy tale before her bedtime. These situations create two different reactions, both of which are undesirable. Tony learns that when he is caught in the future, he should be more devious in order to avoid punishment or to run away. Carol, on the other hand, only learns how to thwart her personal problems through infantile behaviour. Thus she becomes more and more dependent on Warrendale with its baby bottles and bedtime stories.
>
> The dependency factor is one of the major problems that faced Warrendale. Although Tony may run away from his problems, he will learn how to survive in the tougher street-wise aspect of society. People like Carol get drawn further and further into Warrendale's confines. This is a problem similar to that experienced by persons who become involved with cults. After a while, the victim will not be capable of adapting to situations outside of the unit.

Here is a more positive quote from a high school student:

> I don't think I could ever see myself working in an institution like this one. However, I do have some experience working with a child in a daycare who had an emotional disturbance. I really enjoyed working with him. He taught me a lot, but he was very uncontrollable. Like some of the kids in the Warrendale movie, Jayson, (the child I worked with) had a dirty mouth, he had tantrums and he never listened. He only got along with two people in the daycare, myself and another teacher whom I worked with. I believe most of his problems originated at home. He was brought up among women, with no male role model. I feel he was lacking love and attention. He found that support within myself and the teacher. I could see myself working one on one with children with these type of difficulties, but I don't think I could handle working in an institution like Warrendale.
>
> To conclude this essay I will discuss the comparison between the different methods of treatment provided. When watching *One Flew over the Cuckoo's Nest* we saw how some patients were treated with drugs, sedatives and all the way to lobotomies. This was to calm the patient down who lost control. In the Warrendale movie we saw no such use of drugs. The children were talked to and held in a position to calm them down. Both methods work but which one is less harmful? The use of drugs is unnecessary. Some people say "Why do the kids have to be held?" They are only held to stop themselves from hurting others and themselves, and if you didn't notice, it did work.

Developing Investigation Skills?

As readers will surmise, the assumption of typical skills enthusiasts is that in taking courses like these, students are learning investigation skills. To me, the investigation skills must be the servant of the knowledge you gain about social and political conflict in contemporary society. Am I just quibbling about words by saying this? I suggest it isn't, for these three reasons:

1. When we know what technical skills are going to *be used for*, we can tell whether the focus is a worthy cause. I am not saying there won't be lots of debate about whether the focus is a good one or not. Provincial, state and local curriculum authorities in the past always

assumed it was their difficult job to iron out what constituents thought were worthy matters for their children to study. The examination of what is to be taught at least prevents the illusion of many skills people that their system avoids all moral judgements and all preaching in their choice of curriculum.

2. The action of trying to separate skills from knowledge will help to establish whether the "learning paradox" is in operation. The "learning paradox" is a situation where the system designed to help you understand a topic is more complicated than the topic it's meant to clarify. I once shared a platform with an education scholar who said that history could not be understood properly by students until we taught them what he called "Elements in the Structure of the Discipline of History." He correctly identified some basic assumptions about time and change and "historical agency" which lie behind our ability to talk sensibly about change in history.

So long as these points could be woven into a regular history class incidentally (as lots of teachers do already), I had no quarrel with him. Taught as a whole separate scheme (as he insisted it must), it qualified for the "learning paradox" award — a scheme to assist students which was more complicated than the history it was meant to clarify.

3. If we clarify the difference between the "investigation skills" and the subjects they are meant to investigate, we can apply what I call the Frank Smith Test. Frank Smith is the education psychologist I have quoted from time to time in this book, and the author of *To Think* and *Insult to Intelligence*. Smith would frequently say: If a student appears not to understand what we are calling a skill, maybe the student's problem is "lack of knowledge," not "lack of skills."

To help show what I mean, let me first offer a Spectrum of Opinion on Abortion chart which I have used for years in discussions on abortion.

Spectrum of Opinion on Abortion

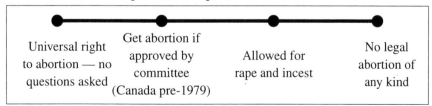

| Universal right to abortion — no questions asked | Get abortion if approved by committee (Canada pre-1979) | Allowed for rape and incest | No legal abortion of any kind |

A similar spectrum of opinion can be set up for many topics, such as capital punishment.

Spectrum of Opinion on Capital Punishment

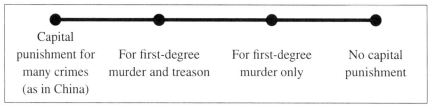

| Capital punishment for many crimes (as in China) | For first-degree murder and treason | For first-degree murder only | No capital punishment |

It so happens that the spectrums I have used in my high school classes have been helpful for many individual students and for class discussion on these topics. The very idea of the rainbow spectrum of light being used as a metaphor for a spread of ideas was very useful. (I readily agree that this is a mental skill which I was teaching *before* we looked at the content of any of our topics.)

Spectrums of Politics Are Highly Complex

It was in my university class that the problem with two spectrums arose. It seemed not to have been an issue before, but this probably meant that I just hadn't noticed it before or nobody brought it up as a problem.

The class, Childhood, Schools and Society, is described in the university calendar as follows:

Childhood, Schools and Society

A battle rages in Ontario today about what is wrong with our families and our schools.

On the issue of families the battle is between those who believe children should be given broad freedom and those who think that firm parental authority and even traditional religion should be restored.

On the topic of schools liberals see methods like whole language, co-operative learning and child-centered classrooms as a must to develop thinking citizens. On the other side many critics say that students are not even being taught the basics of reading, writing and arithmetic any more.

What is the truth in these struggles about families and

schools? This class will explore this debate, keeping a sharp focus on the practical — on how current families and schools actually function.

For a number of years when I gave an overview of this course, I offered two spectrums of opinion. The first was the spectrum of political opinion in Canada — leaving out attitudes about the future of Quebec. (I knew how rough and misleading my spectrum would be when I acted as if we could drop out Quebec and have much of significance to say!)

Canadian Politics Opinion Spectrum

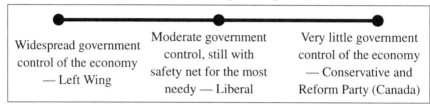

| Widespread government control of the economy — Left Wing | Moderate government control, still with safety net for the most needy — Liberal | Very little government control of the economy — Conservative and Reform Party (Canada) |

The second was about education opinion:

Canadian Education Opinion Spectrum

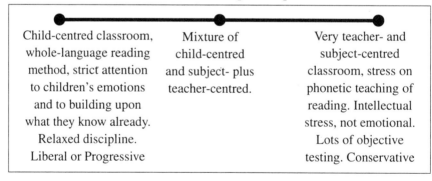

| Child-centred classroom, whole-language reading method, strict attention to children's emotions and to building upon what they know already. Relaxed discipline. Liberal or Progressive | Mixture of child-centred and subject- plus teacher-centred. | Very teacher- and subject-centred classroom, stress on phonetic teaching of reading. Intellectual stress, not emotional. Lots of objective testing. Conservative |

I knew how oversimplified these spectrums were. I didn't even include the left wing in this spectrum because it needs another whole variable: "what classes of people you want well-educated." Then, too, the skills emphasis position was missing; it could only be on a spectrum that included a variable about technology and technique.

But even without these refinements, a handful of my university students were deeply baffled near the end of the course when they went back to their early notes. They were preparing for an exam for which they got the wording one month ahead of time, and which they could spend up to three hours writing, but with no notes or books in front of them. The one handout they had was two pages of the course topics plus all the names of readings and films.

They could also use the month prior to the exam to do sample answers to the questions and get my responses, then rewrite, etc. Some worked in groups doing this. I will come back to the student bafflement after I show you the final exam. It went as follows:

Childhood, Schools and Society (1800.06A)
Summer 1997: Final Exam

1. *"The modern problems with the family such as child and wife abuse, drugs, children defying parents, latch-key children, day care woes, single-parent families, are caused by giving up traditional values such as male authority, women staying home with children, different roles for mothers and fathers, traditional discipline and religion."*

   Discuss this statement, defending your own views with arguments from the course and from your experience and knowledge. Your answer should contain a mixture of general coverage of course topics, readings and viewings with a stamp that is your own, i.e., with enough sections or a general approach which are developed in your own way. (25 marks)

2. *"The lines are drawn in the education battle today. The question is whether education will offer high standards, real teaching, proper basic skills, advanced thinking skills in subjects like science and computers, proper streaming, and all of this controlled by the people who actually pay the taxes — the parents and the public; or will education be progressive, child-centred teaching with vague report cards, touchy-feely curriculum, expecting the least common-denominator of kids in classrooms full of every variety of ability and disability, class, race, language, motivation, and all this controlled by education bureaucrats and teachers' unions?"*

   Explain the ins and outs of this debate, and lay out where you stand and why. As you explain the debate and take your stand, show your knowledge of the course material to illustrate your points. You should also include relevant experience and knowledge of your own. To put this as I did in the previous question, your answer should contain a mixture of general coverage of course topics, readings and viewings with a stamp that is your own, i.e. with enough sections or a general approach which are developed in your own way. (50 marks)

This final exam was 25 percent of the student's final grade.

What was still baffling a handful of students fairly near the end of the course were all the labels like right wing, left wing, conservative, liberal, technocratic, and how one could see the conflict as different responses to the same challenges — or what it meant to describe "the essence" of a problem. I eventually decided that my answer could be found in the good old Frank Smith Test — the problem was more a knowledge problem than a skills problem. Ten years ago most of my class had been teachers in their late thirties, forties and fifties who had already raised families and had taught school for years. They could call on masses of personal reference points and experience about raising kids and teaching school.

Today I have students who mostly come straight from high school to university. Ninety percent of the class have fewer pictures in their minds about school and child-rearing. It was important to draw out as much of what these students *did* know as soon as possible. About raising children, they certainly knew a lot about *being children*. And about school, they had been students. How many in this class remembered most of their elementary classrooms having rows of chairs and the teacher at the front? And how many remember chairs being in small separate groups and you were in small groups most of the day doing different things? Why were there these differences? How did yours work? And so on.

This issue is not unlike the problem my students reading about ancient West Africa had with translating a chart into prose. Partly with the skills question, we are debating how much reality can be simplified, summed up or represented on a map, in a list, in a chart, as a spectrum, in a formula. Lots of reality, for certain purposes, in certain contexts *can* be so represented. But just because we are in an age that has come to represent more and more things, more and more often this way does not mean that touch, taste, smell, hearing, sight are becoming obsolete. It doesn't mean that *how to live* can be neatly abstracted in a chart. And it doesn't mean that we now have a magical shortcut to learning such large and deep issues as how the current conflict in education came about and what it means — never mind the monumental task of how it could be resolved.

Know Your Own People

I have been giving classroom examples from some from my black history classes, since that is what I specialized in my last years of teaching. The methods I have talked about can mostly be used for any class. But I would like to emphasize that in the current debate about what should be taught about race, difference and identity, I am solidly in the camp that says schools *must* provide difference as well as common education. Black students must have the option of studying African and diaspora history and current events in their community, especially local events. There must be the courses everyone must take. Of course we'd like to see eveyone taking these subjects, but while we're fighting for that great day to arrive, the options route for specific groups is also a must. We need specific courses in the history of women and working-class history courses as well.

We must not be intimidated by critics who turn us away from making these courses available by telling us that these courses are dividing people or asking, "What if everyone started demanding such courses?"

Let me take you back to the late eighties, when various parent "quality groups" were getting started with their lobbying and their writing of pamphlets. The ideologues of this right-wing movement were aware of how little interest these parent leaders took in the education of the underdog, of new immigrants and the working class generally. Descriptions appeared in brochures of the poor beleaguered middle-class child in today's classroom surrounded and held back by mainstreamed disabled students, by students of colour (many of whom couldn't speak English) and by "the great unwashed."

As I said in the Introduction, one of the right wing's chief publicists in Toronto, Dennis Raphael, told me in 1993: "Mark Holmes and I are trying to get the quality groups to add the disadvantaged to their concerns." Sure enough, the disadvantaged are found in the television show *Failing Grades* (1993), put together by Dr. Mark Holmes and Dr. Joe Freedman. The disadvantaged appear as one of the four topics along with international comparisons, patterns of effective instruction and effective schools. Interestingly, however, the disadvantaged are handled very quickly and, unlike the other three topics in the video, there are no references to research studies, elaborate statistical charts or clips of American experts to bolster the arguments. It is clearly a tack-on.

Notice, also, this carefully chosen label, "the disadvantaged." A very large mass of working-class, immigrant and disabled students is hereby narrowed to sound like a small handful of difficult kids who deserve nothing but an afterthought.

In the last four or five years, many mainstream thinkers and political leaders both in the United States and Canada have become more and more upset that the schools' multicultural programs are supposedly tearing our countries apart. American books like Arthur Schlesinger, Jr.'s *The Disuniting of America: Reflections on a Multicultural Society*[10] and in Canada, Neil Bissoondath's *Selling Illusions: The Cult of Multiculturalism in Canada*[11] have offered this point of view.

With novelist Bissoondath the attitude is like a variation of the old rhyme:

> The working class can kiss my ass
> I've got the foreman's job at last.

Only with Bissoondath, it's more pedigree than class:

> Trinidad can kiss my ass
> I've been a cosmopolitan from birth.

More recently, Neil Postman's *The End of Education*[12] has picked up the same theme. To Postman it's great to study the history of words, but not the history of peoples — too fragmenting! None of these authors points out that both countries were a lot more fragmented in the 1950s when the lower class and the "ethnics" were "kept in their place." But that, clearly, was a kind of fragmentation (the big bad word) that all three writers would have been more comfortable with. Gary B. Nash, Charlotte Crabtree and Ross E. Dunn put this point very well in *History on Trial: Culture Wars and the Teaching of the Past*:

> One of the peculiarities of today's history wars is that those who believe that particularistic studies of women, African Americans, Asian Americans, religious minorities, and working people will balkanize America do not reflect on whether groups that have been ignored, demeaned or marginalized can expect to feel part of the *unum* when they are not counted among the *pluribus*.[13]

For recent education writing surely the most strident trumpet call of all comes from Peter Emberley, co-author with Waller R. Newell of *Bankrupt Education: The Decline of Liberal Education in Canada.*[14] In a review of *Public School and Political Ideas: Canadian Education Policy in Historical Perspective* by Ronald Manzer, Emberley says, "the issue of multiculturalism is the defining political question of our day, for what cannot be ignored is that the volatility of the appeals to race, gender,

and ethnicity is corroding central metaphysicial ideas of the person, reason, and the public realm."[15] To Emberley these new ideas are
"volatile." In the blunter language of conservative politicians of the
nineteenth century, Emberley is worried that "the natives are getting
restless." He goes on: "By adopting an analysis . . . built on the vagaries
of historical contingency" (that's presumably what blacks and women
are — "vagaries of historical contingency," or the "meanderings of passing fads"), we are going to wipe out that conception of the stable, liberal world of "the person, reason and the public realm." Emberley will
recall that only relatively recently have women in Canada been considered "persons," to use one of his sacred words. And people without
property couldn't vote. I, too, believe we should continue to teach students the evolution of democratic government in Canada, but not without a proper respect for human protest, past, present and future. Blacks
and women are not passing fads.

In fairness to Emberley, he takes a few swipes at skills mania in his
own book. He is a vintage conservative who wants to protect the traditional curriculum from all this boiling up from below. Most of these
writers who accuse feminism, racial liberation and ethnic pride of fragmenting Canada want to solve the problem by an appeal to education as
above all these ideologies, and as an enterprise that passes on the technical skills of writing, speaking, reading and thinking.

Those who were part of the battles of the 1970s for a less class-
biased school system will notice that debates about race and ethnic
group have almost totally replaced the debates about class bias. The
view of racial problems as unconnected to class have ascendancy right
now, even with many leaders in the visible minority constituencies. The
skills language would like to factor away the class, race, gender and ethnic issues, and maintain that all students are equal under the new pedagogy of skills.

Of course, some are more equal than others. Life skills, despite the
comprehensive sound of the term, is mostly about filling in forms, writing letters applying for jobs and preparing yourself for an interview —
as well as "getting them off Caribbean time," one principal in Metro
Toronto confided in private. Finally, and perhaps most significantly, the
skills philosophy has not presented an accurate future employment picture; the worst class-bias feature of this philosophy is its insistence that
following its tenets will equip a mass of students at least for Information Age employment. In fact it equips only a handful.

"Difference" Is There whether It's in the Curriculum or Not

Of course even if we pretend that we're keeping the "damaging ethnic, racial, gender and sexual orientation factors" out of our school, they operate there anyway. In 1975 my high school, Stephen Leacock Collegiate, was basically what my friend Jim McQueen called a mayonnaise-and-white-bread school. Now 20 percent of the population is black and the largest group is Chinese.

There is a lesson I learned from our African Canadian parents and from the Toronto African Canadian leader, Akua Benjamin. In my second year of teaching black history I went out and knocked on sixty parents' doors and we had a meeting at the school of fifty black parents. One thing we reported to the parents was that many teachers complained about black students coming late to class or skipping. "Why aren't we being called about this?" parents asked. "And why aren't teachers *insisting* on proper punctuality and attendance?" I told them that, from the teachers' point of view, teachers got such attitude from the black students that they gave up insisting. When Akua Benjamin spoke at the school a year later she said, regarding police relations with black kids, "One thing we have to deal with on this issue is that our black kids talk back. If we hadn't learned to talk back, we'd still be slaves," Benjamin said.

Teachers need to hear the same message. "Teachers are afraid of us," say many black students. "They're always complaining about 'attitude.'"

For several years in the early 1990s we had an eight-person committee to check out how black students were doing academically in our school. Five of the eight were the African Canadian teachers in our school at that time. What we found was that black kids, on average, were doing more poorly than most other kids. But the committee, staff and principal were not prepared to carry this further and the parents were not at that time organized to push. At the final staff meeting after this survey and discussion, the committee invited Toronto's best-known black parent organizer, Keren Brathwaite, to address the teachers.[16] The result of our survey was not unique, Ms. Brathwaite said. School systems had to examine their practices to discover the cause of this poorer performance.

Most of the staff were furious. It's not our fault, they said. One teacher even wrote Keren Brathwaite that Toronto wasn't Nova Scotia. So people may hope that keeping multiculturalism out of the curriculum will keep out racism. It won't happen. It's there regardless. Better, in my opinion, to meet it head on and get involved deliberately and officially.

Here is an example of this different approach.

Case Study: What Learning about Your Own People's Current Situation Can Mean

Since my namesake Rob Davis, the local African Canadian city councillor, knew about my black history classes, and since we had a connection because I had worked to get him elected even though he was a conservative (!), he called me when topics of interest to my classes came up at Council. Once he called to say he was leading the fight at Council for a new affirmative action hiring policy for the fire department. (An admirably unconservative policy, I thought!)

At first I thought simply of preparing the class with background about the issue and then all of us taking a daytime field trip to the Council for the final meeting that would decide the issue. I was slated to be one of the constituents addressing the meeting, so that would provide another tie-in. Rob Davis would address my two classes in an antichamber before the Council meeting.

Then, because there was so much public interest in the meeting, it was changed to night time. I had too many students with night jobs, so I decided to get the videotape of the Council meeting. Instead of riding the school buses to the meeting, we would pay an afternoon visit to a fire station around the corner from my house. Councillor Davis would then address the classes at my house before the students would bus back to school, and he and I would attend the meeting that night. Then a week later, when the tape of Council was available, the class would see it and study it.

But setting up the meeting at the fire station was not that easy. The stations are used to showing the nice trucks to grade 1 students. "Why did you want to come," they asked? "To discuss the issue that was before Council — the equity hiring issue." I heard a distinct gulp on the phone. The local councillor for my area, Rob Davis, was to address my students, I said. We'll have to talk to head office, I was told. The next day they called back to say that a firefighter administrator from main office would speak to us.

The morning of the event I got a call from the head of the firefighters' union, who was a straight-from-the-hip sort of guy solidly opposed to the proposed law. "Don't you have any fire stations up in

Scarborough?" he asked. Why were we coming all the way downtown just to see a fire station? I said I think he knew the reason. It was the area of my home and the counsellor, Rob Davis, was leading the battle for a new equity hiring policy. "Sounds like a teacher propagandizing his students," he said. I said I hoped he would come to the fire station himself and tell the students why he was against the new proposed law. "I just may do that," he said.

When fifty mostly African Canadian students set off in the bus for the fire station, I told them about the phone call from the head of the union. Because we had studied the background papers given us by councillor Davis and various groups including the union, the students knew that the union's position was that the standard of firefighting would go down with this new policy.

Rob Davis's main argument was backed by a professor of physical education at York University who had been the advisor in the design of both physical and knowledge tests taken by people applying to be firefighters. Davis had told me — and later this is what he argued at Council — that when the city received the expected two thousand applications for six new jobs, and the number was then cut down to fifty applicants from whom the six jobs would be filled, the city would be making choices among people who all achieved high nineties in both tests. Three of the six jobs were to be picked particularly from the target groups of minority races, women and certain disabilities that did not affect the physically demanding nature of the jobs. The professor had said to Rob Davis that, from his knowledge of statistics and firefighting, he honestly could not tell whether someone who scored 93.9 would do a better job than someone who got 93.7.

When we arrived at the station, the fifty of us were greeted by a very tense group of six or eight people, including the union president and a very gold-braided senior officer in the fire department. Did I just want him to field student questions? he asked. "I would actually appreciate if you would speak to the students before questions about what it takes to be a firefighter," I said.

Before the administrator started speaking, one of my students started to talk, very deliberately. "Now let me get this straight. You're saying — am I right? — that if there are more of *us* on the force, the standard of firefighting will go down, right?"

Immediately, the union president jumped up, moved close to the student who had spoken and yelled out, "Who told you to ask that? Your teacher put you up to that, didn't he?" (I hadn't.)

Another student, a bit of a "class enforcer," then rushed to the front, went nose to nose with the union president and said, "What's your name? Who asked for your opinion?"

I spoke up: "OK, let's get down to business hearing the chief tell us what it takes to be a firefighter. There'll be a question and discussion period after that when we can continue these points." The official gave a restrained speech and the question and discussion period went off without any fireworks — so to speak. The discussion with Councillor Davis at my house was exciting because the students were eager to talk about the fire station visit. Davis said the firefighters had probably never seen that many black teenagers face to face before.

The motion passed that night. Fortunately, the conservative mayor made this equity issue *his* issue as part of his cooperation on many issues with my councillor — because of the large African Canadian population in the area. When the videotape of the council arrived, it was too long and too tedious and too strange a process for most students to relate much to. However, they did see their teacher making a presentation and they saw Rob Davis interviewing the York University physical education professor. By the end they understood the issue and the politics behind it quite well.

A Protective Buffer to Ask Blunt Questions

The people who say that the options in African/diasporan and Asian history at Stephen Leacock Collegiate fragment students' loyalty and make them less supportive of their school are dead wrong, in my experience. I say, very confidently, that such students are *more* supportive. Most of their classes are not particularly black-oriented, but the black history classes (with their strong component of "current events," as we called it in the old days) are an essential part of the unity mix. We used to boast that in Canada, unlike in the American melting pot, we had a *mosaic*, where those who were not white could be patriots yet could affirm their own separate identity. We now know that this approach was more honoured in the minds of liberals than practised in reality. But I certainly know that the battles on this issue we have had in the schools for English as a Second Language programs, for Heritage Languages, for ceremonies that honour more than European memories and holidays and for courses which help make a mosaic a reality must remain at the centre of our struggles.

I think of something else as well. Those students who spoke up confidently at the fire station knew they had a protective buffer in the political process with the black councillor who was leading a public battle and their teacher who was more interested in their righteous demand to debate the truth than in some proper and boring field trip. Masses of our students need more opportunities for righteous debate, and we should be prepared to step into the multitude of waiting forums — where students have a better chance to learn what it will take to fight for their place and their rights than in the often-mute walls of their classroom.

CHAPTER 8

Psychology

Know Yourselves, Know Your Families

A technically oriented age like ours should especially stress the importance of self-knowledge. We learned in the 1960s to keep our twin sights on the psyche and the polis, the mind and the state, as two key aspects of existence that could be understood and changed for the better. Technocracy has been telling us and the schools for some time that this is obsolete advice. "Changing things for the better" is now called "fine tuning," and it's thought to be the job of technical experts with their polls, their machines, their behaviour tips and their pills. All that old (Dewey)-eyed sentimentality about citizenship and personal understanding and happiness is thought either quaint or dangerous by an age obsessed with "boundaries," with finding some islands for the rich, including "headspace" islands. Or let's put it a little more politically: an age of power for the few and dependency skills for the rest. Those of us who want schools at their best surely want power for the *many*, and that should include helping students to build strong minds and strong egos. This is not done best with a raft of self-esteem techniques (self-affirmation skills) but by helping students to do well in school, especially in academics.

The specific part of my teaching I'll be describing here is my frequent encouragement of students to write about their personal and family histories and their own feelings. In particular, I will be telling about the class production of books of student writing about themselves and their families. In fact it has been in *history* classes (and one media class) that I have had students do this writing and magazine and book production. "This is a history class and you're now going to write your personal history and your family's." It doesn't matter to me through which discipline this personal topic enters the curriculum.

Right now it enters a high school curriculum very rarely. It's thought to be a valid activity for small children, but unnecessary and even a bit corny for specializing high school students. I call this activity psychology to link it to sociology since, when we go from the group to the individual, we go — in familiar modern categories — from sociology to psychology.

Personal Stories within Societies of Mutual Aid

As you no doubt can guess already, I do not recommend self-knowledge and knowledge of one's family history for the sake of work training skills. The chorus on that one is familiar:

> Employers, before they hire you, want to examine who you are and what you can do in more depth than ever before. And they're paying particular attention to your so-called "soft skills" — how you deal with others, handle difficult situations, your drive and enthusiasm.[1]

Let those who are forced to teach "soft skills," or those who like it, do it. Often the whole thing is gussied up to sound like more of a big deal than it really is. Often it means "be polite to customers" or "cooperate when you're on a team." Big deal! It's certainly not the reason I recommend self-knowledge and telling your own story. I do that for literacy, but mostly to help build strong egos. I also do it to build, if I may use the subversive word, the sense of a *collective* in a class. Eveybody in a class has to contribute to a book. There is plenty of student editing and we have a big class ceremony when the book comes out. A teacher has a strong obligation, when stressing a "class collective," to make sure that rebels or the silent ones don't get ostracized. But that essential obligation doesn't wipe out the old elementary teacher's sense that building a class into a cooperative group is a central part of her task. High school teachers, mostly because they're on a merry-go-round with scores of students and subject specializations, usually give up on class cohesion. Some of us believe we must counter this inhuman tendency and build small societies of mutual support. To paraphrase the African proverb, it takes a village not only to raise a child but to teach her. Especially to tell your own often highly charged personal story, you need a sensitive community you can trust it with.

I shall focus particularly on the student writings published in class magazines and books. These magazines and books have gone all the way from paper sheets folded into 8 1/2" x 11" and stapled, to cerlox-bound booklets to highly professional 8 1/2" x 5 1/2" "perfect-bound" books, well illustrated and sold on the market. For every book or magazine, everybody in a class had to contribute, and all contributions had to be done on computer so they could be fed into the general desktop publishing program.

Partly I have stressed books and magazines for the old reason that school writing usually has only one reader — the teacher. All too often a teacher, busy with marking, doesn't comment much on student writing. A real magazine or a real book, if it's interesting, gets out to people. They react. In fact it's the main reason some students take time to decide whether they *want* to be in a book — especially if the writing is personal.

Back in the second semester of 1989-90, I taught a grade 10 general level English course in a tough high school in North York, Metro Toronto. In the first half of the semester, we published a book called *Views on Abortion*. As has happened on many occasions, the abstracted photos which our computer cameraman from the Tech Department produced brought in several students who were still objecting to participating long after I said I wanted everybody in the book. They liked their abstracted photos and they could now tell the book was really going to happen.

For the second book I strongly encouraged students to tell their personal stories, but I didn't insist. The book had a long title, *Family Backgrounds & Ideas on Racism & Multiculturalism.* One day during a period writing their stories on computers, one girl told me she was going to meet her birth mother that day and was nervous. The next day, behind deadpan eyes, I could tell she wanted to tell me how it went. Yes, she was nervous, she said, but it went well. I asked her, could she make this her story for the book? "No way, Mr. Davis, Are you crazy?" Instead she wanted to write a book review of V. C. Andrews's *Flowers in the Attic.* Then began a two-week drama, especially in computer lab periods, with me asking her how her writing was going, right up to the last day

when she dropped her contribution on my desk after the last period and then ran out. The next day she donned that tell-tale deadpan look again. Of course you've guessed that she did the story about her birth mother. She was now dying to hear what I thought of it and I was overjoyed!

I offer quotations from the student books that are longer than customary because readers need them to get a proper feel for the writing.

The Day I Found My Mother

You see my biological mother was sick in the hospital. She and my dad were on the outs and my dad had a girlfriend like all men do, I guess. So, well, she was in the hospital so I guess they saw less of each other or something. I don't know, but that's none of my business. Well, they got a divorce and about three years after, or something like that, my dad and now my step mom got married.

You know kids, me and Darlene — that's my sister if you don't know — we've been looking for our real mom since we were twelve and thirteen. My sister is older, of course. Well, we were looking for our biological mother and had no luck. We never said anything to our step mom or dad about doing this. So a little while later, we tried like maybe six months ago and we asked our dad if he would get mad if we were looking for our biological mother. He did not seem to mind, so we did, and just the other day — I think it was a Tuesday in the month of February — we found her.

She wanted us to go down and see her on Easter so I told my dad and he told our step mom and she said it was better if we waited a while. So she said, did you think me and Darlene would listen? Well, we did not go down on Easter, but we went to see her two or three times since Easter. She gave me and Darlene 14 carot gold rings with our initial on them — which is D.

We still have not told our step mom that we saw our real mum, but my dad does not seem to mind at all. He said we have a right to see our real mom and he told that to our step mom before or after their marriage.

Well, that's my story.

One of the startling experiences putting together these books is the emergence of pieces I can only call *sacred texts*. Often these wise and pulsing pieces come from totally unlikely sources. Teachers who read the book will say, "Wow! Is that the Lee Ox *I* know? I thought he was just a shallow hellraiser."

Here is Lee Ox, grade 10 general level student:

My Heroes
by Lee Ox

My heroes are not famous, rich or successful by any standard way of measurement.

I have two such heroes. Picture a man wearing only a small Tarzan-like covering. He is standing on top of a huge cliff in the jungle. The fog over the side of the cliff is so thick that he can't see the jungle floor below. This man has no name, he's never needed one. He has no concept of time. Never needed that either. This nameless man has seen few other people in his life.

This isn't really a hero but I do admire him. His worries are few. His only concern is survival. In his world there is no politics, pollution or crime. He has no boss. No need of money, or the things people buy with it. What I admire about him is simplicity. His lack of stress and lack of commitment. His whole life revolves around a few basic needs. The only person able to tell him he can't or shouldn't do something is himself.

My other hero has only one name. That name is "Lethal". He has never gone by any other name. He's my hero because he too doesn't do anything he doesn't want to do. He doesn't care about school, work or money. He just parties, drinks and has a great time no matter where he is. But if he doesn't like where he is, he leaves. No one tells him what to do.

We have done many illegal things together, Lethal and

I. Which I would never have done without him. Even around my friends who are crazy and will do just about anything, Lethal has done some things that they see as "Going Too Far". He doesn't do drugs . . . doesn't have to. He's always on a natural high.

His morals are few. But the few he has, he won't compromise for anyone. You don't ever want to offend him. He hospitalized a man for kicking a cat. It's not that he has a special place in his heart for animals, he just tries to equalize any unfair fight he sees. I have a great deal of respect for him on that. Lethal usually takes as many beatings as he gives. This is due to the fact that he doesn't know when to walk away.

In case you have't guessed yet, Lethal is me. My nickname. But I couldn't do everything he does. I consider him a completely separate entity. Lethal is a state of mind. He is not necessarily me when I'm drunk, just in a mood.

Don't think me egotistical for choosing a part of myself as my hero. Lethal is not really me. He's me acting like the person I want (wanted?) to be. An act. Some of my friends are not my friends, but they *are* his. I think they would find me boring, and I would find them basic.

I see less and less of Lethal and those friends as time goes on. I still like him and enjoy his life. I just don't like seeing him as much. Actually, lately he only comes drinking with me. I miss him. Time to time I'm in a place where Lethal should be and I don't belong. I can feel so out of place with the same friends doing the same things he used to do. Even though I do miss him, at the same time I don't want him around any more.

Sometimes I think I just don't have the time for that shit. I work, go to school, have a very active family life and a girl friend who deserves all the time I can find for her. All that doesn't leave much time to get drunk, PARTY, and be a general shit disturber. I have a life now, a full time life that doesn't give me time to spend living another one on the side.

I guess I'm just growing up, but just a little late. I hope that when Lethal is finally gone for good, I hope memories of him serve to make Lee C. Ox live on the "wild side" every now and then.

I am constantly amazed at what hardships some students will share with their reading audience:

In 1982 my father lost his job at Branson Hospital as a security guard. He's pressing charges on the grounds of racial discrimination. My father was and still is a good man, but at first he felt like a total failure. There was a time when all he talked about was ending it all for himself. I guess he was just overwhelmed with the idea of failing. It's been eight years and his trial is not yet finished. The tension and stress at home used to be unbearable. Everyone took their frustrations out on everybody else. I am glad things have finally settled down.

Or this story, so tragic and so eloquently told:

Living in Glendower? . . . When I was younger I always wanted to be a stuntman. I used to try to do stuff like Lee Majors although he wasn't my idol. I love climbing too. I remember once in Dower I climbed this tree and fell out of it. It must have been a long drop because a lot of people said they saw it. I landed flat on my back and just got up and went home, no crying. Things like this gave people who knew me a feeling that I was a madman.

At age sixteen I went blind. I saw something floating in front of my eye and I went home from school. The doctor said there would be a ninety percent chance that my retina could be reattached and I would be able to see better. Yeah right, I thought, as he said it. I wasn't too pleased to have lazer surgery. He gave me a lot of stats about only one in every ten operations not being successes. I thought what if I'm that one in every ten.

Obviously it didn't work. The doctor tried two more times with no success. He introduced me to patients whose operations were successful. I thought why should I have to be their statistic?

In the same year my brother was murdered. I was mad with grief. When I was younger I was hyper and used to throw tantrums. I threw one the night he was murdered. I miss him. He was the only one that understood me and my only brother. I have four sisters Nicky, Tara, Bridgette, and Renel. I know that in the long run my blindness and my brother's death will be hard to deal with.

Troubles for one student were political, and happened on a trip to her home, South Africa:

The next visit I would make to South Africa would also be for reasons of ill health, this time, my dad's sister. In December 1985, we all went back home. This was a time when riots were very common in South Africa The streets were filled with armoured vehicles, trucks and tanks. It was quite a sight, and I was very scared for my family.

Earlier in the year the student protests and the school bomb-ings occurred, and during one of the riots, my cousins were shot at with rubber bullets as well as tear gas. Things had quieted down over the Christmas season, and my family tried to show us a good time, but no matter where you went, you were always reminded of the fact that this was a police state. Road blocks were everywhere, and there were military officers, police and sharp shooters at every stop.

What they were looking for I don't know, but they were making random stops. That trip more than the last had opened my eyes to the problems of the country. Once again it was time to say good-bye and return to Canada.

Or listen to this story of family violence:

But all of this happiness soon changed. Our family nights were replaced with nights of terror.

They were the nights when my mom and step-dad had their fights. Arguments led to physical abuse. All through the nights all you could hear coming from my house was cursing and screaming. Whenever my step-dad would beat up on my mom, me and my sisters and brother would get scared and run upstairs. We didn't know what to do. My older brother wasn't home most of the times they had their fights; he was usually at work. These fights would usually end with my mom bleeding from a gash on her head and with cuts and bruises. There were even times when the police were involved, but my mom never pressed charges.

I remember a time when they started arguing while a friend of mine was over at the house for a visit. I didn't think it was anything big. Surely they wouldn't fight right in front of my friend — at least that's what I thought. I don't remember all the details, but I do remember that my friend did something that I didn't dare do in those times — she tried to break them up.

The same thing I feared would happen to me happened to my friend. My step-dad threw her against the wall and she was knocked out for a couple of minutes. It was one of the most embarrassing experiences in my life, and I'm sure in my mother's as well because mom was close friends with my friend's mother. From that day on I made sure not to make a practice of inviting my friends over.

This student spent a long time thinking about whether she wanted to leave this violence in the book version of her story. At first she had put it in the version that only *I* read. Then at one point she decided she *did* want to include it in the book as well, because it had strengthened her to write it. (She was also a strong fundamentalist Christian.)

Eventually her Mom also agreed. At that time they had persuaded the father to leave the house. I saw her again after she had finished two years of working after high school and had started university; she told me her father was back home and that things were currently peaceful and friendly.

My Life: Boring Compared to Malcolm X's and Maya Angelou's?

In preparation for writing and publishing *Our Roots 1, 2* and *3* books, the class had spent lots of time with two great autobiographies, *The Autobiography of Malcolm X* and *I Know Why the Caged Bird Sings* by Maya Angelou. Some students were intimidated when I presented these books as a model of people of African origin telling their own life stories. "My life is boring compared to theirs," some said. But in the end the books gave the project a high purpose and were an inspiration.

The time period during which students decided whether any parts of their autobiography that had been included for me as a reader should be edited out for the book version became very important. This student, for example, decided to *leave in* this passage, and he cited an experience of a student from the previous year whose father's violence towards his mother had been the cause of the family's move from Guyana to Toronto.

> It would be only months later that my parents would file for divorce. Although I hadn't known at the time, my sister later told me how it had been a mutually abusive relationship; very violent and constantly tumultuous. My mother had become dependent on valium which had been prescribed for her during some earlier illness and later during her pregnancy with me. My father had become an alcoholic during all the pressure of inheriting an "instant" family, since my mother had my three sisters from a previous relationship.

The Students' Own Stories

Readers need to know that the primary emphasis in writing these autobiographies was the student's own story, not those of their parents or siblings. Some students decided that one consequence of including sensitive stories was that they would not show their piece to their parents. At first this disappointed me, but afterwards I decided that this increased the chance of intimacy and honesty, so I became reconciled to the fact. Also it removed these books from the category of "interview your parents" assignments, with a surface quaintness born of rushed work and parent shyness. This is not to say that some of the greatest gems in these books did not also come from these family interviews — as we shall soon see.

Photos and Sales

For each book, one of the interesting developments to watch for was when students began to believe that "this book was actually going to happen" and was an OK project. At this point, a sizable percentage of the class began bringing in their family photos to illustrate their stories.

Over time, we made decisions about where the books should be circulated and sold. When the first copies of the first book were available in our class, I chaired a hurried discussion in which we agreed that the books could be sold to the school staff but not the school's students. (The students insisted on this because they were sensitive to the reactions of their peers beyond their own class. Keep in mind that only 15 percent of the school is African Canadian.). It was agreed that it could go out to bookstores and universities. It was to be sold at cost.

But this was so hurried (and, I suspect, such a new situation for the students and me) that the understanding was not clear to everyone. Consequently, when I started selling them at cost to my university students, the mother of one of my high school students told her daughter: "Did you know Mr. Davis is making a profit off your writing?" The daughter went to the principal.

So we had another meeting and put all these things in writing. We also added several other points which I suggested: if a change in cost for a new edition was contemplated, as many students as could be reached had to reconvene in a meeting to decide new arrangements. It was also settled that any media that reported on the books should be requested to not use any names from stories quoted or discussed. (There is a possibility, if the first edition of *Our Roots 3* sells out, that students will each get some small amount of cash for the second edition sales.)

Humour

So far I have presented very serious quotations from the books. But there is also wonderful humour throughout these books. Here is one student's earliest memory of childhood in England:

> My very first recollection from Birmingham, England was one night when my mother was making dinner in our tiny kitchen. On that night's menu was crab, which at that very moment had just been put in a huge pot to boil. I still do not know how to cook crab; however, even as a little child it seemed peculiar and inhumane to boil the crab while it was still alive. It was pointless to say anything, however, since, at the tender age of three, my opinion carried less weight than a paper clip.
>
> It was about two minutes later that the pot, roughly the same size I was at the time, started to sway on the fire. All of a sudden it tipped over. In a moment that would be infamous in many family anecdotes for years to come, the crab, which was still alive, began to crawl around the floor, and all hell broke loose in our kitchen. I remember those huge threatening pincers snapping at me as I ran round the kitchen table in an attempt to escape. It seemed like I had sloshed through the sea of hot water for ages in order to avoid the fate that awaited me before I got the bright idea to stand on the table. I was soon joined by my two siblings who had also been caught up in the scene.
>
> As soon as some order had been restored to the pandemonium, it was up to my mother to recapture the wild snapping beast that inhabited the seas below our point of safety. I can still vividly recall her bending over with a small pot in one hand and its lid in the other, vainly trying to capture the creature. She waved the lid as if it was a matador's cape in an attempt to make the miniature bull make a charge and encapture itself in the pot. This furious battle finally ended, the beast was entrapped and kitchen was put back together.

Here is another memory, from a Filipino student, who was alone in an earthquake as a child, yet still managed a joke about it at the end:

> When I was seven years old, we moved to Quezon City. At first, I didn't like it very much because it was away from my friends, but, as time went on, I began to appreciate it. After all, it was my home. I remember a time soon after my house was built and I was lying on the floor watching television. All of a sudden I was rolling to the other side of the room. For a second, I thought

I was being possessed by some spirit so I stood up right away. The next thing I knew, I was being pulled from one side of the room to the other. Then I realized that it wasn't just me, it was the whole house. I felt scared. I was in an earthquake and no one was home. They were all next door. It felt like I was that kid in the movie, *Home Alone*. I started screaming and yelling hoping someone would hear me, but nobody did. I found myself hiding under the stairs until the house and everything inside it stopped shaking. After this event I learned another valuable lesson. I learned that for some parts of my life, I am alone and am left to fend for myself.

For my first earthquake I don't think I did such a bad job, do you?

And finally, on this topic of humour, a sketch one student did of his uncle:

My uncle would pass the time drinking 40 ounces of liquor, even while babysitting my brother, sister and me. He wouldn't get drunk, but he was always buzzed.

It was funny to watch and listen to him. His name is Brandon, but I had to call him Uncle Brandon, until one day when he gave me my first beer and said "call me Brando."

Brandon is 5′ 8″ with a beer belly, but it's gone now. When he talks he finishes every sentence with a burp into the face of the person he is talking to, because he gets right up into your face when he talks.

After two months living with him, I learned to identify the kind of beer he had, the time of day he had it, and if it was cold or warm when he had it. And on a good day, I could tell what hand he held his beer with. After living with us for two months, he moved to California where he now lives with his wife and kids.

He rarely drinks any more but when he lived here in Canada during the 80's he taught me a few things. When he left I became a belly-scratching, fight-instigating, whistling, girl-crazy kid, who gets props from peers because I was the first one of my friends to drink a full bottle of beer by myself.

My uncle Brandon speaks with an American accent and his voice screeches when he talks. My Dad and him didn't see eye to eye, but I would have chosen my uncle over my Dad just because my uncle was more fun.

A week before my uncle left for California, he put geri-curls in his hair because it was the in-thing at the time. Obviously I wanted geri-curls too. He gave me a firm handshake and said, "Make sure you come and see me at my place. But bring I.D. because where I'm staying, you're gonna need to be 19 and over, burrrrrrrp!"

I waved the smell out of my face while saying OK! Bye! and he was laughing, looking at my Mom, his sister.

He is sober now and married with children. I don't know what career he's pursuing, but I know he's livin' large.

This student wrote this sketch in a summer makeup class of thirty students who had all failed grade 11 English!

Range and Variety

The range and variety of the writing startled me. Here is a troubled student's comments on his early schooling. It is all the more poignant because he is convinced his problems are so much his own fault:

It wasn't till I made it to the third level when they felt it was time to take more serious measures to control my uncontrolable urge to beat other children to a pulp. So they put me into that great Special Ed class which made you feel so intelligent.

It just made things worse. I got into more fights, got sent home more often, and I ended up being confused even more because not even the teachers at school knew what was wrong with me.

Of course the school had its own resolution to the problem. Send a social worker over to speak with the child. At first it didn't work because the problem steamed within me, and the worker would just want to talk with my family. She didn't even discuss anything with me. It just made me feel that I was being left out.

When she did want to talk, I would get bored with the questions she asked, so I would just get up and leave the room. My mother would come and yell at me for being so rude. I would then start to cry and she just left me alone. As you can see, I was a very spoiled child who got his own way with just a few tears — even at times when I should have got a slap.

They'd give me anything to keep me from crying. It started before I had troubles in school. I think it started when I was born because my mother left all her troubles behind her and got her new life in Canada, the so-called "land of milk and honey" by Jamaican thinking at the time.

It's still called this even today, but we in Canada know better.

Here are some of their comments on racism, first from the student who lost both his sight and his brother:

> I grew up rugged. I never used to comb my hair, do my chores, etc. I was a "nappy nigger child". I used to listen to a lot of reggae, rap, and slow jams and I was a pretty good breakdancer. My favorite Mc's, reggae artists and singers back then were Ninjaman, Junior Demus, Whodini, Run DMC, Grandmaster Flash, Soul Sonic Force to name a few. As I got older those changed into Bounty Killer, Supercat, Bennieman, Buju Bantan, Ice Cube, Scarface, EPMD, etc. When I used to breakdance I used to do this move called the Suicide. You flip and land on your back in a position as if you were in a coffin. I used to do it on the concrete.
>
> My friends used to call me Bull because I used to charge people with my head down when I fought. I loved fighting. I had to stop that because people used to move and I'd run into things full force!
>
> I remember one of the biggest racial incidents when I was younger. Some white people had moved into Glendower and their son started to pick on a friend of mine, so I beat him up. His brothers came after me to get revenge and in turn I went for my brother. My brother beat up the two brothers that doubleteamed me and the mother came swearing at my mother. My mother cursed them back and the white woman's husband came out with a bat after my mother.
>
> One of my mother's friends saw this and threw a bottle at the husband and came out running. Anyways, it ended up that it was a family feud. My mother grabbed the bat from the white man and hit him with it. My mother's friend hit him on the other side and he ran. My mother threw the bat after him. Meanwhile in the middle of all this my brother and I went back and beat up their sons again. They moved two weeks or so after. My family was always known as a fighting family after that incident.

And to emphasize that I think we have to avoid shying away from the tough challenges of multicultural education, here is the work of a tolerant Jewish student who nonetheless is committed to a tough policy on antisemitism:

> My name is Jonathon Adam Goldberg and I immigrated to

Canada two and a half years ago. My family comes from many different countries. My great great grandparents were from Russia, Israel and England. My parents were born in South Africa and grew up there. My dad died when I was 12, and four years later we came to Canada (my mother, Shirley; Brother, David; and sister, Liza). . . .

By the way, I am Jewish and a few days ago we did some work on antisemitism in this class. We read an article about how in Hungary at a soccer game they started calling out things like "dirty Jews" and they spray-painted the Star of David. Things like this.

I myself feel that things like this should be watched by the government very closely, and should there be any sign of a real anti-semitic build-up, something should be done.

Let me tell you also: the lives of the Jews, they have been put down and picked apart by others, so one more time would not change a thing. However, we are a proud race and will stand up for ourselves come what may. I doubt the Hungarians will try anything, not with the state of Israel, for there is an Israeli army which by far surpasses the standards of any army in the world. Although they are fighting a war they will always watch out for their own.

If push came to shove, well I would for certain go and fight either to help Israel or to stop anti-semitism anywhere in Europe or for that matter anywhere in the world.

There will never be another Holocaust even if I had to die to defend my people. For the Jews stick together, and when the going gets tough, the Jews kick some serious ass.

Black, Brown, White

Several students talked about attitudes they grew up with on the topic of shades of black, brown and white. Here are the comments of one of these students as they appeared in the book *Our Roots 3*:

Moments in Time
by Peta-Gaye Domville

I was born on July 24, 1976 in St Joseph's Hospital on the beautiful island of Jamaica. I was named Peta-Gaye Antoinette Domville, a name I used to hate but grew to like. I was born to the proud parents, Barbara Spencer and Carl Domville. My mom was a single mother, who more than made up for a more-or-less absent father. I lived in the city of Kingston and moved to an area called Elleston Flats when I was three years old. Here I spent probably the best seven years of my life.

When I was five I began attending Alvernia Preparatory School. I can remember all the fun I used to have, and every now and then I actually dream about the good times and wish I was young again. I do, however, remember some negative things concerning skin colour and my insecurities. I found at a young age that even though the majority of the people in Jamaica are black, there is a sick amount of mental slavery around concerning what shade of skin you have. I remember that only the light-skinned, long-haired girls were the teachers' favourites. Only the light-skinned, long-haired girls got the leading parts in a play. Only the light-skinned, long-haired girls were considered pretty.

Peta-Gaye Domville

Eventually, I began wishing I was light-skinned or mixed with so-called "pretty hair" or, even better, white. I remember my mom telling me that I was black. I would get upset and tell her I wasn't black, I was brown. My friends and I would try to think of all the people in our family who were mixed, so we didn't have to say we were pure black. I would talk about my grandmother who is mixed and could pass for white with her grey eyes. Or I would talk about my aunt who is married to a white man or my other aunt who is mixed with Indian and white.

Now that I think about those days, I think I was crazy, smoking something I shouldn't have. What the hell is so good about white people?! I remember this old saying, "If you are black, stay at the back; if you're brown, you can stick around; if you're white, you're alright." It reminds me of a part in a song Bob Marley sang, "Emancipate yourself from mental slavery; none but ourselves can free our minds."

How Much Editing Did These Writings Need?

Before I offer the last selection of quotations from these books, I will try to answer a question that some of you may have considered. Did the first drafts of these student writings not have bundles of technical mistakes and unclear muddles? And the follow-up question: In this light, are you, Bob Davis, not being dishonest writing a book that criticizes skills teaching when the skills cleanup of the students' own book is hidden from readers?

Over and over again in this book I have repeated that I do see an important place for skills in learning. True, I am against calling activities skills that are really knowledge. True, I object to the diarrhea-like inventing of more and more operations as skills that mean "smile at customers" (soft skill) or "watch the screens and deal with other workers at the counter" (multiskilled worker). I am most strongly against the skills *ideology* which says that content and commitment are now obsolete in the great age of portable skills.

I said from the start in the Introduction that teaching basic skills well, especially reading, writing and arithmetic, were very important to me. And here we are talking about the skill of writing.

I have always taken lots of time going over my editorial suggestions with each student and, in cases where a student didn't mind being edited by another student, the writing would have been through that stage as well. But I would never pretend that my editing is a "program" of writing instruction. Fortunately, the school I taught in has a tough English department that is insistent about the "skill of writing." If there wasn't this skills backup, most of the students would have brought back their next piece of writing with all the same mistakes they made the first time.

No, my message in this chapter is only that we resist the skills ideologue's message that the topic we ask kids to write about is not important. Mind you, I also know that learning the skills of writing will often involve some boring exercises. To work out what combination you want of meaningful human writing *and* good skills teaching can only be accomplished with a schoolwide policy of what is to be done, when and how. And of course Deborah Meier (*The Power of Their Ideas*) is right that the cooperative way is the only proper way to do this.

But make no mistake. You will be swimming against the stream for part of this plan: cooperative ways, when they are not considered downright subversive, are thought too slow and risky; second, skill teaching can crowd out the weighty sentiments that the kids want to write about.

So yes, I know this book does not focus on answering how to teach the techniques of good writing. But I think many of you may agree that these mostly alienated students are ready and willing to express searching and wise thoughts — which to me is a giant start in good writing, good thinking and good living.

Maroons, Moms and Grand Moms

I end with quotations showing students' feelings towards their elders, ancestors and parents. The first student talks about his Maroon ancestry and his mother:

> When asked if I am ashamed or wish my family's history were different, it is a question that should not even be asked. Everyone does what is necessary at the time to survive. I believe my family may be descendants of the Maroons, because my great-grandmother lives in the country where she owns land, but she does not pay taxes.
>
> If Maroons are a part of my blood line then I am extremely proud. It is good to think that my family did not sell out and stood for what they believed in. When someone mentions the phrase, "You are making history," I prefer to see it as leading the way to the future. In hopes for a better tomorrow. I know my mother in the past has tried, to the best of her abilities, to create a better life for my sister and me. I'm proud of all she has done for herself and us.

Or read what another writes about his grandmother:

> I looked at my grandmother as my second mother. She would feed me when I was hungry and discipline me when I was bad. The only strong recollections I have of our first house was sitting in front of the television with my grandmother at around 6:00 pm every evening to watch Carol Burnett. I also remember waking up every morning to watch my favourite cartoon, Spiderman.

Not all recollections of family were happy:

> I don't really remember my father that well because he got the double "d", divorced and deported. I never liked my father, because he never kept his promise. While I was in Trinidad, at the emotional age of eight, my father promised me that he was going to take me to the beach. I was really excited because it

was just me and him going, not me and all my cousins. It was supposed to be a special moment for me, because he was supposed to come and pick me up and just take me to the beach.

I was all excited when I heard he was coming to get me. I was bragging to my family, saying how I was going to the beach today, but Tantie told me not to get my hopes up, because he wasn't coming. I didn't believe her. I had faith in my father, so I got all dressed up and sat on the veranda.

He never came to get me, but he called and said that he got stuck in traffic and I believed him. He told me that he would come for sure tomorrow.

I didn't learn. Once again I got all dressed up and went back on the famous veranda, and Tantie said again, "Don't get your hopes up, he's not coming," but I was too excited to hear her. I sat there for the whole day waiting and waiting. Again he called and made up another excuse why he didn't come, but I was too vexed to talk to him. After that incident with my biological father, I cut him off for good.

Here is a bittersweet memory of family:

It was always a very pleasant setting when the family got together. Over the years my family rapidly grew like a small African village. In 1990 my mother's father died and I think my soul died along with him. As I stood over his still wet cemented grave, all the years that we spent together flashed before my eyes. I loved him more than anything because he was one of my best friends. He used to drive my cousins and me to the beach in his gigantic delivery truck even when grandmother told us that we couldn't go.

I remember a time when a sea urchin got stuck in the bottom of his foot and he still managed to drive us home safely. I know that he endured severe agony with the urchin's needles stuck in his foot. I even offered to drive the truck, but he just gave a soft chuckle and told me that it was okay. He used to take me for long walks on the beach, and before we left, he always cracked some almond nuts for us to share. We even shared our birthday parties, candles and cake. He never tried to win my affection with material gifts and believe me, he didn't have to.

My family gradually drifted apart. Everyone had separate lives and moved away. I long for the family reunions because there was always love and reminiscence of the good old days when the family was whole.

Another student looks back even past his grandparents:

> I also thank my great grandparents who as indentured slaves from Kashmir were brave and strong enough to venture to a new land with the vision of making a better life for themselves in Guyana.
>
> Through the years, my parents, especially my mother, have taken an interest in my life and allowed me to try new things and helped me not to be afraid to fail. Most of all she taught me, like my grandma taught her, to respect all people till they disrespect you, and, most importantly, to respect myself.
>
> Thank you.

To close with this tender scene between a mother and her son, I go back to the student who lost his brother and went blind:

Son: How is it dealing with me now that I can't see?

Mom: Oh Jesus, I don't know . . . It's not as if it's harder, it's just the emotions of it. You know, knowing that I'm not going to be around all of the time. You know what a mother's instinct is for her child, and fear that somebody might hurt you or something, and I'm not there. I guess basically that's it. You know? I know you can cope.

Son: What are your expectations of me in life?

Mom: Well, I'd really like to see you reach the point where you are basically self-sufficient and can take care of yourself by yourself in an apartment or house. I know that you are going to need some help from someone, but I just want you to be independent. Isn't that what you want for yourself?

Son: Of course!

Literature Interlocks with Personal Lives

I close this chapter with an account of the oral presentations of two Vietnamese students taking their final year of English in a night school class of twenty-eight students from twelve different countries and every continent. The official OAC provincial rules say that their final mark must include 20 percent for an independent study, which is an essay plus an oral class presentation on a topic of their choice, but which is to include relating two books or two movies, or one of each, to the topic itself.

I urged them to relate the topics to matters in their own lives or at least to choose a topic that intensely interests them. It always distressed me that many students chose topics very remote from their lives, especially topics from typical high school textbooks they think the teacher will like — or they've been told the teacher will like.

The third speaker, a quiet Vietnamese boy, began by announcing that his theme was Sacrifice. His first book, he said was Dickens's *A Tale of Two Cities.* He said that Sydney Carton sacrificed himself for Charles Darnay but my mind wandering off with *Sale of Two Titties* and *Mad Magazine*'s opening for *Moby's Dick*: "Call me Fishmeal" — instead of "Call me Ishmael." I'm not too hot on the school classics. He spoke without notes, and describes the plot of *A Tale of Two Cities* very accurately. He said his second example was Willy Loman, who sacrificed himself to the American dream in *Death of a Salesman.* I wondered if he had taken these works in day school. I asked him and he says no. And then I noticed he spoke very interestedly about *Death of a Salesman* — all very naturally and without notes. He then moves to his third example.

The third example of sacrifice was his own father, he said, who left Vietnam with his mother on a rickety old boat before he or his other siblings were born. The parents nearly starved in the harbour of Hong Kong until they got a chance to get to Canada. His father and mother built a new life and a new home, and raised three children, including him.

The climax crept up on us and caught us by surprise, so unfashioned, so unadorned was his telling of the story. Three years earlier his father had died of cancer. He sacrificed his life for his family, said his son. His voice was tense in the last few sentences but he completed his story and sat down.

A new pulse hit the class. The classroom had become sacred ground.

And then three classes later a very bright Vietnamese girl arrived in class, early as usual, but this time was very agitated. This was the first time she had stayed away from home overnight, she told me. She had stayed for the weekend at her boyfriend's parents' place, and they had eventually persuaded her to sit down for a long chat with her single mother about whether their relationship, which Lora was finding increasingly impossible, could be improved. "I had the chat, Mr. Davis, but I've had these showdown chats before and they just help for about ten days. Nothing I do is right. It's not the best night for me to do my oral, sir, because it's on my relationship with my mother."

I offered to change the night and give her more time; she could change the topic as well if she wanted. "No sir, I'm going ahead with it tonight."

The two works she had chosen were both novels by Amy Tan, *The Joy Luck Club* and *The Kitchen God's Wife*. She had prepared film clips from *The Joy Luck Club* and we were told right away that these two novels were about relations between girls and their mothers. She began the story of her own family, but as soon as she got to her feelings about her mother she couldn't continue and ran out of the room crying. A friend ran out after her and in a few minutes I went out too. "You've done a really good job already, Lora," I said, "and there's no need to go on. Besides, you're giving me the written essay, and I know you're an excellent writer."

Lora was hearing none of this. "I'll be alright in a few minutes," she said.

Sure enough, in a few minutes she returned and finished her story, holding herself together with a steely will. Long applause.

A woman of twenty-eight put up her hand and said, "Me and Rose are both in our late twenties and we know you'll come through this, Lora. You're right to stand up to her."

An Afghani boy was waving his hand. "Lora, in two years you'll discover your mother was right in everything she said." "I doubt it," one Hong Kong boy blurted out.

The class was becoming a village.

Later the next day I thought back to a student who once wrote:

> For some reason everyone in my extended family in Jamaica had the mentality that they were better than everyone else. Now, as I see it, it was like the feeling of superiority that house slaves had over field slaves, as Malcolm X describes them.

She also wrote:

> My parents' families were like the Capulets and the Montagues in Shakespeare's *Romeo and Juliet*. They only associated because of a marriage and most of the time it was plastic smiles and shallow conversations with slight hypocrisy and sarcasm.

I am indebted to this student and to the two Vietnamese students for showing so well that understanding yourself and your world can be deepened by books, plays and films — even classics! Of course this assumes a school system that offers works of art not just as plots and subplots but as illuminators of life itself. And it also assumes you are in a class that has become a community of mutual support.

CHAPTER 9

Strengthening Science as a Subject for All Students — Part I

How Science Crept into the Curriculum of a History Teacher

The last school subject I will discuss is science, to which I devote two chapters. This might seem strange since I'm not a science teacher. I just happen to think that for the good of high school education some of us must keep shouting across the canyons that divide our specialties. Besides, for the good of the education of youth, all people concerned about schooling, regardless of specialty, have a right and a duty to make thoughtful judgements about the curriculum as a whole.

For many decades, science has been the ultimate skills subject. At least ideally. The school might have wanted you to learn a certain amount of science content, but since well before World War II you were always meant to learn mostly what "doing science" was all about. Learning how scientists go-about their work was the number one aim, at least on paper. In a former era, this was the thinking behind getting science teachers to do experiments at the front of the classroom, even though, if you were a student, you probably had to sit pretty near the teacher to see anything. The technique, still in full bloom, of having all students appear to replicate in the lab how each scientist discovered each principle — that whole "hypothesis, controlled experiment, observation, recording, and finally, proof" approach — was meant to teach you the skills of the scientist.

Now plenty of scientists and science teachers knew from the beginning that this lab method was not really teaching many students what it was intended to teach. For one thing, most students knew too well beforehand how each experiment was supposed to turn out. For another, that playfulness of mind which scientists need was missing. So was the ability to try something, leave it, come back to it and then try something different. Also missing was the element of surprise and accident in what scientists do and discover — the rough-and-ready lab method did not reveal these things.

That's what drove science educators in the 1960s to design more open-ended settings and simpler artifacts. More of this later.

I hope you now realize that I'm not talking about the mechanical, lab-period version of the modern skills approach to science. That's the method of teaching science that tries to cash in on the skills fad by suggesting that "doing science" is learning mechanical procedures supposedly followed by scientists. Derek Hodson of the Ontario Institute for Studies in Education has a proper disdain for this corruption:

> In my view, this [skills-based testing] represents an undesirable trend — one that should be strenuously resisted by teachers. It is my contention that the skills-based approach is philosophically unsound (because it is not based on a valid model of science), educationally worthless (because it trivializes learning), pedagogically dangerous (because it encourages bad teaching), professionally debasing (because it de-skills teachers) and socially undesirable (because of powerful hidden messages concerning control and compliance).[1]

I am trying to picture the skills approach to science at its best. This best approach is not trying to teach mechanical procedures which can be memorized; it is saying that since science has shown us the best way to establish truth of all kinds, we in schools must teach children how science works as a method — what the "skills of science," in all their subtlety, consist of. I am saying that we must examine what these skills are anchored in and decide whether the whole science teaching enterprise as a mass subject is on a solid basis, or whether its mass education side needs serious revision.

So what were the anchors of this modern version of learning the skills of science? We know that in the 1950s, both in Canada and the United States, science was given a very high place of honour in the hierarchy of subjects. Chief history inspector for Ontario in 1957, George L. Gray, tells us that students

> will gladly[!] search the past with us in order to know how to meet the future but they ask us not to spend the time poking around in old ruins and antique shops. They do not ask us to inject the term "atomic age" into every lesson. In fact they beg us not to do so. But they do ask us to teach as if we were in that age and open up to them all of man's past experience so that they may be enabled to have some share in making this the greatest of all ages, *as every scientist of repute declares it can become.*[2] (Italics are mine.)

David A. Hollinger, a professor of history at the University of California at Berkeley, has documented well that after World War II science was considered, by intellectual leaders like Harvard President James B. Conant, the essential handmaid of democracy. Science and democracy were the two-fold guarantors of progress. Science was the opposite of superstition. You proved things in science. Often it also had immediate technological consequences. Disease and abject poverty could be conquered with science.[3]

And what were the consequences for schooling when this subject was now to be the guiding religion? Conant thought the populace needed some minimal general science to help them decide who the most reliable science experts were. Others like John Dewey expected more: he had already pronounced, before World War II, that it was essential for the mass of people to get a general grasp of how scientists went about their work. This was because the approach to science was to be the approach to all knowledge. But most leaders also agreed that more specialists in science must be trained, and by the end of the 1950s, after the big Sputnik debate, winning the arms and the space race had mostly replaced Dewey's "Road to Knowledge" as the number-one motivator for science education.

Although the anti-war and environmental movements have presented a rearguard challenge to the mainstream approach to contemporary science teaching, no generally accepted, large-scale alternative to Dewey's aim has emerged since World War II.

Can Science for the Millions Be Recovered?

In mainstream thinking we've come a long way since 1950, and not necessarily in a forward direction. Already in the 1950s Daniel Bell had told us about "the End of Ideology."[4] Today, as we read about "the End of History"[5] and now "the End of Science,"[6] we see how the intellectual underpinnings of restructuring capitalism are driving education to narrower and narrower skills or techniques. If the study of politics, of time (history and science) and space (science and geography) are not useful except as fine-tuning, then we have moved well beyond the visions of Gray, Dewey and Conant of reading history's and nature's secrets for the benefit of humankind. The big secrets are supposedly known already. The current approach to skills, then, starts in the head and ends in the head. The world, for these people who have been announcing the "end of" this and the "end of" that, has no more big secrets so, using our favourite image once again of teaching as helping students look out the window of life and the world, why look out the window any more if there's nothing important to see?

What John Horgan, author of *The End of Science,* thinks *is* possible is ironic science, a kind of bemused elegy about images of the earth and the people of the earth. A brilliant historiographer like Hayden White talks similarly about the giant philosophers of history, like Ranke, Hegel and Marx.[7] To White, these giants are like interesting novelists whose fiction illuminates thinking about thinking, but not thinking about any world out there in time and space which is considerably separate from us, but nonetheless holds secrets about how we act.

Back in the early 1950s when I was an undergraduate in history and philosophy, leading British philosophers like A. J. Ayer and Gilbert Ryle believed they had reduced their subject of philosophy to clever judgements about *language*. This is what postmodernists mean by saying that the only usable reality about any subject is the "discourse" about it. Earlier thinkers of the 1950s, and some people like Francis Fukayama, author of *The End of History*, are not postmodernists, but they share the scepticism about all large-scale theories.

For those who have heard the words "postmodernism" or "post-structuralism," but have not heard them properly defined, here is how Terry Eagleton defines them at their birth in the political context of France, 1968. Consider that both terms mean the same:

> Post-structuralism was a product of that blend of euphoria and disillusionment, liberation and dissipation, carnival and catastrophe, which was 1968. Unable to break the structures of state

power, post-structuralism found it possible instead to subvert the structures of language. Nobody, at least, was likely to beat you over the head for doing so. The student movement was flushed off the streets and driven underground into discourse. Its enemies, as for the later Barthes, became coherent belief-systems of any kind — in particular all forms of political theory and organization which sought to analyze, and act upon the structures of society as a whole. . . . All such total systematic thought was now suspect as terroristic: conceptual meaning itself, as opposed to libidinal gesture and anarchist spontaneity, was feared as repressive. . . . Just as the older forms of 'total' politics had dogmatically proclaimed that more local concerns were of merely passing relevance, so the new policy of the fragments was also prone to dogmatize that any more global engagement was a dangerous illusion.[8]

The mainstream of this postmodernist view of things I have already characterized as "seeing through everything and owing allegiance to nothing." I have suggested that a common political corollary of this has been that "you better stick with the bad you know rather than risk the worse you don't know." The irony these thinkers talk about protects them from the hurt that results from the collapse of large traditional foundations, even the foundations of organized opposition expressed in philosophies like marxism or populism. Writer and media critic Rick Salutin puts the point this way:

For my part I wonder how far you can go with an ironic mindset. If *everything's* ironic, you end up pretty harmless, since if it's all equally ironic, why bother trying to change any of it — which is pretty ironic for a subversive. You're drawn into the mainstream willy-nilly since you accept, albeit scornfully, its premise. . . . You can't do much subverting without an alternative model of how things might be, but then you'd *believe* in something, and that's so unironic. Irony often comes, it seems to me, from not wanting to have your hopes or dreams dashed. One reason Michael Moore really is subversive, is that he believes our world could be different; he's not just saying screw you; his little smile conceals the fact that he can picture a whole other kind of society than this.[9]

Given the coalescence of many forces driving science in the same exit direction as history, is there any revitalization program that schools and science teachers could become part of? Can the elite tide be stemmed which increasingly emphasizes "how difficult" science is and how it therefore should increasingly be limited to students who will specialize in it? Can the uses of science be more widely studied and debated, and can the "skills of the scientist" still be profitably taught?

My Science Memories since the 1940s

In preparation for this chapter I tried to think back by decade to what science memory stands out for me. The fact that science is not my specialty made the choice easier. In fact I only could recall one solid science memory per decade! So the idea worked, and the memories came fairly quickly and weren't consciously thought up in any pattern — but they seem to have a pattern nonetheless, now that they stare back at me.

The 1940s: Wildflowers by Name

What jumped to mind about the 1940s was that my mother was a star botany student at university and had been urged to do postgraduate work, but married my father instead. When we had family trips to the woods around Quebec City, she used to love showing us strange and tiny wild flowers. She called them all by name, which impressed her young son very much.

I'm sure if you had posed the skills issue to my mother, she would have said that the existence of beautiful flowers made the skill of finding them worthwhile.

The 1950s: The Two Cultures by C.P. Snow

But it was with the 1950s that my memories link best with this chapter. When I went to study in Cambridge, England, in 1956, one of the hot topics in universities was C.P. Snow's lecture entitled *The Two Cultures*.[10] I got the book version out of the library when I started to prepare this chapter. Snow was a novelist and a professional scientist who had worked for the British government during World War II.

What he was mainly saying was that science people and arts people couldn't talk to each other. There were deep canyons between us, and I thought, really, it's mostly still true, isn't it? I find in schools we teachers may talk to each other about general school policy or, if we're active in our particular teachers' union, we communicate about that. But it's been my experience that there's not too much communication about our subjects. To us artsy types, the science people have a very esoteric discipline. It has fancy stuff connected with it, and some of us even remember feeling that we weren't really up to the rigours of science, so we took arts instead. I don't find that there's much more talking across the gulf of the two cultures now than there was in the 1950s. There's a *little* more, as represented by these new courses like Science and Society, but more of that later.

Now a very interesting thing about Snow: I had forgotten what he had said his original title was; he was interested in things that really surprised me. It's shown by this quote. This is one of his reactions to the huge controversy about his book:

> Here, in fact, was what I intended to be the centre of the whole argument. Before I wrote the lecture, I thought of calling it "The Rich and the Poor," and I rather wish that I hadn't changed my mind. The scientific revolution is the only method by which most people can gain the primal things (years of life, freedom from hunger, survival for children), the primal things which we take for granted and which have in reality come to us through having had our own scientific revolution not so long ago. [By "us" he means people from Great Britain or from "the West" generally.] Most people want these primal things. Most people, wherever they are being given a chance, are rushing into the scientific revolution.[11]

Snow observed that, in his time, it was the scientists who were more interested in the cause of improving the world than the arts people. The arts people, following authors like T.S. Eliot, were very pessimistic about improving life on this earth. Snow identified the scientists with wanting more equality. I had completely forgotten this part of the book, and I thought: Where would scientists and science teachers sit today on the radical/conservative spectrum? This is an important question, partly because it may decide whether science teachers see their subject as mostly educating future scientists (i.e., a small group) or as educating the millions. I personally don't see why the two have to conflict — but more of this later. Incidentally, Snow was obviously very interested in the scientific method (i.e., the skills of looking at the world), but it was surely the discoveries that this method brought that were helping the world's poor.

The 1960s: Eggs and Poems

I wondered, then, what about the 1960s? What jumped to mind right away was a set of science observations by children which an American teacher, Max Braverman, had set up as poems and sent to *This Magazine is About Schools*, where I worked as an editor. Braverman was working in Massachusetts and studying how to teach elementary science; the Elementary Science Study was the name of his group.

Braverman was also connected with the same group that brought in the new physics course at that time, the P.S.S.C. out of MIT, a project coordinated by Professor J.R. Zacharias. I knew one of the Elementary Science Study people working with Braverman, Eleanor Duckworth, now a professor at the Harvard Graduate School of Education. She is someone you will hear more about in chapter 10 of this book. At that time she was experimenting with how to get away from depending on fancy science materials with small children. She developed lessons in which children would play with readily available things like spools of thread and popsicle sticks to discover certain scientific principles.

What Braverman had done was ask these grade 2 kids to describe what changes they saw in the development over five days of eggs turning into tadpoles. Description should come before explanation, Braverman said. He was quite pleased with what the kids came up with and so were we. We then had somebody do the poems in calligraphy with the bad spellings left in — which I don't usually like doing when printing children's writings, but that was Braverman's decision at the time. And he was so impressed, he made this statement in his introduction to the poems:

> I get the feeling from the poems that time and leisure enough
> exist to look at the world.

That statement surely contains one of the most beautiful aims of science at its best. Just look at what you see. And then he has another amazing sentence:

> The statements embody a crisp clarity reminiscent of Japanese
> haiku.

So he had set them up to look like poems — simple observations by grade 2 children.

> Yesterday I saw some eggs.
> They were gray on the bodum
> and black on top.

And some eggs are going away from the jelly.
The jelly feels funny.
— Stephan Murphy

The eggs are losing the jelly —
are hatching more
But I dot no what they are
But I will soon no.
— James Anderson

Today we onnlee have III eggs
And yesterday we had VIII
I don't understand hoo that can happen.
— Louise Zimberakis

There are two eggs
stuk and there r
three eggs separate.
— David Latham

The first day I had the eggs
I looked at the bottom
I saw grey
Today I looked and there was
more black than the other day.
— Michel le Stovuch

The eggs are bumpyer than yesterday.
and they are losing jelly
and they are separated.
And their is a spek of white on the
bottme.
— Debby Potter

When I looked at the eggs yesterday I saw
that on the bottom of the eggs
they were grey.
But today
They have some very light white.
And they are losing they're roundness.
They have a little point on each end.
— Colleen Happenny

I saw a egg frog
One of the egg will grow.
One of the eggs crakt.
I knew all about eggs
One day the eggs ton into a frog.
— Anon

Reflecting on these poems, I remember what I liked about publishing them. So many people back in the late 1960s were starting to say, "Is the purpose of science just to harness nature or is it also to have respect for nature?" Braverman's student writings illustrated that second purpose by stressing description over explanation and by calling the descriptions poems. Once you call these descriptions haiku you have given them an extra aura, as if there's something special about stopping at description for some aspects of nature.

I think my mother felt the same about wild flowers: "Call nature by name, and don't mess with it." (If we picked any flowers, we were to do it selectively and discreetly.)

I toss this idea out here — developing a respect for nature and an awe in the face of nature — does that have a place in science teaching? Is this a kind of deeper observation skill we could teach more often than we do?

The 1970s: Minamata Disease

When I thought of the 1970s, I recalled an incredible movie I had stumbled upon by accident. It is about Minamata disease (mercury poisoning) in Japan, and it's long.[12] I discovered it because in one of my units for what was then called Man and Society — now Society, Challenge and Change — I had decided on a study of this disease in Northern Ontario. The disease afflicted the Native people of Treaty Three who lived on the English and Wabigoon Rivers in Ontario. At that time the Reed Paper Company (and later the Dryden Paper Company) was using mercury to bleach paper and was dumping the chemical into these rivers.

When I started reading about the disease, I discovered an amazing film produced by the National Film Board of Canada called *Hands Across Polluted Waters*;[13] the title referred to the hands of the aboriginal people of Treaty Three reaching across to the Japanese fisherfamilies who had suffered from the disease in a much more extreme form than the victims in Ontario. The Native people wanted to learn from the Japanese victims about the nature of the disease and about organizing to fight back on the issue.

Photo: W. Eugene Smith

This is a classic experience for some liberal arts teachers. We have a topic about the suffering of a group of people, and if we have some of the reformer in us, as I certainly do, we want to jump in and get busy at the "what-should-be-done" stage. It is easy to miss the science stage, which is so important. And here was this second film, *Minamata,* which took us carefully through the scientific investigation in Japan of the possible causes of the disease. By North American "attention span" standards, the film would have gotten low marks. It contained minute details about the investigation. It also had a sound track with badly dubbed English. It had many lists and charts. Yet, without exception, I always found the film an outstanding success with students. Mind you, it had to be carefully taught — lots of student note taking, lots of stopping the movie, lots of questioning, lots of discussion and testing.

Of course, there were many sequences showing the dreadful effects of the disease. And the Chisso Corporation officials, who were dumping mercury into Minamata Bay, were determined to fight any attempt to trace the blame to them. So the careful scientific matters — right down to a lot of brain research — were set in the context of a fierce human drama, a perfect union of the skill of the investigating scientists and their main motive of helping the fisherfamilies to understand and fight their cause.

The photograph seen here is perhaps the most famous statement from the Minamata tragedy.[14] Scientists discovered that the effect of mercury on a fetus during pregnancy made the children's condition more severe than their mother's. This was not a poison where the womb protected the child from the disease.

It seemed to me so appropriate that the science of this topic should be combined with the politics of how the victims fought back. It was the C.P. Snow view of science — science to relieve suffering. At one point in this movie the victims and their leaders started to organize. They paraded around in the streets with great big signs saying when they caught the disease and where they were from. They stormed the parliament in Tokyo and the Chisso Corporation headquarters in Minamata. The struggle took a long, long time, years and years. In this particular case they actually bankrupted the corporation with the financial compensation they were eventually awarded.

Recalling these classes, I asked myself this question: Why aren't those of us interested in doing battle on these issues, whether history or science teacher, working together? Why do I now know that particular bit of science from the 1970s but very little else, and why have science teachers been taught for so long that the *use* of their knowledge has nothing to do with their profession?

The 1980s: Jacob Bronowski's The Ascent of Man: Knowledge or Certainty?

For years I divided my time between teaching and writing about education. From 1979 to 1985 I published a magazine called *Mudpie: Growing Up in Ontario*. Before the collapse of the Soviet Union and before China discoverd capitalism, there was, as you know, a very large anti-war movement. It was also a time when there was still a fair amount of school board money for unusual conferences. Led by professional-development teacher Myra Novogrodsky, a number of Toronto educators who had written a curriculum on the threat of nuclear war organized a conference in conjuction with a group of Boston experts who had pioneered a curriculum on the Holocaust. Forty of us took part in a weeklong conference. I wrote up the conference in the magazine.

At this conference we were shown a remarkable film. Some of you may know it — Jacob Bronowski's *The Ascent of Man: Knowledge or Certainty?*[15] It has a lot about the Holocaust in it. Its concluding philos-

Photo: Jim Bartley

ophy is that Heisenberg's Uncertainty Principle should be the principle that guides politics. Behind this idea is the experience of certain groups like the Jews who have suffered badly under many different types of regimes. Their analysis is that whenever there is wide acceptance for a philosophy that suggests how everyone should live — and these liberals often focus particularly on fascism and communism — the authorities end up ramming their views down the throats of everyone. All blueprints for a better future are therefore suspect to such people. So what some of these people have said — and Bronowski puts it in this extreme form — is that the government that governs best governs least. In other words, get some basic things organized like roads and police, and otherwise let people be. Organize the things that have to be organized.

Mind you, I've never seen anybody else go as far as Bronowski in saying that a major scientific principle could be the guiding principle of politics. I don't think it's very promising myself, though it is interesting. It represents what some people thought was the development that should happen in the twentieth century — that scientists should run the world. And if they did, they'd supposedly be more humane and more cautious about imposing things on people. I think that C.P. Snow had some hope of that kind, except that his hope for scientific activity had a lot more active social content than Bronowski's. I think Snow thought that the scientists were the ones that were sensitive to the suffering of the world and, if they were in charge, this would be a better place. The skill of the scientists, their way of observing the world, would make them more sceptical and cautious about coming on strong about anything.

The 1990s: David Suzuki's At War with Death

This Suzuki movie was made for CBC television in 1985, but I only became aware of it in 1990. Since then I have shown it perhaps sixty or seventy times, forcing it to fit almost any topic you can imagine.[16] David Suzuki is Canada's greatest popularizer of science, especially as it applies to the environment. The movie compares attitudes towards death and old age in the West with attitudes in places like Madagascar, India and part of the Himalayas in Pakistan. It deals profoundly with our Western scientific focus on prolonging the physical lives of old and sick people even as we shun them or treat them like dirt. The movie brilliantly tells the stories of Barney Clark and the Boy in the Bubble. When Barney Clark was given an artificial heart but died, the doctors stressed that it was human organs that failed, not their artificial heart; the Boy in the Bubble, whose parents agreed to keep him in a plastic bubble twenty-four hours a day because he was born without an immune system, is eventually brought out of the bubble when complications make his death inevitable. Sporting his "space suit" displaying large NASA letters on TV, the movie said that his mother touched him for the first time when he came out of his bubble to die. The film included an amazing sequence of the Hunsicut people in the Himalayas, a group whose old people commonly live to over a hundred years. They breathe good air and have a good diet, but they also are given useful and demanding jobs till they die.

The film had a full budget. Back in 1985 sufficient money was still available to produce lengthy sequences all around the world. The movie was made in the last days of the Cold War, and ends with what Suzuki calls an apparent paradox — that the West spends such huge sums on prolonging life, but simultaneously through the arms programs, on ending it. Suzuki then suggests that this is not the paradox it appears to be, since both activities are in effect "crimes against nature."

Almost no other piece of curriculum I have used in my entire career has produced such deep discussion and writing from young and adult classes alike. It is a film with a message that opposes the idea that science is a set of skills for manipulating the world for our own benefit. For Suzuki, science should make us respectful of our place in nature.

Questions Posed to Science by Environmentalists and Anti-war Activists

Thinking about the Minamata, Bronowski and Suzuki movies, I realized these memories were part of two large protest movements which together had a clear effect on science teaching. Environmentalists and anti-war activists were now asking scientists to look more carefully at the *uses* of their discoveries. It was no longer satisfactory to these protesters to hear scientists say that they just *discover* the secrets of nature and it's not their concern what is done with these secrets. It's been one of the effects of this large stress on science as a neutral skills method that many scientists have talked as if their work was free of moral implications.

The environmental movement has asked: is this what scientific knowledge has brought us to — the destruction of people, eco-systems and ozone layers? And the anti-war movement has asked: Is this what scientific knowledge has brought us to, the possibility of annihilating the world? It's a long way from C.P. Snow's hopes for science. I think these questions have worked their way into the conciousness of a lot of people who now say that scientists and science teachers have got to start getting involved in the *context* of scientific discoveries. I believe this influence is still here, despite the virtual disappearance of the anti-war movement since the end of the Cold War or the setbacks of the environmental movement at the hands of ultra right-wing governments.

Using the Science of Anthropology

While we're talking about the uses of science, here is one example. On several occasions I have taught a comparative religions course, World Religions. One of the useful textbooks, by Huston Smith, was called *The Religions of Man* (reprinted as *World Religions*). There's an amazing statement by Smith in the preface to the first edition. Think of the science he knows as anthropology, religious anthropology. Listen to this use of his knowledge:

> The motives that impel us toward world understanding may be several. Recently I was taxied by bomber to the Air Command and Staff College [the time is 1958] at the Maxwell Air Force Base outside Montgomery, Alabama, to lecture to a thousand selected officers on the religions of other peoples. I have never had students more eager to learn. What was their motivation? Individually I'm sure it went beyond this in many cases, but as a unit they were concerned because someday they were likely to be dealing with the peoples they were studying as allies, antagonists, or subjects of military occupation. Under such circumstances it would be crucial for them to predict their behavior, conquer them if worst came to worst, and control them during the aftermath of reconstruction. This is one reason for coming to know people. It may be a necessary reason; certainly we have no right to disdain it as long as we ask the military to do the job we set before it.[17]

From Smith's own words, I must assume that he supports the job "we ask the military to do," since he accepted the job the military paid him to do. If you know anything about the history of, say, the control of peoples in Indochina (Smith's preface was written in 1958, four years after the French moved out of Indochina and the Americans began moving in), some of the things that were done to the infrastructure of such countries were mind-boggling. I'm not just talking about physical infrastructure like roads and bridges, but about deliberately scrambling people's most basic beliefs, including their religious beliefs. (This is well before the era of Pol Pot.)

In some ways you could call Huston Smith a social scientist selling his knowledge — from my way of thinking — to the wrong people. But are there any *right* people to sell this kind of knowledge to?

I think we have a much more vivid sense now, among science and science teachers, that this use of knowledge is an important question for scientists, not just for politicians, philosophers and theologians.

Is Science Too Hard for the Masses?

What, if any, has been the effect on science teachers of these environmental and anti-war battles? Only a minority has been affected, but they are a very vocal minority. They have demanded that science to be taught with its uses, its historical, technological and political implications as part of the course. In Ontario, the result of this pressure is that we now have one course called Science and Society as an option for the final year of high school. My impression is that a significant minority like this development, but that a much larger group think "it's not really science" and counsel the serious science students not to take it.

It is often the same teachers who talk most about "real science" who also talk about science being too hard for the mass of students. Where has science for everyone gone? The same Englishman who wrote *Mathematics for the Million* wrote another book called *Science for the Citizen*. Are we giving up totally on this dream, except as a means for keeping up science teachers employed?[18]

At times I agree with the idea that some science is too hard for the masses, in this case the masses being me. A few years ago I decided I had to get educated in science, so I tried to read Stephen Hawking's *A Brief History of Time*.[19] Whoops! Totally incomprehensible. I kept going back at it. Maybe I should stop reading it in bed. Try the morning. No luck. After a swim? Nope. Then someone told me it was the most owned and most unread book in history. Someone else told me to read the popular introduction to the book called *Stephen Hawking's Universe*.[20] Just as bad. Finally I tried the comic book version, *Stephen Hawking for Beginners*.[21] What a dummy. Can't even understand the comic book. (I had the same experience with the Martin Heidegger comic book.[22]) The film of *A Brief History of Time* was no better, except as inspiration of the man's incredible courage and accomplishments since his illness.

In the feature movie *Insignificance*[23] I got a little closer to another scientific theory watching "Marilyn Monroe" with her toy trains and flashlight explaining to "Albert Einstein" his theory of relativity. Movies should keep trying.

Recently I tried Stephen Jay Gould's book *Full House*.[24] Now I know well enough that concepts in evolutionary biology are a lot simpler than those in astrophysics, and I know Gould's book is full of great baseball talk, but Gould is also a master of popular writing. I thought I'd check what science magazines said about the book: the review in *Nature* said it was boring because it was too populist;[25] the review in *New Scientist* used language that was incomprehensible to this layman.[26] Only the *Audubon* review called Gould a "national treasure" for "making each of us share his unabashed enthusiasm for scientific inquiry."[27]

Now I can already hear some science teachers getting incensed and saying, look, I educate a few people who can handle these difficult concepts and they're heading into their specialties and getting the prizes at good universities and that's the central part of my work. Science, if done properly, they claim, is an inherently difficult subject and doesn't lend itself to the democratized plan I am recommending. In fact the whole plan sounds like replacing serious learning with mush. Babysit them with pap. Sit around shooting the breeze about why they should pick up their candy wrappers and why car pooling in cities is a good idea.

I am also sympathetic with teachers who feel this way. I don't think we have to choose between training well-educated specialists and the kind of democratized approach I'm recommending. Advanced training is a wonderful thing that science teachers already do. Giving students a superb grounding in these specialty sciences must obviously continue as an essential part of a good science program. What I'm talking about is something different, and it does not need to compete in any way with that specialized work.

I am also very supportive of the resistance to mush, which runs deep among teachers generally. Some social science courses have definitely become mush courses, and some of the government curriculum and many of the textbooks actually invite us into that boring, mushy world. There is also no doubt that Science and Society at lower grades and Science for the Millions is constantly susceptible to the temptation of pap.

But once we are aware of this ever-present danger, we still have a decision to make. Do we roll with the conservative critics who are pushing us mostly to have high standards for the already successful, or do we think we still work in a system that has serious things to say to the masses? This is not rhetoric, friends, it is an absolutely real choice. And my choice is that we should actually DO BOTH.

Unsettled issues of skill hover over this debate about whether science is for the few or the many. Many math skills, for example, which are a necessary part of understanding the higher reaches of some sciences, are difficult for many students. This frustrates many teachers, and they then court the philosophy of soft skillls for the many and hard skills for the few. If, instead, our emphasis on teaching science to the masses were on actual scientific discoveries and their implications (particularly for high school students) and on observation skills of that deeper sort implied by the haiku poems and my mother's hunting for small wildflowers (particularly for elementary students), we would be on a better track. In chapter 10 I turn to these two ideas.

CHAPTER 10

Strengthening Science as a Subject for All Students — Part II

Suggestion #1: For High Schools: More Science and Society Courses

Two Closing Suggestions

It is not my intention to make suggestions about such senior high school specialties as physics, chemistry and biology. I merely suggest that rescuing programs like Science for the Citizen and Science for the Million is currently more important. So I make a twofold suggestion: for high school students we should strongly increase the Science and Society (in the U.S., Science, Technology and Society) version of scientific literacy; and for elementary school children we review successful science teaching programs of the 1960s in order to continue and increase helping small children to observe, name and understand natural phenomena with an emphasis on the ecology of the environment and the human body. For those who feel that this is done already in elementary schools, let me stress that I envision a reinvigoration of elementary science as the learning skills of the scientist in that new spirit of Max Braverman's "eggs and tadpoles" observations. I do not consider Braverman's calling these poems haiku as the clever little metaphor of a good writer but as a new and transformed spirit now confirmed by the environmental movement. The spirit must be the opposite of "the world is our oyster." It must reflect Braverman's statement: "I get the feeling from the poems that time and leisure enough exist to look at the world."

I am suggesting a stress on science content for high school and science process for elementary school. I am assuming in this suggestion #1 for high schools that there is a place in certain science courses — especially those for mass consumption — for making the scientist's skill in *how* they discovered certain principles secondary and for focusing instead on *what* they discovered and the implications for human life. In my suggestion #2 for elementary schools, the reader may be surprised to find me finally giving a central place to process and skills. I do this because I think there is a noble conception of the Way of the Scientist once this Way, Method or Process is linked, as Max Braverman does, to the Eastern religious conception of a Way. That religious Way is about relaxing the mind and the ego until the world can speak directly to us, in part in its own language. The Way of Zen, for example, is a method that provides a check on the pervasive mechanical and egotistical approach at the foundation of most skills ideology. To use Fritjof Capra's title with a different slant, I am recommending not *The Tao of Physics* but the Tao of *learning* physics, or even better, of *learning biology*.

As so often with poets, W.H. Auden saw these issues for science well before most people.[1] What do we want this scientific knowledge for, he asks? Has all this search for knowledge of the entire universe left human beings behind?

> This passion of our kind
> For the process of finding out
> Is a fact one can hardly doubt,
> But I would rejoice in it more
> If I knew more clearly what
> We wanted the knowledge for,
> Felt certain still that the mind
> Is free to know or not. . . .
>> — from "After Reading a Child's Guide to Modern Physics," 1965

For High Schools: Increase Science and Society Courses

I am suggesting that scientific literacy needs the moral and political dimension of a Science and Society course. What has been done with scientific discoveries — good and bad? What can be learned from the history and politics of science? What have been the chief arguments at various times for raising and lowering the funding of science?

As you can tell from my religious anthropology example earlier, I believe social science must be given its place as part of the science content that students will learn and debate. And I don't mean endlessly discussing the difference between natural science and social science — as if social science is some kind of "ugly sister" or "bastard brother" of pure science. I know this component is crucial when I remember how I was flipped by the books of Margaret Mead and Ruth Benedict back in the early 1950s. Why are we not still expanding student thinking with these lively reports of societies where women are the dominant gender or where children were wildly indulged? And did great numbers of my students not benefit from seeing *At War with Death,* including the anthropological comparisons between North American customs surrounding death and those in Madagascar, India and Pakistan? And how could I not want my students to study the benefits to mental health of good psychoanalysis by comparing, say, *One Flew over the Cuckoo's Nest* with the brilliant methods of treating disturbed children shown in, for example, the international award-winning documentary *Warrendale*?[2] I am not bothered by the hard work of having to help our students understand and assess changing views about curing mental illness — from the radical Reichian theory and experiments of the 1960s to the brain and drug theories of today. Let us take our students through these debates that fascinate and challenge them.

Since I first recalled as my 1950s science memory the controversy initiated by C.P. Snow in *The Two Cultures*, I set out to update some of the ongoing debates concerning this science/humanities rift over the forty or so years since 1956. One fact I noticed was that almost nobody was interested any more in what Snow considered the most significant point of his essay; recall that he had meant to title the essay *The Rich and the Poor.* He believed that scientists of his time wanted to use their knowledge to alleviate the suffering of poor and oppressed people, especially in the Third World. Cambridge University Press printed a new edition of *The Two Cultures* in 1993, and the long introduction of seventy-one pages does not mention Snow's declared main point till page sixty-four! Even then, editor Stephen Collini shows that the point doesn't interest him.[3]

In a seminar on Snow's lecture reported in *The Cambridge Review* in 1987, only one of the four presenters connects with the *uses* of science.[4] Steven Rose, with his fellow writer and biologist wife, Hilary Rose, have been active as scientists, scholarly writers and members of the British anti-war and environmental movements. Rose shows — as Collini also shows — that Snow had rather simple notions of the inevitability of world progress that was supposed to arrive via science and sympathetic governments. The ultimate example of this view was Stalin's answer when asked what the Soviet Union would do when the country's mineral resources ran out: "Mine the stars."

But the brilliant insights and the political focus of Steven and Hilary Rose and the Green Parties and the anti-war and the environmental movements have not developed in educational circles into a significant enough lobby for the widespread use of courses that look systematically at both the good and bad uses of science. Scientific literacy most often tries to keep itself separate from Science, Technology and Society. It still tries to act as if the noble view of science is that it just describes and explains. It's above the hurly-burly of real life.

My brother told me that Martin Heidegger had important things to say about the genesis of science and technology back in the fifteenth and sixteenth centuries. Art recovered from the high school funk I described in chapter 4 and later went on to do a Ph.D. thesis on Martin Heidegger.[5] So I asked him to tell me about these views. Fortunately, I understand my brother on Heidegger better than I understood the comic book. (Note: I know my brother is not the last word on everything and neither is Martin Heidegger. There's the old objection about Heidegger, for example, that because he was a Nazi for a good part of his life, everything he said must be suspect. This is narrow and doctrinaire; I don't agree with it. Lots of scientists, including C.P. Snow, have agreed with Heidegger on the point my brother will now present.)

Art: The book by Heidegger that I know best on this question of science and technology is *The Question Concerning Technology*.[6] And one of the main points that Heidegger's making in there is about the close relation between modern science and modern technology. Normally this story is understood in the opposite way to Heidegger's understanding of it, namely that modern technology harnesses pure science. Heidegger's point is that science is anything but pure. It is already guided by what he calls the spirit of technology, the technological approach to the world, the approach which says that nature is there to be controlled by human beings. This approach to nature is part of the very constitution of the great modern sciences — physics, chemistry, then later biology, and finally all the social sciences.

Heidegger liked the image of the Inquisition to describe the attitudes of early modern scientists. Actually, it's an image Francis Bacon used a lot, too. Bacon said this: what we need to do is bring nature to the rack and find out what makes her tick so that we can take advantage of her and get the best out of her. What's implied here is a fierce conquering relationship. Now Heidegger would agree, in opposition to some modern thinkers who want to call science as "arbitrary" as the humanities, that there's a certain givenness to science, it's not just pure arbitrary imposition of some kind of fiction onto reality. It is very much geared to responding to things as they are, but *in this very fierce relationship of interrogation, summoning nature to the bar to give account of herself.* This is an image that Bacon used to emphasize that things have to be forced to give their reasons for existing. And if they can't give any, they don't exist basically or they're worthless to us so it's more or less the same thing, right, that we don't care about them, so let's not even bother with them. What we need is to get things that can give an account of themselves so then we have control over them. We know what they are because they've shown us how they operate.

What I find very revealing about this is the fact that it's similar to calling human beings resources. Remember these phrases like "people are our great resource"? The way of conceiving of human beings as potential entrepreneurs or workers or any form of conception of them that fits them into a plan that will lead to certain goals down the line. It's demanding of them to give an account of themselves according to a plan that usually someone else has set up.

The folksinger and storyteller, Utah Phillips, of "Moose Turd Pie" fame, tells a story about speaking to a huge conference of student writers:

> I was invited to the state young writers conference out at Cheney at Eastern Washington University and I didn't want to embarrass my son, you know, and I was going to behave myself. But I got on the stage and it was an enormous auditorium. There were 2700 young faces out there, none of them with any prospects anybody could detect. And off to the side of the stage was the suit and tie crowd

— the people from the school district and the principals. And the main speaker following me was from the Chamber of Commerce.

Well something inside of me snapped, and I got to the microphone and I looked out over that multitude of faces and I said something to the effect of: "You're about to be told one more time that you are America's most valuable natural resource. Have you seen what they do to valuable natural resources? Have you seen a strip mine? Have you seen a clear cut in the forest? Have you seen a polluted river?

Don't ever let them call you a valuable natural resource! They're going to strip mine your soul. They're going to clear cut your best thoughts for the sake of profit, unless you learn to resist. 'Cause the profit system follows the path of least resistance. And following the path of least resistance is what makes the river crooked. Mmmm!"

Well there was great gnashing of teeth and rending of garments. Mine. I was borne to the door screaming epithets over my shoulder. Something to the effect of: "Make a break for it kids! Flee to the wilderness! The one within if you can find it."[7]

Art: That certainly struck a chord with me. Is that all nickel is — a resource? Are nickel *miners* a resource? Or what about the people of Ontario, are they resources? The use of this word "resource" has now more or less taken over. The Department of Human Resources becomes the term that has replaced the Personnel Department — a word only slightly better.

My brother's comments and the prompting of educator Eleanor Duckworth — who will figure in the second half of this chapter — prompted me to dig out more on the views of Francis Bacon. His frequent and complex sexual metaphors for this process of conquering nature startled me. Bacon even has nature "teasing us" with her secrets. In her *Reflections on Gender and Science*, Evelyn Fox Keller finds other evidence of male metaphors for nature and decides that, for Bacon, nature is not a woman but a hermaphrodite.[8] Despite the nuances of this debate, I suggest, following my brother's comments, that discussing the uses of science as an integral part of science itself is not some prejudice from the anti-war movement or the environmental movement. The linking of scientific discovery to its practical uses is as old as Francis Bacon himself.

It is in this spirit that I recommend that high schools increase the offerings of Science and Society courses. With two courses built up till both are popular, science would move more to centre stage. Mind you, I believe the science component must be strong and demanding, that these courses not be known as bird courses.

I would also note that courses with good scientific literacy are a first step towards the study of Science and Society, and deserve our support.

Even proper Scientific Literacy courses are suspect with many. Those who want more Science and Society courses for high schools need to know what they're up against. Note the cynicism about such courses from an expert in this field, Morris Samos, author of *The Myth of Scientific Literacy*.[9] Unfortunately, important as the book is, Samos's position is almost a parody of that activity we used to call "scientism." Samos says that only if a monumental twenty-year study proved that teaching scientific literacy worked would he support it. But his study is set up to fail. His definition of a scientifically literate person is so exhaustive as to be out of reach. He says as well that when masses of high school students have been tested, they must be tested again as adults to prove they kept the literacy they picked up in high school. The definition of literacy, you may guess, must not be "adulterated" with Science, Technology and Society approaches, since Samos calls these courses "social science" and therefore not really legitimate. For me the final coup de grâce is that after twenty years, if one of Samos's grand-scale studies proved that scientific literacy was attainable, how would we know that what was proven was any help for the new times?

Samos also disposes of the Dewey approach to teaching science as a method or superskills subject by saying that the same training could be produced by studying logic or law. Samos will grab at anything. Science, logic and law surely have very different ways of establishing truth.

Samos's book is evidence of what profound conservatism we are up against with both of my suggestions, popular "uses of science" content for high school students and a Zen-like approach to method (i.e., science skills at their best) for elementary students. Samos is so eager to prove scientific literacy impossible that he even slices up one of the best advanced high school and university science literacy textbooks, *Science Matters* by Robert M. Hazen and James Trefil.[10] The book may not be Science and Society, but we must defend imaginative scientific literacy programs. Regarding Hazen and Trefil, Samos pronounces, "That's just *their* view of what pieces of scientific knowledge should be included." But so is every textbook on any subject, so what's he proving?

An Aside on Old Political Stances and New Philosophies

Of course the left is often not much better — which leads me to a major aside on what's happened to the concepts of right and left. When I noticed that author James Trefil had done another book called *The Dictionary of Cultural Literacy* with E.D. Hirsch, an author associated with defending the European canon, some voice in my head told me I must be siding with the bad guys! Someone once said, "Your criticism of the skills mania sounds conservative at times. Is this a problem?" I don't think so. Some of my principles sound conservative because they *are* conservative. I'm what we in Canada call a "Red Tory," although a "Tory Red" would be closer to the truth. In my opinion, many truths about community are abandoned by both the modern left liberal *and* the right, to our detriment. I also believe that the breakup since the 1970s of the classical left/liberal/conservative polarizations we inherited from post-World War II politics are now so deep that orthodoxies of these kind make little sense any more. For example, most contemporary neo-conservatives have given up old conservative ideas of community and the need for a strong civil society[11] to the point where the market ideas they are pushing actually undermine their cultural policies like family values, etc. "There is no such thing as society, only individuals and their families," said Margaret Thatcher. But families need jobs, neighbour-hoods, community organizations and support at times of special need, such as retirement, unemployment and sickness.

Let me offer an example of the problem of rigidity within current political thinking. Congratulations to Todd Gitlin for raising the classic left analysis of class conflict as the central theme of left vs. right.[12] Con-gratulations to him as well for showing us that those who threw out this class conflict principle have been snookered many times by the powers that be, when the left would win the battle for the headship of social science at some university while the right won the presidency.

But unfortunately he's wrong that this is a time for only one princi-ple for those of us who are on the side of the common people. The bat-tle for identity cannot be shoved aside as if it's gender, racial or sexual-orientation selfishness. People do not currently see viable, third-option class politics, like the erstwhile Rainbow Coalition or an older version of Canada's New Democratic Party or certain trade union coalitions at var-ious times in North American history. At the moment, lacking such gen-uine oppositional forces, many working-class people have focused their attention on matters of culture, identity, education or daily dignity.

Only the example of successful actions of class forces they sympathize with will lure them to combine their identity politics with class politics. Narrow urgings by intellectuals will not.

So I do not apologize in this discussion of science for offering two seemingly contradictory suggestions: morally and politically charged science-and-society content courses for high school children and what I will be calling the Way of Observation for elementary children. If we think of them as irreconcilable opposites (i.e., tough political material and new-age floating), it is only because we are trapped by old clichés. In fact, the combination is a yin/yang that science teaching needs.

Another personal example: when my father graduated from the Anglican (Episcopal) seminary in 1930, he was given marching orders: "catholic at the altar, evangelical in the pulpit and modernist in the study." This mysterious, three-fold motto meant traditional in church rituals, personal in preaching and open in your reading towards harmonizing religion with modern scholarship. (Therefore he found no contradiction between the creation story and the theory of evolution.) I personally wished that part of his marching orders had been "Christian socialist in the streets," but that is not my point here!

If the truth needs two, three or four main principles, then such a position doesn't mean that a person has sold out and become all things to all people. It may mean that the person is on a quest for a new overview that takes all important aspects of reality into account. William Blake understood this issue when he prayed

> May God us keep
> From Single vision & Newton's sleep![13]

Perhaps I will stretch this aside a bit further to suggest the general framework I am currently thinking within and especially what I mean by the term Tory Red. I hope as well that this explanation will clarify my premises for the recommendation I make for elementary science teaching in the second half of this chapter.

Why do I call myself a Tory Red? Red Tories in Canadian history have been Tories who did not share the current mainstream Tory suspicion of state action, but saw a positive role for the state in policies like broadcasting, electricity and supervision of industries like wheat through the Wheat Marketing Board. I prefer Tory Red since I believe the Red Tory philosophy stops well short of hoping for full citizen control of common interests and still contains a fair dose of noblesse oblige.

So why, in the most general sense, am I a Tory Red? It is partly my dualism; I sense that life is both reverence and rebellion, and in this formulation the Tory part is the reverence. The environmental movement, as much as any modern group, has taught us that part of life's quest is to uncover those things *that we try to change only at our peril*, and develop a reverence for them.

I am not saying there's nothing new under the sun. The rebellion side of things is very wrapped up in understanding change, novelty and inventiveness. As I said in chapter 8, we learned in the 1960s that the psyche and the polis, i.e., the mind and the state, could be understood and changed. Unfortunately, however, the postmodernism of the present is a completely shaky foundation for a solid philosophy of change. If there's no firm psyche and no firm polis except for versions of them made up by clever thinkers, then how can one make even a word of recommendation, have even an inkling of any common path, sense even a hint of a Way to pass on to other people? Therefore my approach to rebellion and change inevitably becomes concerned with whether there are any firm conceptions of the psyche and the polis which can become *shared* visions to help us fight for change for the better.

On what basis do I suggest that *my* images of the mind and the state have any firmer basis than those of daydreaming postmodernists?

Because I know that on some level this subjective retreat into current scepticism and its favourite posture, irony, is not the way the earth and the world actually speak to us. That is why modernism, the belief in science, is deeper than postmodernism. I don't mean a modernism that puts nature on the rack. I don't mean "Single vision & Newton's sleep." I don't mean a worship of technology; some of us are proud to be Luddites and some of us fear biotechnology. Neither do I mean the modernism which says that all thought about politics, morality and human action is merely personal "values," nothing more than subjective prejudices.

If we show this maturity about science and modernism, then we need to observe that the scientific way has deep links with, yes, even the old — horror and shudders! — metaphysics, because they both share the notion that the earth and the world will speak their truths to us, not vice versa. How can I say that physics and metaphysics share the same stage? Because both say in certain ways that an understanding of life comes from watching and listening to the earth, including the earthlings. What we bring of our own minds to this understanding is significant, but a prior necessity must be a speaking earth and a speaking time for us to listen to, once we have developed our "listening skills."

But as soon as postmodernists hear talk about metaphysics and eternal verities, they ask why nature has been seen so differently by different people and different eras. Because, I would answer, change and difference are as firm in the earth and in time as the eternal and the unchanging.

Looking at the same point from a different slant, in explanations for the movement from the ancient to the modern world it is commonly suggested that the modern belief in change, and especially the modern belief in change for the better, are beliefs that make obsolete the ancient belief in eternal truth, in primordial anchors.

This is a key assumption we must challenge in our era. The environmental movement challenges this view, so comforting to many modernists and especially postmodernists. Environmental activists know they are dealing with a strange amalgam of deeply embedded truths about human beings and the earth, but also with human evolution and with very contemporary battles with principalities and powers — where newness and inventiveness are a totally key ingredient.

So these are some of my general thoughts. If you share my misgivings about modern skills mania without sharing these general thoughts, that is just fine. I include them here for those who prefer all cards to be on the table.

Suggestion #2: For Elementary Schools: The Way of Observation

If we could name fifty of our neighbours of other species (e.g., twenty-five birds and twenty-five plants), we would be more likely to revere and protect them when they were being threatened.[14]
— Robert Bateman, Canadian painter and naturalist

About ten years ago a nephew of mine, reflecting his love of the more philosophical branch of Karate Do Shotokai (he was to receive his black belt several years later), and reflecting the beginning of his practice of Zen and the Tao, told me: "I know there wouldn't be enough of the right kind of teachers, and I know most students haven't got the concentration, but I still think as an ideal a high school should mostly teach serious meditation and martial arts, and training in living in the present — and what else students want to study will follow in due time. Schools should teach a Way, not a Destination." Gadzooks! At first I thought maybe I should just pack my tent and follow this sixteen year old!

He made me realize that teaching the skills of the scientist in this new ecological form was a far deeper view of skill than skills mania.[15] If in my suggestion about high schools I am recommending some form of Marx's "understanding the world in order to change it," in my suggestion for elementary school I am recommending a form of "looking at the world in order to look after it better." The two seem totally contradictory but are not. I suggest them for concentrated programs at the two different levels of high school and elementary school because neither gets the proper emphasis at the moment.

The former is more appropriate for concentration by older students. Students of this age are beginning to understand the issues of politics and public morality. Eventually I would hope science for all ages would have both strong emphases, but for the pioneering of the Way of Observation, small children are generally acknowledged to be more open to it. Let's learn with small children before we stumble into the high schools and fall on our faces.[16]

I will also present a series of extended quotations in this section. Once again I need to go beyond the convention of short quotations to give a proper glimpse into this final and most important of my suggestions.

For a start, I believe that the Bateman vision of making potential naturalists of children needs to be extended with some thoughts from Herbert and Judith Kohl. The Kohls contrast the ecological vision of scientific observation by small children with what behaviourism would want them to do:

> There are several different ways of studying animal life. One way is to isolate an animal in a laboratory and do things to it. Then one merely observes how the animal responds and reports on those responses. This approach which is usually called behaviorism concentrates on what is done to an animal and how the animal responds. What the animal thinks or how the animal organizes experience is not of immediate concern. Behaviorists usually take animals out of their natural environments and isolate them in laboratories. They are not concerned with the rhythms of an animal's life, with its social world, or with its sense of space or time. The animal is put in an experimental situation. It might be taught to run through a maze, avoid an electric shock, or push a lever to get food. In any case, what is studied is the behavior of the animal in the experimental situation. It makes no difference whether one is studying a pigeon or dog or rat — what is important to behaviorists is the animal's reaction which is isolated from the rest of its life and its experience.

There is a completely different, more respectful, approach to the study of animal life which is called ethology. Ethology is concerned precisely with how an animal experiences the world and organizes the environment. It too is concerned with behavior but in the context of an animal's overall experience. Ethologists acknowledge that one can never get into the head of another living being, can never experience the world exactly as animals do. However, there are clues we can use to help build up an intelligent model of other forms of experience. These clues are provided by animals' senses and by the range of things in the environment that these senses make it possible for the animal to perceive. The clues are also provided by observations of how animals act in their natural environments and by occasional laboratory experiments that attempt to reproduce natural conditions in a controlled setting.[17]

This is the Way of Observation I am suggesting for elementary children. Samos takes a swat at this kind of thing, warning us that nature study is different from the study of nature. Did the ecology revolution pass him by? Does he want us to summon nature to the rack, Bacon style? Does he want that for small children? The gulf between the Reverential Way of Observation and the Science and Society approach I suggest for high school students is not a gulf I will deal with much in this chapter. For one thing, the vast accomplishments for human good won by traditional science are a must for high school students to learn and debate. For another, both insights are needed by children, what good and what harm has resulted from the harnessing of nature and, secondly, what pleasure and what peace can come from the acceptance of nature. The two *are* contradictory but are both necessary. They are a yin/yang of the deepest kind.

More on the Way of Observation and more of *The View from the Oak*. The Kohls picture a science experiment that children can do with their pets:

If you have a pet, watch it when it wakes up; when it's ready to go to sleep; when it hasn't eaten for a time; after it's had a good meal; when it seems restless and wants to move and play. An interesting experiment is to offer your pet food at all these times and see if the food is refused. Another experiment is to offer it a toy at all these different times, and see what happens. You can also observe how it responds to people when it's hungry or sleepy or exhausted or full of energy and wants attention or exercise. We've noticed that Sandy (the Kohl's own pet), who's the gentlest of dogs, will growl at anyone if he's hungry and has a bone. He also goes crazy and chases his tail jumping and running in circles if he sees us pick up the car keys or his leash. He gets jumpy on rainy days when he sleeps inside and doesn't move around. Bit by bit we're piecing together a picture of his moods and needs.[18]

The Kohls end their book with the same defense of this approach that Bateman offers in the quote which opens this segment:

> The human view of the world is only one of many. It enriches our understanding of ourselves to move away from familiar worlds and attempt to understand the experience of other animals with whom we share common ancestors. The respect for other forms of life we can gain from these efforts might in some small way help us work toward preserving the world we share.[19]

What I am saying is very different from the insights of some of our heroes of the 1960s, like Jerome Bruner. Because Bruner had been such a hero of mine for stressing the mental capacity of small children, when his *The Culture of Education* came out in 1997 I was excited, because I saw a new stress on the whole institution of schooling and on "narrative" in teaching. What did he mean?[20]

Reading this book, I found the chapter on science particularly disappointing. It's all so *mental*, so much emphasis on *constructing* the physical world with mind. "Narrative," a key point in his new thinking, is just an aid to forming mental speculations about the physical world. Whether or not they're true, he hardly appears to care. None of the great aims of the Tao is present, i.e., to relax all mind, all mental effort, till the world becomes your home. Where is the mind as *vates*, as mirror of the world? Nineteenth-century English poet Gerard Manley Hopkins sees the World and the Beholder differently from Bruner:

> Summer ends now; barbarous in beauty the stooks arise
> Around: up above, what wind-walks! What lovely behaviour
> Of silk-sack clouds! Has wilder, wilful-wavier
> Meal-drift moulded ever and melted across skies?
> . . . .
> These things, these things were here and but the beholder
> Wanting: which two when they once meet,
> The heart rears wings bolder and bolder
> And hurls for him, O half hurls earth for him off under his feet.
> — from "Hurrahing in Harvest"[21]

Bruner's view of narrative made me think he had given up his older dismissal of narrative history. But the change in attitude was minimal. The narrative he's talking about in 1997 is completely different from real history which has an out-there givenness, a frame beyond an individual mind. I know this would all sound very metaphysical to Bruner, but his world sounds very lonely to me. At one point he says that his view of narrative in science is a bit unusual in that it doesn't really imply, as most narratives do, much interaction of *people* with *people*. It doesn't even seem to include "picking wild flowers and calling them by name." He's another thinker formed by physics as the main science, little affected by biology, warm bodies and reproduction.

This mental trip had its point in the 1960s when the enemy was behaviourism and rat mazes. Today we are surrounded by skills and information enthusiasts who are quite happy to agree with Bruner that mind is all, that living with other people is just a matter of people skills. In such a world we need more meat on the old bones than we get from Jerome Bruner. In such an era we must listen not only to the grass-roots political fighters but to the poets, philosophers and saints who know about reverence, openness and meditation and, first of all, about letting the earth speak to us rather than vice versa.

What we need is the spirit of French philosopher Simone Weil, who talked about the right kind of "attention" needed for proper observing and problem solving:

> Most often attention is confused with a kind of muscular effort. If I say to one of you: "now you must pay attention," I often see you contracting your brows, holding your breath, stiffening your muscles. If after two minutes I ask you what you are paying attention to, you will not remember. You have been concentrating on nothing. You have not been paying attention. You have been contracting your muscles.
> What does attention consist of? Attention consists of suspending our thought, leaving it detached, empty and ready to be penetrated by the object.[22]

The object waiting to penetrate the minds of children is the world of people, living beings and things, "endless forms most beautiful and most wonderful," as Darwin put it. Albert Einstein put it this way: "Where the world ceases to be the scene of our personal hopes and wishes, where we face it as free beings, admiring, asking and observing, there we enter the realm of Art and Science."[23]

But is the physical world still firm enough to be the object of schoolchildren's science? These days we are being cornered by some philosophers to adopt a new scepticism about the possibility of proving anything whatsoever, so that the "endless forms most beautiful and most wonderful" have no more firm marvels, no more firm secrets for us. More and more scientists are being put on the defensive these days with the suggestion that claims about the physical world are more like creations of the imagination than provable theories.

But science is fighting back. Scientist Alan Sokol published a sophisticated spoof of science-à-la-postmodernism in a key postmodernist journal in 1996; then he exposed the spoof publicly.[24] Until fairly recently, old-style scientists have been ignoring this questioning of their basic premises since such scientists had not found their grants and prestige shaken. Lately some of the widespread university cutbacks have begun to affect grants to traditional science programs.[25] Sokol's clever mimicking of the postmodernist style describing his view on a most esoteric subject ("Transgressing the Boundaries: Towards a Transformative Hermeneutics of Quantum Gravity") can therefore be seen as partly a political act.

Also taking part in this battle is Stephen Jay Gould, who has spent many hours in court defending the theory of evolution as true science and not just as one of many equally good theories of the earth's development. (Creationists, cashing in on this new postmodernist attempt to undermine science's authority, have used this argument to get "creationism" onto science courses.) Many cowardly boards of education have capitulated to fundamentalists and have allowed creationism to be taught in science classes. Might one hope that more science teachers would see the need to get more political and defend their subject in the face of this attack?

I want readers to be very clear that the Way of Observation I am recommending as a widely expanded program in elementary schools is the farthest thing from hocus-pocus. It is not a secret gate to some religious trip. In focusing on the earth itself as the place of study, I am one with both traditional and ecological science. In fact, I agree with G. K. Chesterton that on some very primitive level young children are most closely in touch with the marvels of the physical world:

> This elementary wonder is not a mere fancy derived from the fairy tales: on the contrary all the fire of the fairy tales is derived from this. Just as we all like love tales because there is an instinct of sex, we all like astonishing tales because they touch the nerve of the ancient instinct of astonishment. This is proved by the fact that when we are very young children we do not

need fairy tales: we only need tales. Mere life is interesting enough. A child of seven is excited by being told that Tommy opened a door and saw a dragon. But a child of three is excited by being told that Tommy opened a door. Boys like romantic tales, but babies like realistic tales — because they find them romantic. This proves that even nursery tales only echo an almost prenatal leap of interest and amazement. These tales say that apples were golden only to refresh the forgotten moment when we found that they were green. They make rivers run with wine only to make us remember, for one wild moment, that they run with water.[26]

Beyond Observing and Naming

There remains only the job of showing that the Way of Observation goes beyond observing and naming things.

> Once the whole is divided, the parts need names.
> [But] one must know when to stop

says the *Tao Te Ching*.[27] Knowing when to stop with naming can also begin to help children see some mathematical connections. I learned this from Professor Eleanor Duckworth, author of *"The Having of Wonderful Ideas" and Other Essays on Teaching and Learning*.[28]

Obviously I did not pick Ms. Duckworth's book because we agree on everything. There are many features of her work and ideas that do not fit my premises here. (By now I think that this is a virtue!) For one thing she has the same constructivist premises that I have already declared wanting in some thoughts on Jerome Bruner's latest book. For another, very few of the science experiments with children in Ms. Duckworth's book fit the ecological mold. Most are physics experiments and the majority do not even hint at environmental questions. The children and the teachers work on things like the moon; on pendulums; on magnifiers made of cardboard, water and a match box to see tiny things; flashlight batteries, bulbs and various wires to understand circuits; music and time; simple arithmetic; simple geometry.

The fit between Ms. Duckworth's ideas and those I've been calling The Way of Observation comes in her extraordinary respect for children making their discoveries in their own way at their own speed. This excellent quality — presented in a time which damns such a view as teacher-absent teaching, an utterly false representation of this method — is practised in a style that David Hawkins called "not covering a subject, but uncovering it."[29] As they help children uncover something that is already there, teachers in Eleanor Duckworth's Way are very active midwives helping children to have "wonderful ideas," to experience the excitement of puzzling through problems where the answer is not known ahead of time. The metaphor of the midwife has been well explored in *Women's Ways of Knowing: The Development of Self, Voice and Mind*:[30] someone who is not pretentious, who respects you and helps you give live form to an idea that you yourself put together. I am also reminded of *The Power of Their Ideas: Lessons for America from a Small School in Harlem* where principal Deborah Meier talks about working to create a culture where "having an idea," a theory, is the proudest boast.[31]

With her method, Ms. Duckworth is training children in the skills of a real scientist while remaining a staunch foe of modern skills mania.

> I react strongly against the thought that we need to provide children with only a set of intellectual processes — a dry, content-less set of tools that they can go about applying. I believe that the tools cannot help developing once children have something real to think about; and if they don't have anything real to think about, they won't be applying tools anyway. That is, there really is no such thing as a contentless intellectual tool.[32]

I found that at first I had some resistance to reading about these experiments, mostly done with small children. It wasn't the writing style, which is completely natural and accessible. I think it was the detail and the precision of it all, and especially the step-by-step building of a picture of kids doing the experiments and their supervisor doing the careful thinking about what is happening at every stage. She applies that same respectful, Zen-like patience and acceptance of children's observations that ecology-minded teachers have. Eventually I learned to slow down and take it "a step at a time," like the children have to do. Gradually I decided that Bateman is stage #1 and that the Kohls and Duckworth are stage #2, because they start taking the children beyond observing and naming and get them puzzling about the physical world and doing some "mathematizing" where it fits.

Duckworth is also very clear that children have a nature we need to understand in order to help them learn. The new competitive, conservative parents, for example, want their children to *learn the outcomes* and they're not very fussy about how kids get there; *how kids get there* sounds to them like the dreaded enemy, process. Some of the looser progressives, on the other hand, sometimes imply that all these particulars of "when you learn what" will eventually fall into place by themselves. Duckworth's view, unlike both of these positions, is a very grounded attention to the child-as-scientist with a careful focus, like her mentor Piaget, on the fact that a child is a separate being whose stages of thinking the teachers must understand to be helpful.

This sensitivity implies too much of a relationship between teacher and student and too much human emotion to be of interest to the skills movement. Hand the kid the operational tools and drill 'em. Duckworth mentions her disagreements with Siegfried Engelmann on this point.[33] About some of these behaviourist experiments, which speed up children's learning, she says that "the children had learned a verbal overlay, but their deep-seated notions had not evolved." Many conservative parents are obsessed with speeding up their child's education. In a chapter called "Either We're Too Early and They Can't Learn It or We're Too Late and They Know It Already," Duckworth counsels us to listen to children's own rhythms and not give in to our rush and competitiveness.

In short, Eleanor Duckworth's subtlety about children and how they can be encouraged to examine the physical world complements the new stress of the environmentalists on looking into new places and respecting our sister bear and our brother fox. This subtlety comes out all through her book, but perhaps most beautifully in one of her sessions with teachers. One student-teacher who was "struggling to make sense of a morass of observations and models" had just made a key jump in understanding. "I needed time for my confusion," said the student teacher. Says Duckworth in reply:

> That phrase has become a touchstone for me. There is, of course, no particular reason to build broad and deep knowledge about ramps, pendulums, or the moon. I choose them both in my teaching and in discussion here, to stand for any complex knowledge. Teachers are often, and understandably, impatient for their students to develop clear and adequate ideas. But putting ideas in relation to each other is not a simple job. It is confusing; and that confusion does take time. All of us need time for our confusion if we are to build the breadth and depth that give significance to our knowledge.[34]

Lastly, from this comment you can tell how important teacher training is to Eleanor Duckworth. Teachers must become more like Zen masters who learn to ask the equivalent of one-hand-clapping questions. She knows that the teachers themselves have to go through the same

Way of Observation they expect the children to go through. She takes us through a number of her teacher classes doing just that. Regarding a group of teachers watching the progress of two children called Timmy and Sandy, Ms. Duckworth notes

> the surprise, puzzlement, dogged pursuit, resistance or suscepti-bility to suggestion, doubts, conviction, and so on, all of which gives us an appreciation of a mind at work. It was all of these aspects of the session with the children, not to mention ges-tures, facial expressions, and eye movements, that contributed to the teachers' understanding of Timmy's and Sandy's thinking.[35]

Needless to say, Duckworth knows that teacher-proof textbooks are the exact opposite of what she is recommending.

Teacher training and retraining in depth are also essential for the proper carrying out of my first suggestion, the expansion of Science and Society courses for high schools. Note, for example, that the difficulty of teaching about the splitting of the atom, and its connection with Hiroshima and the Cold War, or about the discoveries that drastically reduced fatal childhood diseases is the combination of information, poli-tics and morality that tempts busy teachers either to lay on nothing but memory work or to turn morality and politics into indoctrination. But many teachers know the way to avoid these mistakes, and their knowl-edge must be more widely acknowledged.

But there is also a newer approach that I have stressed in this book which is as bad as the memory work and indoctrination, i.e., to turn the whole business into a critical thinking skills, armchair discussion, where the participants see through everything and owe allegiance to nothing. The group with the best things to say on this issue were the teachers from Boston who produced curricula about the Holocaust and Decision Making in a Nuclear Age.

In my own area of Toronto, Canada, the most intelligent, sensitive and thorough teacher training on matters like this has been done under the supervision of gifted teacher trainer Myra Novogrodsky. We so asso-ciate teacher retraining workshops and courses and professional devel-opment days with the travelling gurus selling various forms of snake oil ("Increasing Your Facilitation Skills," "How to Teach Metacognitive Reflection") — lubricants of skills-capitalism? — that we forget the unsung artist-professionals like Novogrodsky who constantly fight for training programs to be longer than one hour and who offer topics that *question* capitalism. Such teacher-artists offer the opposite of snake oil;

they have thought long and hard about the details of good curriculum and have practised it themselves, not just for topics like Science and Society but for racism, feminism, labour, fine arts, war and genocide, peace and politics. (Here in Ontario a short, province-wide experiment in destreaming grade 9 has now been cancelled — to the cheering of middle-class parents and teachers. Apart from the deep class disagreements on this issue, the second-biggest stumbling block to securing more destreaming has been the lack of any broad teacher-retraining on how a destreamed class could be run without losing both the faster and slower students. Yet big corporations, which spend millions retraining staff in attitude shifts, will cheerfully advise governments that teacher retraining is an unnecessary frill!)

Such science curriculum changes as I am suggesting will not work without long hours of teacher retraining from people like Myra Novogrodsky. Neither will they work without networks within which teachers can get inspiration from each other and help each other out of difficulties. I am thinking here of networks like the one produced by the fine magazine, *Green Teacher, Education for Planet Earth*, a Canadian publication which now has a large following of writers and readers across North America.[36]

The Star Trek Factor

Some readers may wonder why I have talked about the teaching of science for the masses without building on the public fascination with space travel. Surely when we see on TV a serious actor like Jodie Foster (in connection with *Contact,* a science fiction movie she stars in) discussing the possibility of life on other planets, are we not in touch with something teenagers like to discuss? Doesn't what John Horgan (*The End of Science*) calls the *Star Trek* factor — the love of science fiction movies and books, the excitement about the landings on Mars and the moon and the interest in telepathy and genetic engineering — suggest our leads for school science for the masses? I don't deny that these matters should figure in the kind of high school Science and Society courses I am suggesting, but I do not believe the above interests are primarily *scientific* interests for common people. They are mostly religious interests: space wars between good and evil, making contact with spirits, creating the perfect species — these are first of all deep, mythological expressions with only a very secondary care for *whether it will really happen one day.*

John Horgan, for all his fascination with the psychology of professional scientists, is little interested in the attitudes to science of average citizens. "Science and Society" is barely mentioned in his book. He says correctly that public fascination for scientific wonders eventually wears down. But one of Horgan's problems is that he thinks of the "wonders" as the central features of traditional science. No wonder those who think of science as traditionally a series of kicks want to slap the wrists of ordinary people when they lose interest.

This fading interest is not because common people are stupid but because they are smart. Most are no more impressed these days by flashes in the sky than they are by miraculous flashes in the Bible or the Koran. No, the commoners are looking for improvements in their lives, not for kicks about a universe that feels removed from them. Whether science in Horgan's sense is dying makes not a spot of difference to the masses of people: not because science is too difficult, but because masses of people aren't sure any more whether science and technology are bringing things that are helpful or hurtful. That's why many people can be both fans of the *Star Trek* mythology and complete sceptics about science itself.

As a consequence, if we educators are not trying to transform science teaching so that the natural awe of small children for nature is nourished and so that the sense of justice in older children is fostered, then let's pack it all in or just let elitists prepare the "bright kids" for their physics and chemistry exams for university entrance and the rest be damned. This may in fact be where the current crisis in science teaching is headed; and if ordinary parents are prepared to let this happen, a few teachers or projects here and there will have little effect.

Closing Meditation

On a more restful note, I'm going to end by summing up my two suggestions with a prayer that I've used before about curriculum. It's from Pope Gregory, and I don't recommend it for its religious side but because I think it's a useful framework for thinking of the ways that science in particular can be divided — an alternative way of looking at the subject. The prayer goes like this — some of you undoubtedly know it:

> Lord, help me to change the things I can change, to accept the things I cannot change, and give me the wisdom to know the difference.

Notice the three-fold sum-up, the yin/yang/yung, if you will, of curriculum reform. Now I see the "things that I can change" in the science curriculum context as the ways in which nature can be harnessed for the good. But bad uses need also be studied to make the good more obvious. Maybe — this is just a personal hope — some of the spirit that C.P. Snow saw in science in the 1940s and 1950s could return, the spirit that says that an understanding of the world could be applied to help alleviate suffering. Some of the really valuable roots of some aspects of science could be restored if it was seen in this way — "help me to change the things I can change."

"To accept the things I cannot change" — I see this as the respect for the earth side of science. This side is represented by those haiku written by grade 2 children, by my mother's love of wildflowers which she called by name, by *uncovering* the topic instead of covering it, and by Eleanor Duckworth's teachers as midwives, watchful, skillful and ready for the labour times and the birth times — in this case the birth of "wonderful ideas." This is the side that says don't harness nature, contemplate it and understand it — with a certain reverence. Both of these approaches are the kind of living spirit that I think Einstein thought should be behind any learning of skills.

And finally, "teach me the wisdom to know the difference." That's why I suggest widespread discussions at local schools and on the conference circuit. It is a chance to think through our work, and think through what we're trying to teach children about the world and about nature.

CHAPTER 11

Why We Should Turn Away from Skills Mania, and What We Should Try Instead

On June 27, 1997, Rick Salutin wrote an incisive column in *The Globe and Mail*, in which he dropped a piece of the news of the day into our mindpool and, as a great columnist can, then showed us the vibrations outward till they eventually include this society's entire agenda for kids and schooling. He opened with a squeegee kid called Outback who was asked by a radio reporter why he thought the police were giving the squeegee kids a hard time. "Because they're fascists," said Outback. This bluntness made the interviewer uncomfortable, and his reaction became Salutin's way into the wild and angry attitude of drivers towards squeegee kids.

But soon the vibrations moved outward:

> The Outback clip is also a great riposte to the cultural barrage of *faux* concern for kids we see everywhere. Have you noticed how no social issue can be broached now except in terms of kids? A Globe and Mail front page last week had four of five stories on or around kids (Liberal spending plans, child poverty, tobacco crackdown and Quebec child care) plus a big photo of a boy

hero. Jean Chrétien said one of his goals at the Denver summit was "children": when Bill Clinton wanted to say something nice about France, he praised its health care for kids. They sound like Anna in *The King and I* singing, "The children, the children, I'll not forget the children." The money from tobacco companies in the US is supposed to go to Medicare for uninsured kids. What are the parents of these kids — debris? Are there no adults in the world worthy of compassion any more? American "child advocate" Marian Edelman writes that 10 years ago "support for whatever was labeled black and poor was shrinking and . . . new ways had to be found to articulate . . . continuing problems." She hit on kids and, says another lobbyist, "cleverly . . . shifted the focus from poverty to children." This is at best speaking in bad faith for the sake of good causes. It's as if some people afraid to express care for others, in our mean era, get to sneak it in under cover of kids (as one sometimes suspects about animal rights). Meanwhile others, who really *don't* like or respect their fellow humans, can cover *that* by saying they love kids or animals.

The case of the squeegee kids blows any such cover. What you hear is hate and fear: "Here I am driving my posh car from Oakville to Bay Street and — Omygawd, who's on my windshield? Get 'em outta my sight, I don't care how!" It's odd how official effusions about kids coincide with attacks on the school system that call for rigid standards, punitive methods (failing students), bigger classes and badmouthing teachers; and treat education strictly as "training" . . . so kids can be fed straight into the great digestive tract of the economy. If these people like kids so much, why are they determined to turn them into the precise opposite of kids, namely adults, i.e., people lacking exactly what kids generally have: exuberance, spontaneity, a high degree of creativity, a deep seriousness about issues of life and justice. The power of the resolve shows in the way so many adults, all of them former kids, try to wipe out those very traits through what a recent Globe editorial called "Reality school." You'd think adults who felt real affection for kids would nurture a continuity rather than a chasm, between these two phases of life. . . .

The *Globe and Mail* pitch for *Reality School* is the skills/outcomes/standardized-tests approach to Reality. This Reality is, in fact, Unreality:

It is complete unreality to tell our high schools that all students retrained in the skills approach will get jobs.

It is complete unreality to continue to cut back subject after subject where students can ponder the large questions, where students can make music and art, which go beyond job training.

It is complete unreality to suggest that all content, substance and commitment are inevitably propaganda or obsolete the minute they're learned.

It is also unreality to suggest that limiting education to a barrage of skills does not itself have a reality principle behind it, one called technocracy.

The difference comes down to this: Are we making a serious examination of the world out there and inside ourselves, or are we mostly examining techniques for examining that world? The thinking skills proponents are suggesting the latter and I am suggesting that techniques should be grounded or anchored by keeping the emphasis on the former.

Once again let me offer what Albert Einstein had to say on this subject: *"All means prove but a blunt instrument if they have not behind them a living spirit."*

It is this spirit, these anchors in people, in their minds, in their history, in their common bonds, in their lives as integrated wholes, that the skills zealots are eroding from education. They are asking us to produce T. S Eliot's hollow men, with headpieces filled with straw. They are suggesting that our job as teacher is entirely technical or instrumental. They are asking us to train people who are *mentally skilled but mindless.* They are saying, "the information age showers us with information and we're going to give you the skills to sift the useful from the useless." But this discernment is not primarily a technical matter. In this connection Neil Postman quotes Edna St. Vincent Millay:

> Upon this gifted age, in its dark hour,
> Rains from the sky a meteoric shower
> Of facts. . . . They lie unquestioned, uncombined,
> Wisdom enough to leech us of our ill
> Is daily spun, but there exists no loom
> To weave it into fabric.[1]

Postman goes further, saying that most information is garbage and teachers are being asked to be garbage collectors.[2]

George Martell, in *A New Education Politics: Bob Rae's Legacy and the Response of the Ontario Secondary School Teachers' Union,* calls this kind of education "neo-taylorism for the 21st century." At the turn of the century, Frederick Taylor showed business owners how to break down industrial processes so that *people's* work could be calculated as mechanically as machine work. One of the challenges and tangles of this current education/business package is that its proponents (as I have shown earlier) want to represent their philosophy as the *opposite* of Taylorism. Lena Dominelli and Ankie Hoogvelt make this point about Taylorism in an article in *Studies in Political Economy* 49: "Ironically, just when it [Taylorism] is disappearing as a tool for controlling *manual* workers, it is being introduced as an instrument for reorganizing *mental* labour!"

Martell says that this new educational Taylorism has three main features: First, what the Ontario Royal Commision on Education (1994) calls the "love of learning" is actually "the love of process, floating free from the substance of what is to be understood and what is to be done. Actually very few of us love this kind of learning," continues Martell, "which is often boring and abstract."

Second, says Martell, values themselves are now thought of as skills. They have "little to do with what we understand as human morality, rooted in our experience of life." In practical terms what this approach teaches are the "skills" of working "co-operatively" in a company to produce financial success regardless of the human casualties resulting from downsizing, the selling of shoddy goods, the undercutting of Canada, the closing down of a community dependent for years on a particular business or the ruining of an area's ecology.

Third — a development of the first two features — Martell suggests that the downplaying of a larger social vision (the part of the old curriculum represented, albeit in very conservative terms, by reading literature of substance, by citizenship training and by progressive ideas of teaching social reform), are central to this "neo-taylorism of the 21st century." In commenting on this third feature Martell probes the hidden curriculum implications of North American school philosophy since World War II:

> Implicit purposes and informally learned ideologies (the socialization of the hidden curriculum) have always been on the table for those who have constructed our school system, and they have always mattered a lot. They still matter. But those who have had the most say in our schools have always judged an explicit conservative or pro-business curriculum too explosive a proposal to put before a potentially unruly populace. Such a curriculum would have to be slipped in unobtrusively, when that was possible, or at particular moments when the tide was running favourably. Otherwise one must trust in broader social norms, brought forward by church, state and media, to shape

the creation of local curricula and the manner in which they are taught. But under no circumstances was an alternative social vision to be taught. This position has been consistently resisted by many teachers and parents and community activists, but it has largely carried the day over many generations of curriculum development and many forms of "progressive" reworking of old texts and old pedagogies. Official school curriculum has come to be imbued with a conservative aversion to social critique tempered with a liberal rhetoric of individuality."[3]

This muting of the system's main philosophy has certainly been more true in Canada than in the United States. But for both countries this is how the proponents of skills mania want it to remain. The skills obsession is a new twist on an old idea that education is strictly about work and jobs and preserving the capitalist market, but part of the new muting process is to say that the system is now about technology or the Information Age.[4]

I would like to return to a compelling point about totalitarian education, made by Hannah Arendt in 1964, which fits our current technocratic education as well: "The aim of totalitarian education has never been to instill convictions but to destroy the capacity to form any." Technocratic education increasingly does the same thing by keeping students busy with skills and thereby pre-empting all struggle with content, topics and convictions — except as soft commodity discussion skills or values education.

So whether it is in Hannah Arendt's piercing insight, Martell's probes about Ontario education, titles like *People and Skills in the New Global Economy* or *Failing Grades: Canadian Schooling in a Global Economy*, we see that this skills mania philosophy is not the disinterested New Way it's cracked up to be. Its exponents are telling us that *restructured global capitalism can be the "living spirit" Einstein talks about.*

Remember as well that I'm saying the scheme does not command respect even on its own terms. The new capitalism does not need the jobs it says it needs,[5] and the jobs it has, even in its newly emerged service and technical sectors, are routine and repetitive, not mentally challenging. Here's another emperor with no clothes, but so far not enough people have noticed. This is not a popular position right now, but it is urgent to speak plainly since the lives of an entire generation of youth are at stake.

The Friendly Side of Skills Mania?

As we do battle with technocratic education we will continue to encounter those who call us paranoid, the old and current colleagues who latch onto the teamwork and discussion skills.

Here is a statement from an important book of pedagogy called *Brave New Schools: Challenging Cultural Illiteracy* by Jim Cummins and Dennis Sayers:[6] "Should teachers continue to transmit officially approved information and skills as if they were neutral reflections of objective reality, or should they help students to analyze issues critically from a variety of perspectives?" Sounds warm and friendly. Of course, if put this way, who could be against the second half of the statement? But we're back to the armchair, in my opinion. We're back to the implication that merely "analyzing issues from a variety of perspectives" by itself will lead to enlightenment. Now obviously I thoroughly approve of students "analyzing issues critically from a variety of perspectives." But what I have been contrasting throughout this book is this: To some people ideas, strongly held, have consequences; to others such ideas are merely things to toss around in discussions. Teachers with grounded ideas who are also enthusiastic about this new approach enliven their class discussions with their own strongly held convictions, thus giving the discussion skills approach a serious purpose, *a purpose that is not in the method itself.* The purpose for teachers who feel this new method to be genuine is usually to discuss in order to get a deeper grip on reality. The purpose of the method itself, on the other hand, is to teach free-floating, portable discussion skills.

The difference is crucial.

One Person's Experience of the "Living Spirit"

Perhaps I could illustrate what I mean by anchors, by the "living spirit," through telling a story told me by a friend who travelled with three fellow teacher-union executive members in the summer of 1995 to Harare, Zimbabwe, for a meeting of the world teachers' organization called Educational International. It was a long journey, first from Toronto to London, England, and then even longer to Harare. When the four teachers got off the plane, two of the party were talking and my friend noticed that the other executive, who was black, was standing to one side and had tears in her eyes. "Have you been to Africa before, Pat?" he asked. "No, first time," answered Pat. "Home at last, eh?" my friend said. The tears flowed down Pat's face. Later Pat herself said to me: "You know the experience was even more dramatic because I didn't know *myself* that I felt that strongly until I stepped off the plane."

That's what I mean by the living spirit. I counted on that spirit teaching my two black history courses at Stephen Leacock Collegiate in Scarborough, Ontario. I counted on the skills I taught in essay writing, critical reading and exam writing being anchored in the student need and desire to learn their roots and sort out how to live in a difficult contemporary world. If that spirit does not hover over our work, then the work is a waste of time.

I also counted on these anchors when I helped students to understand the current battles between Quebec and Canada. Can they really understand why 50 percent of Quebec voters wanted to separate from Canada when no serious provincial history program traces this development of Quebec thinking? Is some bias exercise like reading short pieces on both sides of the issue followed by a brief discussion or a formal debate really an adequate substitute for a proper study of the history of the country?

Skills Mania's Attractive Wrapping

My colleagues are sincere in their defense of skills mania. The starry-eyed version, however, the one linking school teaching to the swinging new version of teamwork capitalism, has been passed on in spades by the gurus of modern schooling. One such guru, Robin Fogarty, outdoes herself in spreading this warm and fuzzy approach to teaching, particularly in her book, *The Mindful School: How to Integrate the Curricula*.[7] Listen to her chapter headings:

Fragmented (the bad old way)
    Connected
        Nested
            Sequenced
                Shared
                    Webbed
                        Threaded
                            Integrated
                                Immersed
                                    Networked

This teacher-training book presumably encourages education students to prepare their future charges for all that teamwork down at Office Building X. Could this feeling possibly emanate from the self-same, lean and mean corporations which, for a very large portion of their workday, use a very different set of words from Ms. Fogarty's?

Rationalized

Downsized

Restructured

Reallocated

Refocused

Privatized

Liquidated

Fired

The Peter Druckers who says that education workers are running things these days and, as we shall see in a moment, the Edward de Bonos, see no inconsistency in these two languages. For one thing, their theories require neither of them to take any responsibility for the unemployment resulting from the new age of business. This means that the wry meaning of words like "downsized" produce from them only pious teardrops about human waste, not the kind of outrage that would start getting them de-invited as gurus for the high-paying management seminars. Secondly, they insist on seeing a revolution in specific, limited parts of business as a complete transformation of capitalism itself.

Yes, there have been important changes in capitalism as a result of robotics and computer technology. Yes, there have been extensive changes in the ratio of machinery to labour costs. Yes, capital is able and does move from place to place all over the world at a much faster pace. Yes, more use is made of "teamwork" in many firms. Yes, there is a new worker in some fields called the "multiskilled" worker. Yes, "just-in-time production" places new requirements on many workers.

But ask workers what these revolutionary-sounding terms mean in practice. I think you would hear from honest workers that, except for the handful of superstar computer geniuses, even the clever, thinking students are meant to be superior drones, superior hollow people who do lots of de Bono's lateral thinking, lots of lithe mental tricks, but in the unthinking service of the marketing, transportation, labour, production and information policies of the corporations they work for. And as I asked earlier: Are the Nortel teams given big decisions like whether to move whole programs out of Canada? The answer was no, but they *are* likely to be tossed the decision of how to break the grim news to the workers. Do secretaries who move to teams get appropriate pay raises? Not at Nortel. But they *do* get all sorts of new pressure to work at times that were fomerly protected under their union contracts. Do multi-skilled workers all do the range of important, demanding jobs implied by the way management gurus use this term? Not at all. Often a multi-skilled job will be monitoring a set of computer screens and using "people skills" when talking to people who come to the counter for routine requests.

And no, these changes in business do not add up to a decisive transformation of capitalism if you include in your definition of capitalism a pretty basic conflict between workers and management. Management experts who say this antagonism is gone mean that they would like to persuade their workers that it's gone. Such workers will then cooperate better than the old union folk did. De Bono wrote his early books in the 1960s as if he were talking about new ways of thinking for people in general. With his recent books we see nothing but advice to management, the kind of stuff he preaches in his seminars for CEOs. In *Handbook for the Positive Revolution,*[8] he says towards the end that "in a highly competitive world in which no one owes a living to anyone else, the destructive model of union behaviour has become less relevant. There is a general move to the constructive model." Would De Bono really be as prepared to argue this at a seminar of unionized workers as he is at his usual seminars for CEOs?

This is management talking. It's part of management and school talk where change, change, change and innovation, innovation, innovation are presented as inevitable and also good.

Begging is not negotiating. The power is all on one side. The fact that the union movement the world over is having to rethink how to exert its influence does not mean that the rosy, exterior wrapping of skills capitalism is the true definition of the new business. Robin Fogarty's chapter headings are the public relations pitch for business, and school systems who say they are switching to the skills emphasis to help train students for modern business need to take off the shiny wrapping and examine the goods inside. A little conversation with workers currently working in modern corporations will reveal this difference between shiny wrapping and nasty goods.

What Direction for the Future?

But what direction *should* we go? The narrative side of this book has been mostly about teaching black kids, but it has been 100 percent about teaching working-class kids. It's about students with a strike or two against them in our school system. It's about students who still register statistically in the lower streams or tracks of the academic hierarchy. They aren't the neat little group that conservatives like to call "the disadvantaged," whose needs can be met by a few special ed. experts, and then everything will turn out fine. They're a very large group, an ill-served majority.

This book is addressed mostly to people who want to tackle or are already tackling how we're teaching or not teaching this very large percentage of our student population. Mind you, I believe the kind of program I have been describing is a good education for everyone, but the particular group I have described here needs it most. I am also saying that the skills emphasis, because of its hollow base, is not a satisfactory long-term answer to this ill-served majority. It is also my view that, except for outstanding exceptions of the type represented by remarkable inner city experiments — some of which are documented in the video series *Every Child Can Succeed*[9] — the performance of most such students is a universal disgrace to the school systems of North America. That's why I do not belong to the school of thought, espoused by some teacher unions, which says that the public school system is not broken, so it doesn't need fixing.

Yes, there's been a need to analyze carefully some of the shoddy statistical comparisons with Japan and Germany to make North American schools look worse than they are. Yes, it has been useful to show the steady rise in the literacy rate of youth as a whole over the last few decades. And, yes, it has been important to show rising rates of literacy in minority populations over the last decades. But if these facts lead us to the smug conclusion that what Jonathan Kozol called the "savage inequalities" of schooling both in Canada and the United States are somehow wiped out, then we are gripped by a terrible illusion.[10]

The Green and the Red

The only educational approach I know that is up to the job of tackling such a giant problem seriously is a model that is still full of resilience and vitality when practised with breadth, firmness and patience. I call it the educational philosophy of the Green and the Red.

It is a Green educational movement because it teaches children to protect what is good. It acquaints children with those features of the earth and of history that we mess with at our own risk. It also builds schools where the right ecological mixture of classes, health, sports, drama, music, art, community work and school government give children a taste of that shared knowledge, pleasure and participation which is the right of all classes, colours, genders and orientations. This last part of the Green philosophy reminds us that knowledge, pleasure and participation keep competition solidly in check, and that classroom learning need not be sacrificed for other school activities.

If the Green side teaches children to protect what is good, the Red side teaches children to fight for what should be better. It is committed to the very best education for everyone (in reality, not just in rhetoric) with a message that skills must be taught seriously, but with the purpose that students be inspired to use them to find out what's wrong with the way this world is run and join in movements for its betterment. Since the powers that be consider this a dangerous philosophy, part of the Red approach must be that teachers, parents, students and the public work together in strong groups to protect those whose teaching challenges in this way.

Mastering Existing Tests

These are aims for an improved schooling which we in the Green and Red movement must fight for. Meanwhile back at many school ranches, a very different system is often at work. How do we combine the struggle for a better system with the promotion requirements of the existing system? To explain my position on this point I need to return for a moment to the video series, *Every Child Can Succeed,* and its consultants, Dr. Barbara Sizemore and Dr. Asa Hilliard. This series of seventeen videos, three handbooks and one full background text is inspired by a very simple proposition, and by the evidence for its truth: i.e., "We've got to get busy and teach inner city kids (of all colours) to have as good a chance to get into university as kids from other areas, and here are the examples of schools and methods that prove it can be done." The stress I have been putting in this book on purpose, conviction, content, blueprints for social change and what's worthy of contemplation are almost entirely absent from these videos. The authors are right that there need be no agreement on these matters to accomplish their main task as described on the videos — top student performance as measured by current public standardized tests. In this series, only spokesperson Louise McKinney of Seattle espouses the full Information Age skills philosophy, and readers of this book will understand why I feel the absence in the videos of a full-blown skills philosophy is a virtue.

It's an interesting example to me of the "two worlds" philosophy of the best black education — and what I would say is the best working-class and anti-racist education in general. It's a version of the old religious idea that you're of this world but you're also *not* of this world. You're trying to do two things at once (very contradictory in many ways): organize systems that push hard to get your people ahead in the official ways, and also push for visions that give students beacons to present and future fights for a better world. The second aim forms no part of the *Every Child Can Succeed* video series. That's fine with me — we all do different things in different places at different times.

But I know from attending four National Association of Black School Educators conferences in the United States that educators like Sizemore and Hilliard push the visions as well. And they don't call them "the vision thing," as George Bush did. With them visions are born of the deepest struggle. The distinction is essential. Sizemore and Hilliard don't want soft visions — a black history class here and a Martin Luther King, Jr. Day there — when the school system is not committed to top education for black students. But they also feel that black people have every right to the deepest visions in their school education. One of the exciting moments at one NABSE conference was Barbara Sizemore's description of her trips to Egypt and the Sudan.

I bring this dual aim to the fore at this late stage to remind you that although this book has not been about how to push hard to get oppressed kids ahead *by the current ways of this world* (including the skills mania), I nonetheless consider that, for poor kids, it is a completely essential corollary of what I have been saying. Our criticism of testing systems can be no excuse for not helping our students to master them. Analyzing them and fighting politically to have such systems abolished or significantly changed is a completely worthy project, but meanwhile our students must be served by teaching them to master such systems and do well with them.

This need for the left to draw some clear lines yet reach out to all inventive new education ideas reminds me of another place that insight can be found. It's tucked away in unlikely places, like a fifteen-hour series of radio interviews on education by CBC *Ideas* producer David Cayley. Represented among the interviewees are educators as diverse as A.D. Hirsch and Carl Bereiter. Even homeschooling gets serious attention.[11] As I noted in my aside in the previous chapter, even those of us who have allegiance to what liberation theology calls "the preferential option for the poor," i.e., we identify with "ordinary people," or as the old language said, with "the masses," we nonetheless need to listen to Blake's caution about avoiding "single vision & Newton's sleep." Sensitive and probing ears like David Cayley's will take us to places we feared to listen. This is an age when a new revolutionary combination is needed: solidarity with the masses but with an utter openness to what Simone Weil saw as "paying attention" to reality as a whole. Both sides in their smug isolation may call us fools, those of us who know that this schizophrenic double ear is our necessary calling.

The Teacher as Midwife

For me the main points I have been making in this book are best summed up in the school battles of British author and teacher Chris Searle, whether he is acting as a midwife for school kids' writing at home in working-class England or fighting alongside revolutionary governments in Mozambique and Grenada.

I have just finished reading his story, "The Gulf: Between a School and a War." It's about the writing and public speaking of his students and their parents talking about their attitudes to the Gulf War of 1991. A large percentage of students at Chris Searle's school in Sheffield, England, was Arab from the Middle East, yet through their writing, their public speaking and through community organizing, a passionate and bridging dialogue took place about the Gulf War in this working-class school where Searle was both principal and an English teacher.[12] A year later the same strategies were put to work to prevent their Sheffield school from being closed.[13]

Almost my favourite book of Chris Searle's is called *Carriacou and Petite Martinique: In the Mainstream of the Revolution*.[14] These are 128 pages of the most carefully edited conversations in 1982 with Prime Minister Maurice Bishop and twenty-three of the citizens of Carriacou and Petite Martinique, islands which are part of the political jurisdiction of Grenada. Here is Searle in another of these midwifery roles, this time recording, transcribing, editing and publishing the sensitive, detailed reactions of people who were seeing their poor and forgotten islands being transformed by a revolutionary government — soon to be wiped out by a combination of ultra-left reaction and American invasion. Helping the dumb (those robbed of their voices) to speak, and their friends and compatriots to hear — this is maybe the most important bread and butter contribution that a teacher can make to social change.

But finally, the approach I am recommending is found in bridging thinkers like Eleanor Duckworth,[15] who bring unique and intimate teaching insights to a left approach, a left which has often not taken learning theory seriously enough, especially in teaching science. The left has traditionally had such faith in science (remember C.P. Snow) yet has had little imagination about *schooling* in science. Most of the official left, furthermore, has rightly assumed Deweyism and progressive education as an essential part of its inheritance. Yet when reviewing the details of learning pedagogy — which must now include shedding parts of this progressivism that are too precious and not useful in an atmosphere of siege and "savage inequalities" — we have hardly begun to do the thinking this age presses upon us. This is the terrain that true progressive pedagogues like Eleanor Duckworth inhabit, and we must let them teach us to inhabit it with them. Otherwise, we will not defeat the conservatives and the technocrats where the education arm of our movement must defeat them — in the classroom itself.

What kind of school, then, do these people and I envision?

- It is a school which, first of all, need apologize to no right-winger for the toughness of its reading and writing program, which links student literacy to telling one's own story and the stories of struggling people around one.
- It is a school whose curriculum is a window on the world outside and on the world inside ourselves, which stresses vigorous, school-wide debate focused on finding truth, and stresses that there's a world to build beyond school walls.
- It is a school, in the words of radical Canadian educator George Martell, that "educates all students for personal integrity, challenging work, meaningful citizenship and the pursuit of social justice."[16]
- It is a school that does not, in columnist Rick Salutin's words, treat parents as debris, but strives to have its parents, teachers, educational workers and students in regular dialogue, and to have these four groups share major input into school policy and community action.
- It is a school that keeps its feet wet in the local community and uses the community as a place to give political education to its students through contact not with Whittle Corporation but with courts, councils and daily commerce.
- It is a school whose program — again to quote Salutin — will develop "what kids generally have: exuberance, spontaneity, a high degree of creativity, and a deep seriousness about issues of life and justice."
- It is a school that considers teacher and educational worker unions a valid part of the battle for good schooling. But when parent and student interests clash with teacher and educational worker interests, such a school identifies with Milwaukee teacher Bob Peterson of that great magazine flagship of progressive schooling, *Rethinking Schools*: "Social justice unionism," Peterson suggests, knows how, at key times, to thrash out strategies and plans with parents, teachers, education workers and students to solve conflict within the ranks of fighters for school justice.[17]
- And finally, it is a school that is aware that the left has no corner on

total educational wisdom. Those great educational issues — like ideal school size, multiculturalism, the environment, social class, the community vs. the individual, school variety and choice, and, yes, skills vs. content — these and other issues do not yet have worked out and balanced answers. As they swirl around in the great cauldron of debate, you find our school people at the centre of these debates, stirring up the pot and stoking up the fire.

* * *

We do not know yet in our battle for the millions what new metals will emerge from the great cauldron. To use a different metaphor, the Heidegger image I used earlier, many gods are absent for a time, but the pulse of life is not absent. Meanwhile, we must find the pulse in the fragments. The Canadian poet Dennis Lee, drawing on Canadian philosopher George Grant, puts well a central part of what this search among the fragments is about:

> There are certain things that speak to us at the core, but that scarcely exist within the assumptions of modern thought. I have in mind the kind of reality people once pointed to with terms like "good," "evil," "the sacred."
>
> It is not that we have lost contact with such things in our lives, but rather that educated thinking no longer recognizes them as having any substance. Over the last few centuries our traditional languages of meaning have largely faded; they seemed passé in the world described by science. And the language of fact that superseded them has no place for evil or beauty — except as subjective "values," which we project onto a neutral universe. This account of facts and values is taken for granted in most modern thought; we have trouble thinking of things that matter without adopting its substance. . . . What we know by living our lives, and what we can think within the categories of educated discourse, are no longer on speaking terms.
>
> This is a sorry state for a civilization to be in. We need a more sophisticated form of thinking: one that can deal with both fact and meaning, proceed with rigour and awe at once. But that won't materialize overnight. And until it does, it seems to me, it's worthwhile just sitting still. Swapping stories of what does claim us even if we have no concepts in which to formulate it. Like travellers in unmapped territory, exchanging descriptions of the landmarks they've discovered.[18]

That's half the story.

The other half is about taking hold of horrors and hangups, discriminations and exploitations and the crimes of the mighty who put chains on the weak. It's about taking hold of these things and working serious transformations.

To do this we must develop new ways, new paths, and even new blueprints — flexible blueprints, it is true, but blueprints nonetheless. Blueprints for our larger future and blueprints for our individual futures and our community futures.

And of course we must constantly resist the pronouncements of triumphal neo-conservatives (but since they have given conservativism a bad name, let us call them neo-liberals) who say that all blueprints are wicked government plots or communist hangovers.

And as with Dennis Lee's first insight, so with this second insight, we are cobbling fragments. We are "like travellers in unmapped territory." We must often be limited to "swapping stories" of exploitation and building a good future. Yes, half our time we should be "sitting still," but the other half we should be hammering out new realities.

For me these two necessary approaches cannot be neatly unified — which makes me a hamfisted dualist. As I see it, we are destined to both reverence and rebellion.

In this search among the fragments, our best curriculum guide, our best school policy guide and our best school wars guide is this adaptation of Pope Gregory's prayer — which applies to all education, not just science:

Help us to understand those parts of life and history that can be and were changed for the better, and help us to learn different possible ways to accomplish this change.

Help us also to respect the parts of reality that call for reverence and acceptance.

And give us the wisdom to weigh the distinction between these two different but mutually necessary philosophies of life.

Appendix A:
Africa and the West Indies

Curriculum material for the first
half of the semester, with a
special focus on pre-white
Africa and early imperialism in
the Caribbean

1. *Dr. Leakey and the Dawn of Man*, documentary film supporting the predominant "Eve" theory of the origin of humans. Also a clipping from *The Toronto Star*, July 1992, entitled "Asian skulls rattle African 'Eve' theory" *Dr. Leakey and the Dawn of Man*, movie, 26 minutes, National Geographic, discontinued. Try libraries. On the same topic, *The Man Hunters*, movie, 51 minutes, Films Incorporated, no date available.

2. Basil Davidson, *Different But Equal*, first part of an eight-part film series on Africa. An overview of ancient Africa even back to pre-Sahara cave-painting days. *Africa*, eight-part video series, 1/2 hour each, written and presented by Basil Davidson. Produced by John

Percival. Mitchell Beazley Television. R. M. Arts, Channel Four. London, England, 1984.

3. Molefi Kete Asante, *Classical Africa* (about Egypt, Nubia and Axum) pages 1-92 (Maywood, NJ: The People's Publishing Group, 1994). A four-unit textbook coverage of these areas by the famous African American scholar. A discussion of the Afrocentrist position in relation to other African history perspectives such as that represented by the best-selling high school text by Sharon Harley, Stephen Middleton and Charlotte M. Stokes, *The African American Experience: A History* (Englewood Cliffs, NJ: Globe, 1992).

4. *A Glorious Age in Africa* by Daniel Chu and Elliott Skinner — the story of the West African empires of Ghana, Mali and Songhai. A 120-page book which highlights the flowering of high civilization before the Europeans arrived in the very area from which the highest concentration of slaves were taken. Daniel Chu and Elliott Skinner, *A Glorious Age in Africa: The Story of Three Great African Empires* (Trenton, NJ: African World Press, 1990).

5. Forty-five slides of art from all parts of Africa and from many periods, showing the remarkable artistic achievement of Africans before European influence. I invite to class the right kind of knowledgeable guest to comment intelligently without too many technical comments on styles and historical periods. Collected and produced by students from art books.

6. "They Came before Columbus," speech by Dr. Ivan Sertima. Cassette tape in Black Education Series, 1988. Distributed in Toronto by Dr. C. Sandy, (416) 282-1084.

7. *1492: The Conquest of Paradise* (feature movie starring Gérard Depardieu) portrays Columbus in heroic, epic proportions. Only a very few of the crimes of Columbus are revealed and even these are attributed to one of his lieutenants. Despite the title, there is no sense that the biggest crime of all was that this conquest was a major step in the history of European imperialism. Ridley Scott, director.

8. *Rethinking Columbus,* by the Rethinking Schools collective. Scores of fine ideas of how to take up this issue in class, plus lots of reading suitable for students, including the classic articles by Bill Bigelow. Bill Bigelow, Barbara Miner and Bob Peterson, eds., *Rethinking Columbus: The Next 500 Years,* 2nd expanded edition, 1999. Available from Rethinking Schools, 1001 East Keefe Avenue, Milwaukee, WI 53212.

9. *The History Book,* a Danish cartoon film history with English dubs

on the subject of world history from the 1400s to the 1970s. The first seven of nine fifteen-minute animated cartoons that I find highly successful teaching the history of class, racial and imperial struggles from before 1500 and over seven centuries. I do not use the last few episodes since they are too time-bound and too optimistic about the trend represented by the successful African revolutions of the 1970s. The rest are outstanding and cover a huge sweep of history at a student's level with humour and passion. *The History Book*. Made in Denmark by Jannik Hastrup and Li Vilstrup, 1973. Available in Canada from Idera Films, Vancouver, British Columbia. In the U.S. From Tri-continental Film Centre, New York City.

10. *The Cimaroons* by Robert Leeson, a ninety-one-page book for young people featuring Jamaica's maroons, but covering many places on the mainland as well (including Florida). It shows why Jamaicans who have Maroon ancestry are so proud of it. Robert Leeson, *The Cimaroons* (Toronto: Wm. Collins, 1978).

11. The successful Haitian Revolution of 1791-1815 as presented by guest visitors to our class and by myself from my own reading of C.L.R. James's remarkable book, *The Black Jacobins: Toussaint L'Ouverture and the San Domingo Revolution* (New York: Vintage, 1989). This stirring past is contrasted (via newspaper clippings and magazine articles) with modern Haiti, sometimes called the poorest country in the Western Hemisphere. Also covered: the career of Aristide and the colonial dependency, modern-style, of this country.

12. *Burn,* feature movie about an initially successful slave revolt in a Caribbean island (mid-1800s). Although the revolt was later put down, the movie offers a subtle presentation of the meaning of long-term struggle beyond this particular revolution. *Burn,* feature movie, originally called *Quemada,* directed by Gillo Pontecorvo, starring Marlon Brando. Produzioni Europee Associates/ Les Productions Artistes Associes, 1970.

Appendix B:
Africa and the West Indies

Curriculum material for the second half of the semester, with a special focus on the invasion of Grenada, 1983

1. *Annie John,* a novel by Jamaica Kincaid. I include this book, set in recent Antigua, to show that history is personal stories, not just political and cultural stories. Half the class usually decides that young Annie is lesbian. The book is what teacher language calls an excellent "teaching tool." Jamaica Kincaid, *Annie John* (New York: Penguin, 1986).
2. *Personal Profile* of the class on the topic of why each family left the West Indies. With most it's "to make a better life," where making a better life *financially* is usually central.
3. *El Norte,* made in 1983, the same year as the invasion of Grenada. Two teenage Guatamalans whose father has been murdered for being part of the opposition to the government in their homeland flee to the U.S. Los Angeles, the mythical North (El Norte), where everyone was supposedly happy and wealthy, does not come through for

them. *El Norte.* Director, Gregory Nava, starring Zaide Silvia Guttierez and David Villa Ipando. Celebrity Videos, 1983.

4. *Americas in Transition 1980.* This film is about how, in this century, the U.S. has jealously kept control of Latin American and Caribbean neighbours. Commentators Sister Peggy Healy, plus a former U.S. ambassador to El Salvador, a former CIA director and a former Mexican ambassador to the U.S. (accompanied by graphic visual footage) talk about twelve U.S. invasions of this region since 1900 (now fifteen) and about how local problems of poverty, land distribution and hunger are always ignored and Soviet and Cuban infiltration blamed instead. *Americas in Transition 1980.* Movie, directed by Obie Benz, narrated by Ed Asner, 29 min., colour, U.S., 16 mm.

5. *Nubian Nawledge, From Negro History to Black Liberation Month,* Volume 1, a cassette tape, edited and with interviews by Otis Richmand of Abdul Alkalimat, Maya Angelou, Maurice Bishop, Jan Carew, bell hooks, Yuri Kochiyama, Kwame Nkrumah, Robert F. Williams, Kurt Huggins. MKO Productions, Toronto (416) 408- 2817.

6. *Mudpie* Magazine, special issue on the invasion of Grenada and the Third World, 1983. This magazine contained a Torontonian's eyewitness account of the coup and the invasion, plus Reagan's and Fidel Castro's official speeches about the invasion. It also contained the "Domino Theory" diagrams contained here to teach students the meaning of that theory. *Mudpie* Magazine: *Growing Up in Ontario* 5,4 (April 1984). Toronto. Contact the author via the publisher.

7. *Grenada: The Future Coming Towards Us, 1983.* A well-made, hour-long film giving the official government's position about Grenada under Maurice Bishop and the New Jewel Movement (1979-1983). It was completed just months before the assassination of Bishop by leaders of the coup — Bernard Coard and Hudson Austen. *Grenada: The Future Coming Towards Us,* with John Douglas, Carmen Ashurst and Samori Marksman, The Caribbean Resource Institute and New York Cinema, 55 minutes, 16mm, colour, 1983.

8. *Operation Instant Fury:* TV Frontline Investigation, 1988. An American investigation that suggested that U.S. intelligence about Grenada was next to nil and that "saving the 600 American medical students from becoming hostages" was a venture that possibly put the students in even more danger. A former U.S. ambassador to Grenada during Bishop's time suggests that the whole story of the "Grenada airport threat" was a U.S. government fabrication. *Operation Instant Fury:* movie, P.B.S. Frontline, produced by Mark Obenhaus, narrated by Seymour Hirsch, 1988.

9. I only discovered *Heartbreak Ridge* in 1998. It's directed by and stars Clint Eastwood, and it ends with Eastwood's platoon taking part in the invasion of Grenada. Eastwood plays Sergeant Highway, a macho man supreme, who is invincible with his fists and is not afraid to tell private and general alike where to get off. If I took up the movie, I would ask whether Hollywood was saying that the U.S. saved Grenada from the Maurice Bishops in order to hold up the Sergeant Highways as a better way of life. *Heartbreak Ridge*, director and lead actor, Clint Eastwood. Warner Brothers, 1986.

Notes

Introduction

1 "The Publisher's Perspective," An interview by Paul Bennett, *History and Social Science Teacher* 23, 4 (Summer 1988): 200-206.
2 Ontario Premier's Council, *People and Skills in the New Global Economy* (Toronto: Government of Ontario, 1990), 85.
3 Robert B. Reich, *The Work of Nations: Preparing Ourselves for 21st Century Capitalism* (New York: Knopf, 1994).
4 David Livingstone, *The Education-Jobs Gap: Underemployment or Economic Democracy* (Toronto: Garamond,1999), xii.
5 Bob Davis, *Whatever Happened to High School History? Burying the Political Memory of Youth: Ontario 1945-1995* (Toronto & Halifax: Our Schools/Our Selves & James Lorimer, 1995).

Chapter 1: How the Skills Philosophy Thrives in New Fields

1 William Spady, at Grassroots Education Services Conference run by the Ontario Secondary School Teachers' Federation. Toronto, December 1993.
2 Dr. Barbara Sizemore is Dean of the School of Education at DePaul University and Dr. Asa Hilliard III is Professor of Urban Education at Georgia State University. See especially the video series they were chief consultants for: *Every*

Child Can Succeed (Bloomington, IN: Agency for Instructional Technology, 1992). It is available from the A. I. T. in the United States and from Magic Lantern in Canada.

3 See Hilliard's stress on solid academic content even for elementary teachers in Kathy Checkly and Laura Kelly, "Toward Better Teacher Education: A Conversation with Asa Hilliard," *Educational Leadership,* 56, 8 (May 1999).

4 William Hart, "Against Skills," *Our Schools/Our Selves Magazine* (September 1992).

5 Joan Baer, Ann Lacey and Esther Sokolov Fine, *Children As Peacemakers* (Portsmouth, N.H.: Heinemann, 1995).

6 Tim Kearns, Carol Pickering and John Twist, *Managing Conflict: A Practical Guide to Conflict Resolution for Educators* (Toronto: Ontario Secondary School Teachers' Federation, 1992).

7 *Media Literacy, Resource Guide, Intermediate and Senior Divisions, 1989.* (Toronto: Ontario Ministry of Education, 1989).

8 Douglas Rushkoff, *Playing the Future: How Kids' Culture Can Teach Us to Thrive in an Age of Chaos* (New York: Harper/Collins, 1996).

9 See my wildly optimistic speculations in *The Harvard Educational Review* 38, 3 (1968): 553-57. Reprinted from *This Magazine is About Schools* 2, 2 (Summer 1968): 1-5; for more dreams about youth and revolution see my introduction to the Education Section of *The Cosmos Reader* (New York: Harcourt Brace Jovanovich 1971): 743-52.

Chapter 2: Collaboration and Collaborators

1 Check out this excellent series of easy-to-read historical novels from Canadian history. Bill Freeman, *Shantymen of Cache Lake* (Halifax: James Lorimer, 1975) By the same author: *The Last Voyage of the Scotian* (1976) and *First Spring on the Grand Banks* (1978).

2 Stanley A. Brown, *Total Quality Service* (Scarborough, ON: Prentice-Hall, 1992), 53.

3 See Douglas D. Noble, "Let Them Eat Skills," *The Review of Education/Pedagogy/ Cultural Studies* 16, 1 (1994): 15-29. See also Julie Davis et al., *It's Our Own Knowledge: Labour, Public Education and Skills Training* (Toronto: Our Schools/ Our Selves Publications, 1989); also Andre Bekerman et al., *Training For What? Labour Perspectives on Skills Training* (Toronto: Our School/Our Selves Publications, 1992).

4 Tom Peters and Robert Waterman, *In Search of Excellence* (New York: Warner Books, 1984), 81.

5 Tom Peters, *Liberation Management: Necessary Disorganization for the Nanosecond Nineties* (New York: Knopf, 1992), 453-58. A newer book, *The Circle of Innovation: You Can't Shrink Your Way to Greatness* (New York: Knopf, 1997) is another series of hymns to business folk who go with the flow — and it contains high praise for Howard Gardner's idea of multiple intelligences.

6 See articles by both Sizer and Littky in *Educational Leadership* on the topic of Personalized Learning, 57, 1 (September 1999). See also Theodore Sizer and Nancy Sizer, *The Students Are Watching: Schools and the Moral Contract* (Boston: Beacon, 1999). See also another report on Littky's more recent work "Finding New Ways to Assess Students' Learning," *Education Update*, 40, 8 (December 1998), Association for Supervision and Curriculum Development Conference on Teaching and Learning. (This is the organization that publishes *Educational*

Leadership magazine.) For older classics see Theodore R. Sizer, *Horace's Compromise: The Dilemma of the American High School* (Boston: Houghton Mifflin, 1984). Also Theodore R. Sizer, *Horace's School* (Boston: Houghton Mifflin, 1992). About Littky see Susan Kammeraad-Campbell, *Doc: The Story of Dennis Littky and His Fight for a Better School* (Chicago/New York: Contemporary Books, 1989).

7 Ontario Premier's Council, 44.

8 Judy Clark, Ron Wideman and Susan Eadie, *Together We Learn: Co-operative Small Group Learning* (Toronto: Prentice-Hall, 1990), 44.

9 Stanley Brown, 66.

10 *The Globe and Mail,* Feb. 25, 1993.

Chapter 3: Collaboration Part II

1 "The Story of the Eagle: A West African Folk Tale," retold by Edward Robinson from Linda Goss and Marian E. Barnes, eds., *Talk That Talk: An Anthology of African American Story Telling* (New York: Simon and Shuster, 1989); also Michal Wynn, *The Eagles Who Thought They Were Chickens, A Tale of Discovery* (Marietta, GA: Rising Sun Publishing, 1993).

Chapter 4: English

1 See also Scott Bates's poetry collections, *The ABC of Radical Ecology* (revised 1990) and *The ZYX of Political Sex* (1999) both from Highlander Research and Education Centre, 1959 Highlander Way, New Market, TN 37820. Bates dedicates the first book to Miles Horton and the Highlander Folk School. For Miles Horton's biography, see note 17 in chapter 10 of this book.)

2 Charles William Goldfinch, *The Prodigal Teacher: The Life and Writings of Charles William Goldfinch* (Toronto: Mudpie Press, 1994). Available from Mudpie Press at 11 Lauder Avenue, Toronto M6H 3E2, Canada. $20 Canadian.

3 Lionel Trilling, "Reflections on a Lost Cause: English Literature and American Education," *Encounter* 40, 3 (September 1958).

4 Rewey Belle Inglis and Josephine Spear, *Adventures in English Literature* (New York: Harcourt, Brace, 1958).

5 Edmund Kemper Broadus, *The Story of English Literature* (Toronto: Macmillan, 1936). The quotation my brother remembered is on page 623!

6 Howard O. Sackler, director, *Hearing Poetry*, vol. 1: Chaucer through Milton; vol. 2: Dryden through Browning. Narrator: Mark Van Doren; Readers: Hurd Hatfield, Frank Silvera, Jo Van Fleet. (New York: Caedmon, 1958).

7 Donald Gutteridge, with a teaching unit by Ian Underhill, *Stubborn Pilgrimage: Resistance and Transformation in Ontario English Teaching 1960-1993,* (Toronto: Our Schools/Our Selves, 1994), 13,14.

8 Gutteridge, 14.

9 Herbert Kohl, *36 Children* (New York: New American Library, 1988).

10 Chris Searle, *Classrooms of Resistance* (London, U.K.: Writers and Readers Publishing Cooperative, 1975).

11 Frank C. Baxter, *The Nature of Poetry* (New York, Spoken Arts, Inc., 1958). I am grateful to Donald Gutteridge and several of his colleagues at the Althouse Faculty of Education, University of Western Ontario, for tracking down this and the *Hearing Poetry* records for me.

12 Johan Huizinga, *The Waning of the Middle Ages* (New York: Doubleday, 1956), 10.

13 Judith Barker-Sandbrook and Neil Graham, *Thinking through the Essay* (Toronto: McGraw-Hill, Ryerson, 1986).

14 Malcolm Ross and John Stevens (eds.), *Man and His World* (Toronto: J. M. Dent, 1961). By the same editors, *In Search of Ourselves* (Toronto: J. M. Dent, 1967).

15 *Paths of Glory*, starring Kirk Douglas. Directed by Stanley Kubrick (United Artists. 1957).

16 Charles Yale Harrison, *Generals Die in Bed* (Hamilton, ON: Potlatch Publications, 1975 [1930]).

17 Frank Smith, *To Think* (New York: Teachers' College Press, 1990), 90.

18 Barbara Ehrenreich, *Blood Rites: Origins and History of the Passions of War* (New York: Holt, 1997).

Chapter 5: History

1 James W. Loewen, *Lies My Teacher Told Me: Everything Your American History Textbook Got Wrong* (New York: Simon & Schuster, by arrangement with The New Press, 1995).

2 The international negotiations called the MAI (Multilateral Agreement on Investment) are a later extension of this undermining. For a lively version of this story in Canadian history see David Orchard's *The Fight for Canada: Four Centuries of Resistance to American Expansionism* (Toronto: Stoddard, 1993).

3 Jack Granatstein, *Who Killed Canadian History?* (Toronto: Harper Collins, 1998).

4 Francis Fukuyama, *The End of History and the Last Man* (New York: The Free Press, 1992).

5 See Francis Fukuyama, "The Great Disruption," *Atlantic Monthly*, May 1999. Fukuyama's 1999 modification of his "end of history" theory is modest enough that it does not diminish him as a reflector of the U. S. notion (with Canada solidly onside) that it is the modern watchdog around the world of neo-liberal triumphalism.

6 Michael Bliss, "Fragmented History, Fragmented Canada," a condensed version of the 1991 Creighton centennial lecture, "Privatizing the Mind: The Sundering of Canadian History, the Sundering of Canada" (Toronto: The University of Toronto Magazine, 19, 2 (Winter 1991): 8.

7 See Ken Osborne, *In Defense of History: Teaching the Past and the Meaning of Democratic Citizenship* (Toronto and Halifax: Our Schools/Our Selves and James Lorimer,1995) Also with the same publishers: *Teaching for Democratic Citizenship*, 1991; *Educating Citizens: A Democratic Socialist Agenda for Canadian Education*, 1988. For the American "Standards" documents see Gary Nash and Charlotte Crabtree, *United Sates History, World History* and *History: Grades K-4* (Los Angeles: UCLA, 1994).

8 Nathan I. Huggins, "The Deforming Mirror of Truth: Slavery and the Master Narrative of American History." *Radical History* 49 (Winter 1991).

9 Christopher Friedrichs, "The First-Year Course: The Case for Content," *History and Social Science Teacher* 24, 3 (Spring 1989): 128.

10 C. L. R. James, *Black Jacobins: Toussaint L'Ouverture and the San Domingo Revolution*, 2nd ed. (New York: Vintage, 1989).

11 Walter Rodney, *How Europe Underdeveloped Africa* (Washington, DC: Howard University Press, 1982).

12 See, for example, Luigi Luca Cavalli-Sforza and Francesco Cavalli-Sforza, *The Great Human Diasporas: The History of Diversity and Evolution* (New York: Addison-Wesley, 1995).

13 *Our Roots 2,* Personal and Family Histories by Stephen Leacock Collegiate's OAC Black History Class; 176 pages, including 64 photographs from family albums (Scarborough, ON: Scarborough Board of Education, 1994). Out of print. Also *Our Roots 3*, the sequel by another class of students (Available from Mudpie Press, 11 Lauder Avenue, Toronto, ON M6H 3E2, Canada).

14 Bob Davis, *Whatever Happened to High School History?*, 210-12.

Chapter 6: Citizenship Education

1 I agree with Andrew Hughes (Citizenship Education Conference, Fredericton, April 5-7, 1995) who said that when a policy is declared to be "across the curriculum" as in "English across the Curriculum," it is usually a pious hope rather than a reality. In contrast, I am describing something that was not piously planned but just happened. It is a precise reality in Ontario's high schools.

2 Christopher Lasch, *The Revolt of the Elites and the Betrayal of Democracy* (New York: Norton, 1995), 11-12.

3 Isaiah Berlin, "John Stuart Mill and the Ends of Life," from *Four Essays on Liberty* (London: Oxford University Press, 1969). This particular essay was first written and published in 1959.

4 General Smedley Butler's own words are found in the documentary film, *Americas in Transition.* See Appendix B, Item 4.

5 Alan Sears and Andrew S. Hughes, "Citizenship Education and Current Educational Reform," 6, 7 and ff. Available from Alan Sears, Chair of Studies in Canadian Citizenship and Human Rights, St. Thomas University, Fredericton, New Brunswick, E3B 5G3.

6 See Bob Davis, *Whatever Happened to High School History? Burying the Political Memory of Youth, Ontario:1945-1995*, chapter 1.

7 Tom Wayman, *For and Against the Moon: Blues, Yells, and Chuckles* (Toronto: Macmillan, 1974). "The Country of Everyday" section contains sixteen poems of which the one I quote is only one. All are well worth reading, as indeed are all Tom Wayman's poems.

8 Ken Osborne, Supplement called "History Programmes in Canadian High Schools," from "I'm Not Going to Think about How Cabot Discovered Newfoundland When I'm Doing My Job: The Status of History in Canadian High Schools." A paper presented to the Annual Meeting of the Canadian Historical Association, Calgary, June 1994, page 3 of the Supplement.

9 Noel Annan, *The Curious Strength of Positivism in English Political Thought* (London: Oxford University Press, 1959), 21.

10 Ken Osborne, *Teaching for Democratic Citizenship*, 3.

11 John Ricker and John Saywell, *How ARE We Governed?* (Toronto: Clarke, Irwin, 1961). Despite this promise to show how politics *really* works, Ricker and Saywell begin with the same kind of desert island story found in *A Reader in Canadian Civics* by Stewart Wallace (Toronto: Macmillan, 1935). The message of the story in each case is that politics is not rooted in the big ones eating the little ones (Shakespeare's *Pericles*), but in the convenience to everyone of sharing.

12 Neil Postman, *Technopoly: The Surrender of Culture to Technology* (New York:

Knopf, 1992), quoted in Maude Barlow and Heather-jane Robertson, *Class Warfare: the Assault on Canada's Schools* (Toronto: Key Porter Books, 1994), 148, 149, 152.

13 See a sensitive and brilliant story on this topic by Kate Lyman, "Staying Past Wednesday," *Rethinking Schools* 13, 1 (Fall 1998).

14 Isaiah Berlin, *The Hedgehog and the Fox: An Essay on Tolstoi's View of History* (Chicago: Elephant Paperbacks, Ivan R. Dee, 1993), 3. The book was first published in 1953. See also Bob Davis, "The Death of Isaiah Berlin: Drumroll from the New Right and the Third Way," *Our Schools/Our Selves* 9, 5 (February/March 1999). Updated version from the author: 11 Lauder Avenue, Toronto, Ontario M6H 3E2 Canada.

Chapter 7: Sociology

1 Gerald Graff, *Beyond the Cultural Wars: How Teaching the Conflicts Can Revitalize American Education* (New York: Norton, 1992).

2 *Attica,* full length documentary directed by Cinda Firestone, Attica Films, Inc. Distributed by New Cinema, New York, 1973.

3 Tom Wicker, "The Men in D Yard," *Esquire* magazine 83, 3 (March 1975).

4 Tom Wicker, *A Time to Die* (New York: Quadrangle, 1975).

5 Roger Caron, *Go Boy!* (Toronto: McGraw-Hill Ryerson, 1978).

6 *Quicksilver and Slow Death: A Study of Mercury Pollution in Northwestern Ontario* (Guelph, ON: The Ontario Public Interest Research Group, 1976).

7 Carol Coulter, *Are Religious Cults Dangerous?* (Dublin: Mercier Press, 1984).

8 *Democracy on Trial: The Morgentaler Affair,* documentary movie directed by Paul Cowan, National Film Board, Ottawa, 1984.

9 *Silent Scream,* narrated by Dr. Bernard Nathanson. American Portrait Films, New York, 1985.

10 Arthur Schlesinger, Jr., *The Disuniting of America: Reflections on a Multicultural Society* (New York: Norton, 1991).

11 Neil Bissoondath, *Selling Illusions: The Cult of Multiculturalism in Canada* (Toronto: Penguin, 1994).

12 Neil Postman, *The End of Education: Redefining the Value of School* (New York: Knopf, 1995).

13 Gary B. Nash, Charlotte Crabtree and Ross E. Dunn, *History on Trial: Culture Wars and the Teaching of the Past* (New York: Knopf, 1997), 102.

14 Peter Emberley and Waller R. Newell, *Bankrupt Education: The Decline of Liberal Education in Canada* (Toronto: University of Toronto Press, 1994).

15 Peter C. Emberley, "Storming the Barracades," *The Literary Review of Canada* (September 1995): 22, 23.

16 See Keren S. Brathwaite and Carl E. James, *Educating African Canadians* (Toronto: Our Schools/Our Selves Publications, James Lorimer Publishers, 1996).

Chapter 8: Psychology

1 Janis Foord Kirk, " 'Soft skills' now needed for most types of jobs," *The Toronto Star,* November 1, 1997, Careers Section, 1.

Chapter 9: Strengthening Science as a Subject for All Students — Part I

1 Derek Hodson, "Against Skills-Based Testing in Science," *Curriculum Studies* 1, 1 (1993): 127-48.

2 George L. Gray, Toronto: *History News Letter*, May 1957, 1.

3 David Hollinger, "Science as a Weapon in *Kulturkampfen* in the United States Since World War II," 1994, unpublished.

4 Daniel Bell, *The End of Ideology: On the Exhaustion of Political Ideas in the Fifties* (New York: Free Press, 1960).

5 Francis Fukuyama, *The End of History and the Last Man* (New York: The Free Press, 1992).

6 John Horgan, *The End of Science: Facing the Limits of Knowledge in the Twilight of the Scientific Age* (New York: Addison-Wesley, 1996).

7 Hayden White, *Metahistory: The Historical Imagination in Nineteenth-Century Europe* (Baltimore: John Hopkins, 1973); also *Tropics of Discourse: Essays in Cultural Criticism* (Baltimore: Johns Hopkins, 1988).

8 Terry Eagleton, *Literary Theory: An Introduction* (London: Blackwell, 1983).

9 Rick Salutin, *The Globe and Mail*, December 20, 1996.

10 Snow, C. P., *The Two Cultures*, with an introduction by Stepan Collini (Cambridge, UK: Cambridge University Press, 1993).

11 Snow, 79-80.

12 *Minamata*, Japanese documentary with English subtitles, directed by Noriaki Tsuchimoto. Monument Films, 1974.

13 *Hands Across Polluted Waters*, Noriaki Tsuchimoto, producer. University of Saskatchewan, 1975.

14 See this remarkable collection of photographs in W. Eugene Smith and Aileen M. Smith, *Minamata* (New York: Holt, Rinehart & Winston, 1975).

15 *The Ascent of Man: Knowledge or Certainty?* Episode 11, featuring Jacob Bronowski. B.B.C. Series, 1973.

16 *At War with Death*, from *A Planet for the Taking* with David Suzuki. CBC Enterprises, 1985.

17 Huston Smith, *The Religions of Man* (now entitled *The World's Religions*) (San Francisco: Harper, 1958), 7, 8.

18 Lancelot Hogben, *Mathematics for the Million: A Popular Self Educator* (London: Allen & Unwin, 1951); also *Science for the Citizen* (London: Allen & Unwin, 1956).

19 Stephen Hawking, *A Brief History of Time: From the Big Bang to Black Holes* (New York: Bantam, 1988).

20 John Boslough, *Stephen Hawking's Universe* (New York: Avon, 1985).

21 J. P. McEvoy and Oscar Zarate, *Stephen Hawking for Beginners* (Cambridge, UK: Icon, 1995).

22 Eric LeMay and Jennifer A. Pitts, *Heidegger For Beginners* (London: Writers and Readers, 1994).

23 *Insignificance*, Director, Nicolas Roeg. Warner Bros., 1985.

24 Stephen Jay Gould, *Full House: The Spread of Excellence from Plato to Darwin* (New York: Harmony Books, 1996).

25 Christian de Duve, "The Gospel of Contingency," *Nature* 382, 6603 (October 31, 1996).

26 R. McNeill Alexander, "The Game of Life," *New Scientist* 152, 2050 (October 5, 1996).

27 Nancy E. Smith, "It's Just That Simple," *Audubon* 98, 5 (September/October 1996).

Chapter 10: Strengthening Science as a Subject for All Students — Part II

1 W. H. Auden, "After Reading a Child's Guide to Modern Physics" from Edward Mendelson, ed., *Selected Poems* (New York, Vintage International, 1979), 246.

2 *Warrendale*, a documentary, directed by Alan King, Toronto, CBC, 1967.

3 Snow. See introduction by Stepan Collini, lxvii-lxxi.

4 Steven Rose, "The View Across the Snow-Line," *The Cambridge Review*, (March 1987): 9-12.

5 Arthur Davis, "Freedom and the Fourfold in the Thought of Martin Heidegger," Ph.D. thesis, McMaster University, 1974. Also Arthur Davis, "Justice and Freedom: George Grant's Encounter With Martin Heidegger," found in Arthur Davis, ed., *George Grant and the Subversion of Modernity* (Toronto: University of Toronto Press, 1996).

6 Martin Heidegger, *The Question Concerning Technology, and Other Essays* (New York: Harper, 1977).

7 Utah Phillips and Ani Difranco, *The Past Didn't Go Anywhere*, CD, Buffalo, NY: Righteous Babe Music, 1996.

8 Evelyn Fox Keller, *Reflections on Gender and Science* (New Haven: Yale University Press, 1985), 33-42.

9 Morris Samos, *The Myth of Scientific Literacy* (New Brunswick, NJ: Rutgers University Press, 1995).

10 Robert M. Hazen and James Trefil, *Science Matters* (New York: Anchor Books, 1990).

11 I mean "civil society" in the way Christopher Lasch uses the phrase. See early in chapter 3 and note 2 of that chapter.

12 Todd Gitlin, *The Twilight of Common Dreams: Why America Is Wracked by Cultural Wars* (New York: Metropolitan Books, 1995).

13 Letter to Thomas Butts, 22 November 1802, found in Geoffrey Keynes, ed., *The Letters of William Blake, with related documents,* 3rd ed. (Oxford: Clarendon Press, 1980), 43-46.

14 Quoted by Alex Fischer, assistant to Robert Bateman in correspondance with the author, May 23, 1997.

15 His name is Simon Vigneault and he has now written a first novel, *Tales from the Infinite Living Room.*

16 To see how even a cool establishment magazine gives a nod to the kind of Way of Observation I'm talking about — of course it's got to appear in a special issue on "the spirit of education," i.e., religion as an education issue — see Richard C. Brown, "The Teacher as Contemplative Observer," *Educational Leadership* 56, 4 (December 98/January 99).

17 Herbert and Judith Kohl, *The View from the Oak: The Private Worlds of Other Creatures* (New York: Sierra Club Books/Charles Scribner's, 1977), 53-54. Of Kohl's over thirty books, the current favourite with my university classes is *I Won't Learn From You.* Two versions are available, one from the New Press, New York, 1994, the other from Milkweed Editions, Minneapolis, 1991. See also Miles Horton, *The Long Haul, An Autobiography,* with Her-

bert Kohl and Judith Kohl (New York: Doubleday, 1990) Also *36 Children,* note 9, chapter 4. For a recent title see *The Discipline of Hope: Learning from a Lifetime of Teaching* (New York: Simon and Schuster, 1998).

18 Kohl, 89.
19 Kohl, 109.
20 Jerome Bruner, *The Culture of Education* (Cambridge, MA: Harvard University Press, 1996), 115-129.
21 Gerard Manley Hopkins, "Hurrahing in Harvest" from Roberta A. Charlesworth and Dennis Lee, *An Anthology of Verse* (Toronto: Oxford University Press, 1964), 163.
22 Simone Weil, "On Being Attentive," from an essay entitled "Reflections On the Right Use of School Studies with a View to the Love of God," carried in *This Magazine is About Schools* 2, 5 (Winter 1968): 101-104.
23 Helen Dukas and Banesh Hoffmann, *Albert Einstein: The Human Side, New Glimpses from His Archives* (Princeton, NJ: Princeton, 1979), 37.
24 See Alan D. Sokal, "Transgressing the Boundaries: Toward a Transformative Hermeneutics of Quantum Gravity," *Social ·Text* (spring/summer 1996): 217-52. See also Sokol's revelation of the hoax, Alan D. Sokol, "A Physicist Experiments with Cultural Studies," *Lingua Franca* (May/June): 62-64. An interesting review of the episode is Steven Weinberg, "Sokal's Hoax," *New York Review of Books*, 43, 13 (August 8, 1996): 11-15.
25 For an interesting discussion of this issue see Steven Ward, "The Revenge of the Humanities: Reality, Rhetoric and the Politics of Postmodernism," *Sociological Perspectives* 38, 2 (1995): 109-28.
26 G. K. Chesterton, "The Logic of Elfland," found in Malcolm Ross and John Stevens, *Man and His World: Studies in Prose* (Toronto: Dent, 1961), 338.
27 Lao Tsu, *Tao Te Ching,* a new translation by Gia-Fu Feng and Jane English (New York: Vintage, 1972), verse 32.
28 Eleanor Duckworth, *"The Having of Wonderful Ideas" and Other Essays on Teaching and Learning* (New York: Teachers' College Press, 1987).
29 Duckworth, 7.
30 Mary Field Belenky, Blythe McVicar Clinchy, Nancy Rule Goldberger and Jill Mattuck Tarule, *Women's Ways of Knowing: The Development of Self, Voice and Mind* (New York: Basic Books,1986), 217-19.
31 Deborah Meier, *The Power of Their Ideas: Lessons for America from a Small School in Harlem* (New York: Beacon, 1995).
32 Duckworth, 13.
33 Duckworth, 33-34.
34 Duckworth, 82.
35 Duckworth, 92.
36 *Green Teacher: Education for Planet Earth,* Tim Grant and Gail Littlejohn, eds. Toronto. Address: 95 Robert Street, Toronto, ON M5S 2K5

Chapter 11: Why We Should Turn Away From Skills Mania, and What We Should Try Instead

1 Edna St. Vincent Millay, *Huntsman, What Quarry?* (New York: Harper, 1939).
2 Report from *Utne Reader*'s New York City Town Hall meeting, *Utne Reader* 70 (July-August 1995): 35.
3 Martell, George, *A New Education Politics: Bob Rae's Legacy and the Response of*

the Ontario Secondary School Teachers' Union (Toronto: Our Schools/Our Selves & Halifax: Lorimer, 1995) 260-63.

4 Two fine books which expose the false claims of the "Information Age" hype are Theodore Roszak, *The Cult of Information: The Folklore of Computers and the True Art of Thinking* (New York: Pantheon, 1986) and Bill McKibben, *The Age of Missing Information* (New York: Random House, 1992).

5 Recall from the Introduction David Livingstone's book, *The Education-Jobs Gap: Underemployment or Economic Democracy,* in which he shows with massive statistical evidence the absence of jobs promised by skills mania.

6 Jim Cummins and Dennis Sayers, *Brave New Schools: Challenging Cultural Illiteracy through Global Learning Networks* (New York: St. Martin's Press, 1995).

7 Robin Fogarty, *The Mindful School: How to Integrate the Curricula* (Palatine, IL: Skylight Publishing, 1991).

8 Edward de Bono, *Handbook for the Positive Revolution* (New York: Viking, 1991). I owe the observation of de Bono's change in focus to Professor Bob Luker of George Brown College in Toronto. By 1999 Peter F. Drucker was getting more cautious about how much knowledge workers were *actually* running the world and how much they would *eventually* run the world. See especially page 57 of "Beyond the Information Revolution," *Atlantic Monthly,* October 1999.

9 *Every Child Can Succeed,* see note 2 in chapter 1.

10 Jonathan Kozol, *Savage Inequalities* (New York: Crown, 1991).

11 David Cayley, *The Education Debates.* Fifteen one-hour cassettes, *Ideas,* CBC, Radio, Toronto, 1998.

12 Chris Searle, "The Gulf Between: The School and a War," *Race and Class* 33, 4 (April/June 1992.) The article is also found in Satu Repo, ed., *Making Schools Better: Good Teachers at Work* (Our Schools/Our Selves Publications and James Lorimer: Toronto, 1998), 169-86.

13 Chris Searle, "Campaigning *Is* Education," *Race and Class* 35, 3 (January/March 1994). The articles about the Gulf and about keeping the school open are both in Chris Searle, *Living Community Living School* (London: The Tufnell Press, 1997). For a sweep of Searle's whole career and work thus far see *None But Our Words: Critical Literacy in Classroom and Community* (Buckingham & Philadelphia: Open University Press, 1998).

14 Chris Searle, interviews and editing, *Carriacou and Petite Martinique: In the Mainstream of the Revolution* (St. Georges, Grenada: Fedon, 1982).

15 See note 28 in chapter 10.

16 See Canadian radical educational magazine edited by George Martell and Satu Repo, *Our Schools/Our Selves,* October 1988-June 1999. (Formac Distributing Ltd, 5502 Atlantic Street, Halifax, Nova Scotia B3H 1G4).

17 Bob Peterson, "Social Justice Unionism: A Call to Education Unionists," *Rethinking Schools* 9, 1 (Autumn 1994). See also Bob Peterson and Michael Charney, eds., *Transforming Teacher Unions: Fighting For Better Schools and Social Justice* (Milwaukee, WI: Rethinking Schools, 1999). For the magazine itself, contact *Rethinking Schools: An Educational Journal,* 1001 E. Keefe Ave., Milwaukee, WI 53312, USA.

18 Dennis Lee, *Body Music* (Toronto: Anansi, 1998) vii, viii.

Index